For Rachel and Tumsifu,
with thanks.

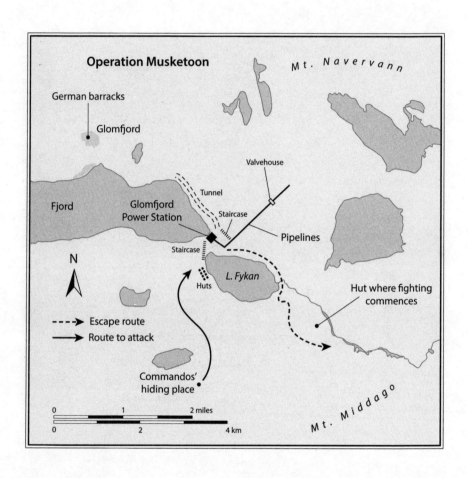

Operation Musketoon

Mt. *Navervann*

German barracks

Glomfjord

Fjord

Glomfjord
Power Station

Tunnel

Valvehouse

Staircase

Pipelines

Staircase

N

L. Fykan

Huts

Hut where fighting
commences

- - -> Escape route
——> Route to attack

Commandos'
hiding place

Mt. *Middago*

0		1		2 miles
0		2		4 km

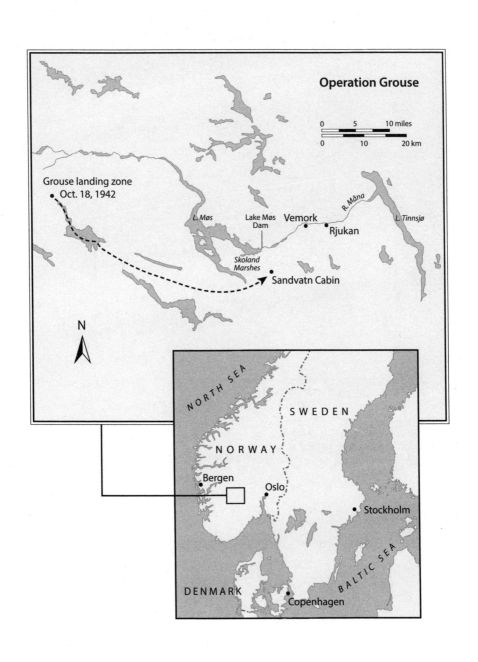

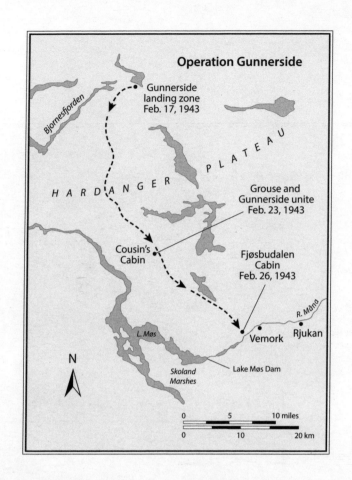

Operation Gunnerside

Bjørnesfjorden

Gunnerside
landing zone
Feb. 17, 1943

H A R D A N G E R   P L A T E A U

Grouse and
Gunnerside unite
Feb. 23, 1943

Cousin's
Cabin

Fjøsbudalen
Cabin
Feb. 26, 1943

R. Måna

L. Møs

Vemork   Rjukan

N

Skoland
Marshes

Lake Møs Dam

0   5   10 miles
0   10   20 km

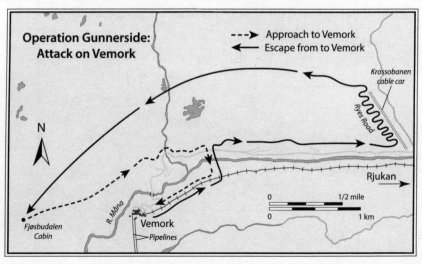

**Operation Gunnerside:
Attack on Vemork**

- - -▶ Approach to Vemork
◀——— Escape from to Vemork

Krossobanen
cable car

Ryes Road

N

Rjukan

R. Måna

Fjøsbudalen
Cabin

Vemork

Pipelines

0   1/2 mile
0   1 km

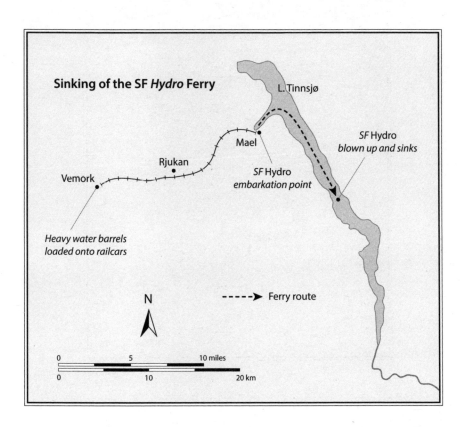

Sinking of the SF *Hydro* Ferry

L. Tinnsjø

Mael

SF Hydro
blown up and sinks

Rjukan

Vemork

SF Hydro
embarkation point

*Heavy water barrels
loaded onto railcars*

N

- - - - -▶ Ferry route

0   5   10 miles

0   10   20 km

'In the high ranges of Secret Service work the actual facts in many cases were in every respect equal to the most fantastic inventions of romance and melodrama. Tangle with tangle, plot and counter-plot, ruse and treachery, cross and double-cross, true agent, false agent, double agent, gold and steel, the bomb, the dagger and the firing party, were interwoven in many a texture so intricate as to be incredible and yet true.'

—Winston S. Churchill

'They did nothing less than save the world.'

—Charles Kuralt, CBS News correspondent,
on the SOE nuclear saboteurs.

Author's Note

There are sadly few survivors from the Second World War operations depicted in these pages, or of the Norwegian resistance, or of the Linge Company. Throughout the period of the research for, and the writing of, this book I have endeavoured to be in contact with as many as possible, plus surviving family members of those who have passed away. If there are further witnesses to the stories told here who are inclined to come forward, please do get in touch with me, as I may be able to include further recollections on the operations portrayed in this book in future editions.

The time spent by Allied servicemen and women as Special Operations Executive (SOE) agents, Special Duty volunteers, and working with the Resistance was often traumatic and invariably wreathed in layers of secrecy, and many chose to take their stories to their graves. Memories tend to differ and apparently none more so than those concerning operations behind enemy lines. The written accounts that do exist of such missions also vary in their detail and timescale, and locations and chronologies are often contradictory. That being said I have done my best to provide a coherent sense of place, timescale and narrative to the story as depicted in these pages.

Where various accounts of a mission appear to be particularly confused the methodology I have used to reconstruct where, when and how events took place is the 'most likely' scenario. If two or more testimonies or sources point to a particular time or place or sequence of events, I have opted to use that account as most likely. Where necessary I have recreated small passages of dialogue to aid the story's flow.

The above notwithstanding, any mistakes herein are entirely of my own making, and I would be happy to correct any in future editions. Likewise, while I have endeavoured to locate the copyright holders of the photos, sketches and other images and material used in this book, this has not always been straightforward or easy. Again, I would be happy to correct any errors or omissions in future editions.

Preface

A strange sequence of events – serendipitous, perhaps – brought me to the writing of this book.

The first was an enquiry that came from out of the blue. My esteemed researcher, Simon Fowler, himself an expert in all things concerning the Second World War, put a tantalizing query to me, one that typified his unerring instinct for what might pique my curiosity, coupled with his mastery of under-statement: 'I don't know whether this might be of interest?'

The correspondence attached pertained to Adolf Hitler's last will and testament. I'd never even conceived that he might have made one. What had the Führer to bequeath to human kind, other than sixty million deaths and a world convulsed by war, not to mention the advent of a new barbarism – the industrialized mass killing of entire races of peoples?

Yes, I replied, I would be interested in seeing Hitler's will.

It wasn't the easiest of documents to access at first hand, but eventually we succeeded. The two original papers, entitled simply 'My Political Testament' and 'My Personal Will', can be viewed in a special invigilation room at the National Archives. An odd sense of heightened sensitivity still surrounds those six closely typed pages, which were signed by A. Hitler at 0400 hours on 29 April 1945 in his Berlin bunker – twenty-four hours before he took his own life.

What might one expect from Hitler's will and political testament, written on the very eve of Germany's defeat? A smidgen of remorse? A sense, perhaps, that the war hadn't been . . . a very smart idea? A sense of bitter loss, especially of Germany's status in the world, and of the reputation of the German people? A suggestion, maybe, that Hitler had got it all wrong? A hint of an apology for the abject suffering and evil unleashed by the Nazi regime?

Not a bit of it.

The first few lines give the lie to any such expectations. 'It is untrue that I or anybody else in Germany wanted war in 1939. It was wanted and provoked exclusively by those international statesmen who were of Jewish origin and worked for Jewish interests.' The document goes on in such a vein, dripping delusional hatred and resonating with a misguided, almost childish sense of injustice.

Repeatedly, Hitler rails against 'the Jew, the race which is the real guilty party in this murderous struggle', describing how the Second World War 'will one day go down in history as the most glorious and heroic manifestation of the struggle for existence of a nation . . . Centuries will go by, but from the ruins of our towns and monuments, hatred of those ultimately responsible will always grow anew. They are the people whom we have to thank for all this: international Jewry and its helpers!

'I die with a joyful heart,' Hitler declares, 'in the knowledge of the immeasurable deeds and achievements of our soldiers at the front, of our women at home, the achievements of our peasants and workers and of the contribution, unique in history, of our youth which bears my name.' He was referring, of course, to the Hitler Youth, at a time when the German nation was gripped by terrible suffering and lay in ruins.

On the final day of his rule over the Third Reich, the Führer urged 'no surrender'. Not ever and not on any terms. His people should 'not give up the struggle under any circumstances, but carry it on wherever they may be against the enemies of the Fatherland . . . I myself prefer death to cowardly resignation or even to capitulation . . . the surrender of a district or town is out of the question . . . above everything else the commanders must set a shining example of faithful devotion to duty until death.'

Those words were penned even as Russian troops advanced to within 500 metres of Hitler's Berlin bunker, and his commanders petitioned to be allowed a last chance to break out, for they would soon be out of ammunition and at the enemy's mercy.

The mind boggles.

The documents are less a conventional will and testament, leaving worldly possessions to named individuals; more a political and ideological last gasp that Hitler intended to bequeath to the world, albeit a twisted and deluded one. And that pretty much accounts for the rest of the documentation held alongside Hitler's final written testament – a plethora of letters, telegrams and memos from various individuals in Allied high command, debating what on earth should be done with such material.

On the eve of Hitler's death three individuals had been sent out from the Berlin bunker, charged with getting the documents into the hands of Hitler's supporters, wherever they might be. They were tasked to spread the word and to keep the Führer's message alive. With war's end two of those individuals seemed to have realized how hollow their mission was. The third, Heinz Lorenz, a journalist long attached to Hitler's staff, kept the will sewn into the lining of his coat, with a view perhaps to preserving its twisted legacy.

It was that copy which fell into Allied hands.

In the early autumn of 1945 Lorenz, living under a false name, was arrested in the British zone of occupation in Germany, and the documents were recovered. MI5 handwriting experts analysed the signature, and found it to be genuine. A debate followed as to whether the documents should be made public or suppressed. The question was confounding: on the one hand, the papers revealed Hitler to be deluded and utterly unrepentant until his final hour; on the other, the Führer's final words might perhaps inspire a long-lived Nazi resistance movement.

The British Foreign Office was consulted. A press briefing was prepared, summarizing the contents of Hitler's last will and testament. But by December 1945 urgent and 'Top Secret' cipher messages were flying back and forth between Washington, London and Supreme Allied Headquarters Europe, stressing the need to 'take every possible measure to limit possible leakage' of the documents.

The British Foreign Office issued its decree that 'the less public notice the documents receive in Germany or outside the better'. The US State Department concurred. But news of Hitler's will and testament did leak out, and from highly placed Allied sources. A witch-hunt followed.

By January 1946 the Foreign Office had asked for all copies of the documents to be sent to London, for 'internment in their official archives'. Directives were circulated to the few already in the know, urging them 'not to disclose anything about the matter' and 'to keep quiet on the subject'.

Of course, I viewed these documents with the benefit of seventy-odd years of hindsight, yet I couldn't say for certain whether those who wanted to suppress Hitler's will and its perverse message had got it wrong. Who knows: it may well have served as some sort of rallying cry for any remaining Nazi die-hards. But it wasn't that which struck me most powerfully. It was this: what would the author of such a document not have been capable of, had he secured the means to win the war?

Which got me thinking, how close had Hitler come to doing so? I was aware of the great advances made by German scientists during the war years in so many fields – the technology under-pinning the V1 and V2 rockets, to name but one. Nazi Germany was assessed as being a decade ahead of the Allies. In short, what would Hitler not have been capable of, had he secured nuclear supremacy?

It was then that the law of unintended consequences came into play.

I was invited to the Royal Marines Commando Training Centre, in Lympstone, Devon, which overlooks the estuary of the River Exe. TV adventurer and former SAS man Bear Grylls – who is an honorary colonel in the Royal Marines – was joining some recruits on the thirty-miler, the final stage of the punishing commando selection course, in which they have to complete a thirty-mile forced march over Dartmoor, carrying crushing loads.

Afterwards he gave an inspirational talk to a packed audi-ence in the main hall, following which there was a dinner in the mess. I happened by chance to sit next to two charming and fascinating individuals – Lieutenant Colonel Tony de Reya MBE, who was then chief of staff at Lympstone, and Major Finlay Walls, one of Lympstone's resident experts in mountain warfare. Over dinner they asked what book I was presently working on.

I replied that I was thinking about writing the story of the race to stop Hitler acquiring a nuclear weapon, an idea that had been triggered by reading Hitler's will. Both men knew the story well, for it encompassed some of the most iconic and daring commando operations ever undertaken. To my amazement, Major Walls was actually in the process of organizing an expedition to retrace some of the operations carried out by British and Norwegian commandos against one of Nazi Germany's key nuclear facilities, which was based in occupied Norway.

Those missions were the nub of Allied efforts to thwart Hitler's nuclear ambitions. High-octane, high-drama heroics abounded, as small groups of men fought and died and eventually prevailed, such that the Third Reich's nuclear dreams might be vanquished. That evening's conversation, and the realization of how significant those commando operations remain to this day, convinced me that this was a story that needed to be told.

Those two seasoned Royal Marine commanders exhibited such enthusiasm for the story that it proved contagious. I returned to see them some time later with a first draft of the manuscript for this book, and was able to use it to help talk Major Walls through his coming expedition to retrace the main commando operations, helping him to refine and clarify exactly what he intended to do. He had named his forthcoming expedition Return to Rjukan, after the main town in the area where the commandos operated.

In the spring of 2017 Major Walls ('Fin' to all who know him) plans to take twelve young commandos into Norway's Hardangervidda – the Barren Mountains plateau, a vast area of snowbound wilderness – to retrace some of the routes and missions carried out in Operations Grouse and Gunnerside, two of the key stories that feature in this book. This Royal Marines expedition was in part inspired by our discussion over dinner. Prior to that it had been an aspiration; after we had spoken, Fin went out and made it a reality.

As they had inspired me to write this book, so I had inspired them to mount a historic expedition. None of us had gathered for that meal with any of this in mind or with the faintest notion that such might be the outcome. Serendipity indeed.

I'm hugely grateful to both individuals, and to those who in due course did so much to help with the research for and writing of this book (all of whom are mentioned in the Acknowledgements). One individual wrote to me with a poignant quote, concerning his uncle who died on 'special duties' during the war. It is by the poet John Maxwell Edmonds, and sums up the sacrifices manifested in the pages that follow:

> Went the day well?
> We died and never knew.
> But well or ill,
> Freedom, we died for you.

Every book has a journey to its beginning – something that reels the author in, like a fish on a hook. This was one of the most unusual and compelling. I am glad that I undertook it. The story in the following pages is one of extraordinary heroism and achievement against all odds, as a small body of men gave their all so that the free world might remain free from a dark and malevolent tyranny.

I am sure there is more to tell about the battle to stop Hitler acquiring a nuclear weapon and achieving nuclear supremacy, and I look forward to whatever revelations may result from the publishing of this book.

But first, let me take you to a lone submarine slipping stealthily into the coastal waters of occupied Norway, in the early autumn of 1942.

Chapter One

Six nautical miles off the autumn coast of Norway a sleek grey shape cut a stealthy path beneath the snow-flecked swell of the sea. The distinctive form of the *Junon* barely moved with the rise and fall of the waves.

Slowly, silently, a black metal tube extended itself from the submarine's conning tower. Lieutenant Commander Querville, the captain of the *Junon*, grabbed his periscope and did a rapid, three-sixty-degree scan of the surrounding sea. He could see that not another ship was in sight, which was just as he wanted it.

The captain downed periscope, ordering his vessel to the surface.

From the bridge, lookouts scanned the horizon as Commander Querville tried to locate his route into the Bjærangsfjord – the intended drop-off point for the team of clandestine warriors that his vessel was carrying.

'No craft in sight,' the navigator reported, as the *Junon* pushed ever closer towards the jagged profile of the Norwegian coastline.

To left and right sharp mountains towered before her, their lower slopes cloaked in dense, dark pine forests, the higher reaches encrusted with snow and ice that blazed a burnished gold in the fine morning light.

Suddenly, there it was: a plunging V-shaped slash yawned before them. Typical of these Norwegian inlets, the Bjærangsfjord

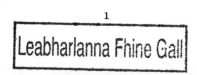

was a long, narrow, steep-walled arm of the sea, one seemingly sliced from the mountains by a giant's hand. But of chief concern to Querville was that the Bjærangsfjord had only been chosen as the *Junon*'s destination during the final stages of their long and storm-tossed voyage.

One of those that his vessel was carrying – a Norwegian commando with intimate knowledge of this coastline – had argued for a last-minute change of plan. He'd suggested a new drop-off point, one that would entail scaling a glacier-clad mountain to reach their target, for the enemy would never suspect an attack from that direction.

It was probably the right decision, but Querville carried few detailed charts of the Bjærangsfjord, and possessed little information as to currents, depths or the state of the fjord's bottom, and almost no intelligence on German defences that might be sited along its length. He would have to edge his craft into the knife-cut fjord with utmost care, feeling his way into her icy embrace.

The *Junon* had been chosen for the present top-secret mission for the simple reason that, with her sharply raked prow and streamlined conning tower, the Free French submarine resembled, in silhouette at least, a German U-boat. If an enemy warship spotted the *Junon*, with luck those aboard would mistake her for one of their own.

One of the few things that might mark the submarine out as suspicious was the rubber dinghy lashed to her casings, but an enemy warship would have to get decidedly close to spy that. And Querville didn't intend to let that happen.

For now, the surrounding waters seemed empty of shipping,

and the *Junon*'s commander took the opportunity to give the dozen commandos that he was carrying a glance through his periscope.

'*Voilà, mes amis. C'est beau, très beau. Regardez.*'

They were steaming towards the coastline, which was indeed beautiful, breathtakingly so, and especially for the two Norwegian saboteurs. This was the first glimpse of their homeland for more than a year – a nation that had been ground under the heel of the Nazi jackboot.

Ground, bowed – but far from broken.

The spirit of resistance was rising within Norway, as it was in so many of the occupied nations of Western Europe, and the present mission was designed to help invigorate that spirit. As Winston Churchill had urged, when unleashing his 'hunter troops for a butcher-and-bolt reign of terror', no German in occupied Europe should feel able to sleep soundly in his bed at night. He had demanded of his chiefs of staff that 'specially trained troops of the hunter class . . . develop a reign of terror down the enemy coast.'

It was 15 September 1942, and the flagship of the 1st Free French Submarine Division was about to launch a daring sortie in Churchill's cause. The present mission, code-named Musketoon, was intended to be one of the very first sabotage operations of the war, designed to hit back hard against a seemingly invincible foe.

It took an hour or more for the *Junon* to creep into the jaws of the Bjærangsfjord, where her captain ordered her to periscope depth. They were drawing too close to land – and prying eyes – to remain on the surface.

But even as the last of the commandos took his turn at the periscope, a fishing boat chugged out of the shadows cast by the towering peaks behind her. She looked innocuous enough, but in the bitter war being waged between Britain and the German forces occupying Norway, the fishing flotillas had come to perform a dual role.

Britain had raised the 'Shetland Bus' flotilla, a fleet of Norwegian fishing vessels headquartered in the Shetland Islands and converted into 'Q-ships' – seemingly innocent trawlers, but which bristled with hidden weaponry and defences. The role of the Shetland Bus flotilla was to ferry men, weaponry and wireless equipment into and out of Norway, and to defend themselves and their charges resolutely if detected by the enemy.

The Germans had responded in kind. They had raised their own flotilla, press-ganging local fishermen into the service of the Reich and tasking them to help rebuff any Allied incursions into Norwegian waters. The vessel now turning into the *Junon*'s wake could easily be one of those.

The captain of that fishing boat was tired. He'd been at work for many hours. Yet still his eyes were sea-spray sharp. The form of the vertical black pole cutting through the waters drew his gaze. For a second he thought he had to be dreaming, before he threw open the wheelhouse door and gave a yell. To his rear a second fishing boat emerged from the shadows, but her captain was still too distant to properly hear his cry.

As the first vessel bore down on what her captain now knew had to be a submarine, the commando at the *Junon*'s periscope finally relinquished it to the vessel's navigator. Taking the handles, the navigator executed a quick three-sixty-degree scan, spotting what the commandos, mesmerized by the dramatic sweep of the shoreline, had failed to see: directly to the submarine's rear were the two fishing vessels bobbing in their wake.

He gave a shout of alarm, and Querville ordered an emergency dive. The nose of the *Junon* tilted sharply and she sank to a depth of thirty metres, which was as much as her commander felt he could risk in the uncertain embrace of the Bjærangsfjord.

Querville reduced her speed, and at a painful snail's pace she nosed her way up the centre of the V-shaped chasm. Above, the throbbing of the fishing boats' screws rose to a deafening crescendo, before fading away on the dark waters.

Everyone was silent and tense.

The *Junon*'s trim officer kept an eagle eye on his instruments as the depth gauges registered a constant thirty metres. For a further two painstaking miles the submarine crept into the Bjærangsfjord, until the shore to either side crowded in to less than 500 metres.

There, Querville ordered the *Junon* to dive for the bottom – whatever that might entail. Forty metres, fifty, fifty-five; the descent was barely perceptible, as all held their breath for whatever might follow. Finally, at sixty metres dead the 870-tonne vessel settled upon what the captain knew from sound and feel alone had to be the flat, sandy bed of the fjord.

Querville – a smart, sanguine fellow – gave a brief but reassuring smile. Everyone sighed with relief. It was one thirty in the afternoon, and Querville planned to wait out any search in silence, his vessel's distinctive outline masked by the Bjærangsfjord's sandy bottom.

An hour later the submarine's bulbous steel hull resonated to the sound of powerful propellers on the surface. The rhythmic beat faded away, but it was audible again forty minutes later. For the next seven hours the mystery vessel quartered the waters above at regular intervals, steering what had to be a search pattern.

By now it was approaching dusk, and Querville intended to release his sabotage party unnoticed and undetected in the night hours. It was time for the force of commandos – nine Britons, two Norwegians and a Canadian – to make their final preparations.

What lay before them was a doubly daunting proposition.

As the official logs would record, the *Junon*'s storm-tossed crossing had rendered all but one of the commandos seasick: 'The effect of the submarine journey under very bad weather conditions reduced the physical conditions of the party.' Ahead of them lay a night paddle to their intended landfall, followed by a punishing trek carrying crushing loads over uncharted, ice-clad mountains.

But today's long and silent sojourn at sixty metres depth had rendered the *Junon*'s air particularly foul, and not a man amongst the sabotage party could wait to get off her and set foot on Norwegian soil.

At nine fifteen the *Junon* surfaced, her form like a great black whale slicing apart the silvery gleam of the fjord's calm. Querville was first up the ladder, conscious of his responsibility to get these brave men safely ashore.

He scanned his surroundings. Moonlight glinted off the snowy peaks, beneath which blinked the odd sliver of light from dwellings clustered at the shoreline. The waters seemed deserted of any other vessels, and the only noise Querville could detect was the gentle slap of ripples against his vessel's hull.

Querville called the raiders up to join him. From the conning tower two figures crept along the deck towards the rubber boat lashed to the stern. They bent over it with an oxygen canister. A sharp hiss rang out across the still water as the gas was released, and moments later the semi-inflated dinghy broke free from her bounds.

'Hell!' a voice whispered. 'What a racket!'

'I hope no one heard it ashore,' came the muted reply.

Querville felt certain the noise of the escaping gas would have reached the shoreline, but there was little point worrying about that now. One by one the raiders made their silent way to the boat. The French crew brought up their bulging rucksacks, each weighed down with fully ninety pounds of war materiel, the vast majority of which consisted of explosives.

They passed the heavy bundles across to the waiting men, all twelve of whom were by now crammed into the 'cow boat' – so named because the first such inflatables were fashioned from rubberized animal skins. With whispers of '*Bon voyage!*' from Querville and his crew, the commandos pushed off. Moments later the dinghy was adrift on the moonlit waters.

Six men set to the paddles, as their captain plotted a course due east, and soon the craft was swallowed up in the emptiness of the Bjærangsfjord. From behind there came a faint snort and a gurgle, and when the men glanced behind them the *Junon* was no more.

They were alone now, in the vast, star-spangled expanse of the Norwegian wilderness. The dozen figures crammed into that dinghy would be for ever in Querville's debt: he had taken them further inland than any had dared hope for. Just six kilometres separated them from the headwaters of the Bjærangsfjord – land-fall.

The crew nosed the dinghy along the fjord's southern shore, moving silently as ghosts and skirting past the odd fishing boat moored to a rickety wharf. The Norwegian coastline is so pockmarked and indented that its total length would encircle fully one half of the earth. The Musketoon raiders were sneaking a tiny rubber craft into just one of its myriad inlets: what chance was there that they would be seen by anyone, or detected by the German occupiers?

The dinghy was almost past Bjærangsjoen, the last of the tiny settlements that ring the fjord, when an old lady – the village insomniac; some believed her a little crazed with it – thought she heard something. Her tiny wooden house lay right on the shoreline. There had been a splash out on the midnight water, she was certain of it.

Putting aside her knitting, she crossed to the window. As she peered into the darkness, she did indeed spy something: silhouetted on the moonlit waters, a small, unlit craft was creeping silently past. What on earth could it be, she wondered? Who could be out on the water at such an hour? And why the need for the dark silence and secrecy?

She decided to raise it with her neighbours in the morning. They'd doubtless think her crazy. It wouldn't be the first time. But there was a war on, and it made sense to be vigilant. She knew what she'd seen. She'd convince them.

The dinghy rounded the end of Bjærangsjoen, and only the emptiness of the night beckoned.

'Right,' rasped Captain Black, Musketoon's commander, in his gravel-edged Canadian drawl, 'steer her in here.'

Moments later the bulbous rubber prow bumped into the first of the boulders lying half submerged in the shallows. The leading commandos – the two Norwegians – jumped out, and began to drag the craft ashore. They'd landed on a rocky beach, where a straggly, orange-tinged grass grew almost to the waterline.

Barely fifty yards away the cover of the trees beckoned: first birch, their silver trunks sleek in the moonlight, and behind those the taller, darker forms of firs.

Quickly, they unloaded the inflatable, hefting rucksacks onto eager shoulders. With the dinghy deflated, they rolled it up and carried it towards the forest. There they dug a hole and lowered it in, throwing the oars after, and covering the grave with rocks and moss. The dinghy had served them well. She deserved a decent burial.

'Right, let's move inland,' Black ordered, as he signalled the others to follow his lead and ready their weapons. It might look and sound utterly deserted, but from now on they would be moving through the territory of the enemy. 'Keep close together. And no noise.'

With the two Norwegians guiding, the file of well-trained fighters moved further into the trees. Once a safe distance from the open coast and in good cover, Black ordered a halt. Sleeping bags were unrolled and the party settled down to rest.

They would move off at dawn, for they would need daylight to find their way over the maze of jumbled ice and jagged peaks that lay between their present position and their target.

Captain Black found that sleep just wouldn't come. He dozed fitfully, the excitement of what lay before them fizzing through his mind.

As with all nine of his British troops, Black hailed from No. 2 Commando, a force formed entirely from volunteers who'd answered Churchill's call to arms. Barely two years into the war proper No. 2 Commando had earned a fearsome reputation, taking part in the famous raid on Saint-Nazaire, amongst other daring sorties.

What, Captain Graeme 'Gay' Black wondered, had drawn him – a Canadian – to his present situation: leading a bunch of British and Norwegian commandos on a mission as desperate as this? Growing up in Ontario, in southern Canada, Black had been an average student at best. He'd preferred snowshoeing in the woods in winter, shooting game, or rafting the wild Ontario rivers.

His thirst for adventure whetted, Black had worked a passage to England on a cattle boat, cleaning the stalls to earn his fare. In London he'd drifted from job to job, before founding a ladies' handbag company, together with a London leather worker he'd befriended. Black knew nothing about leather or the craft, but he was charming, energetic and good-looking – with a shock of unruly blond hair above laughing eyes – and he knew how to sell.

He married a Scottish girl and in time Black & Holden thrived, supplying handbags to the fashion houses frequented by royalty. On the day after Britain declared war on Germany, Black decided to enlist in the British Army. The handbag business could go hang: there was a war to be fought and won.

He promptly volunteered for hazardous service, joining No. 2 Commando. There he earned the reputation of being something of a daredevil, in part because he seemed to reply to just about every order with the 'cowboy'-sounding 'Check', as opposed to 'Yes, sir'.

Black was known to be independent-spirited, which at times rubbed his senior commanders up the wrong way. But having gone on to fight with real distinction and to earn the Military Cross, few could doubt his credentials as a commando officer.

Oddly, it was Black's second-in-command, Captain Joseph 'Joe' Houghton, who was the chief mover behind the present mission. But while Musketoon was Houghton's brainchild, it was Black who had been charged to lead it. Typically, Joe Houghton hadn't seemed to mind.

A former public school boy (Marlborough College), Houghton – pudgy faced, with a thick mop of black hair – was easy-going and likeable, and something of a prankster. In a sense, he was far from being the archetypal commando: he enjoyed grouse and pheasant shooting, but he wasn't exactly a natural athlete. He had got through commando selection and training by dint of sheer will and bloody-minded determination.

Yet, as Black knew, there was cold steel beneath Houghton's affable surface. Black and Houghton had both been on the raid on the French port of Saint-Nazaire, in which a force of commandos had rammed the dock with a ship packed full of explosives, blowing the gates to smithereens under the noses of the Germans. In the ensuing action Houghton had fought like a lion and been wounded.

But it was Houghton's prior experiences in Norway that had brought him to the present mission. Before the war Houghton had worked in this part of the country, in the mining industry. Following the German invasion, in May 1940, he'd joined the fight against the enemy, demonstrating the intense camaraderie that he'd forged with the Norwegian people.

The battle for Norway having been lost, Houghton had been evacuated to Britain. He'd long feared how Norway's rich natural resources would fuel the German war effort, and he'd sold the present mission to the British high command on the basis that it would deprive the Nazi war machine of a vital source of raw firepower.

As the first light of dawn filtered through the trees, Black's men were up and readying breakfast: a thick soup made of pemmican – dried meat mixed with dried fruit – washed down with hot tea, and all heated on the team's shared Primus stove.

Black drew his pipe from his commando smock and thumbed some tobacco into it. As he did, he eyed his men, appraising each in turn.

Cyril Abram – the tallest in the team – was considered by some to have movie-star good looks. A keen Scout before the war, he'd volunteered for service at the earliest possible opportunity. His pal, Rex Makeham, was a fellow lover of camping, cycling and scouting. Both were fine outdoorsmen and Black figured they would endure the coming rigours of the Norwegian wilderness well.

Easy-going Makeham was a stark contrast to the third of Black's men: Fred Trigg. Trigg was a squat, throaty-voiced, barrel-chested Londoner and an amateur boxer of some repute. His was a quiet, brooding presence, with a distinctly argumentative bent, but Black appreciated the man's hunger to take the fight to the enemy.

His fourth man, Miller 'Dusty' Smith, was a typically dour, still-waters-run-deep Yorkshireman. Unique amongst the Musketoon party, Smith had seemed quite at home on the *Junon*, having gone to sea as a merchant seaman when he was fourteen. With his rangy frame and broad shoulders Smith exuded a quiet toughness, and Black was glad to have him along.

Jack Fairclough – number five – was a tall, rakish guardsman. A career soldier, he seemed to bear no resentment towards anyone, the Germans included. Fairclough was here simply because his country was at war, and he felt it his duty to do his part. That was enough for Black: he needed cool, professional, duty-bound soldiers like Fairclough, as a foil to the more fiery-spirited amongst his men.

His sixth operator, Eric Curtis, was the real odd man out. Bespectacled, and studious to a fault, he'd won scholarships at school, and he could speak decent French and German. An accountant by trade, he was a lover both of cricket and of animals. Though he was normally quiet as a mouse, Black had learned that when Curtis was roused to anger he was a force to be reckoned with.

Bill Chudley, commando number seven, was Curtis's opposite: a through-and-through action man. A Devonshire lad and a former dispatch rider, Curtis was a crack shot on the Lewis gun – a light .303-calibre machine gun. He was about as far from your average accountant as it was possible to get, which made it all the stranger that he and Curtis were the best of friends.

Black didn't doubt that when push came to shove – as it doubtless would on this mission – Chudley and Curtis would fight back-to-back. Not that he and his men had a great deal to *fight with*: the target would require such a weight of explosives to destroy it, they had been able to carry precious little weaponry or ammunition.

So be it.

Black's eighth man – Richard 'Dickie' O'Brien – was the senior non-commissioned officer (NCO) on the team, and another veteran of the raid on Saint-Nazaire. Thick-necked and muscular, with a calm, level gaze, O'Brien was a real soldier's soldier, and a great support to Black and Houghton. He was also an accomplished mountaineer, having spent six months instructing his fellow commandos on the Cumbrian fells. With a new and uncharted route lying before them, O'Brien's specialist skills were sure to be crucial.

Lastly, there were the two Norwegians – the late additions to Black's team. Strictly speaking, these men weren't commandos; they had been 'attached' to his unit at the behest of a highly secretive and shadowy organization known as the Special Operations Executive – the SOE.

Under Hitler, Europe had vanished into the darkness of a tyranny without precedent. Churchill's riposte had been to form a secret organization charged to use all necessary measures to wage guerrilla warfare and foment the rise of resistance across Nazi-occupied territories.

One of Churchill's key strategists and long-time friends was the wealthy Canadian industrialist, WWI flying ace and now spymaster, William Stephenson. At the outbreak of war Stephenson had issued a stark warning about how the Allies – Britain, with America's covert backing – should respond to the threat posed by Hitler's war machine. It had left little to the imagination.

The Führer is not just a lunatic. He is an evil genius. The weapons in his armoury are like nothing in history. His propaganda is sophisticated. His control of the people is technologically clever. He has torn up the military textbooks and written his own. His strategy is to spread terror, fear and mutual suspicion.

There will be a period of occupation when we shall have to keep up the morale of those who are not taken to the death and slave camps, and build up an intelligence system so we can identify the enemy's weak points. We'll have to fall back upon human resources and trust that these are superior to machines.

Churchill had taken Stephenson's admonition and built upon it, creating the SOE. For the SOE, the recruitment of the peoples of those nations now under occupation was a first vital step towards liberating them. Since the outbreak of war hundreds of Norwegians had fled to Britain to join the Free Norwegian Forces, under the command of the London-based Norwegian government in exile. In Scotland, in terrain most closely resembling their home country, the Norwegians had established a commando-style training camp.

They'd named the unit 'The Linge Company', after its then commander, Martin Linge, who had sadly lost his life during its first ever mission. On 27 December 1941 the men of the Linge Company had teamed up with British commandos for Operation Archery, a daring raid against the German island fortresses of Vågsøy and Måløy, off the Norwegian coast. The operation had proved a stunning success, but Martin Linge had been killed by a German sniper as he had rushed the enemy headquarters.

The Norwegian saboteurs attached to Black's team were both Linge Company veterans. During the German invasion of Norway, Sverre Granlund and Erling Djupdraet had fought on the front line, the latter manning a heavy machine gun battery. Since fleeing to Britain, Djupdraet had been put through the SOE's wireless school. He'd proven an ideal recruit, for his father was a railwayman who'd taught his son to operate a radio and to use Morse code.

Granlund and Djupdraet were united in their intent to drive the German invaders out of their homeland. But of the two of them, it was Granlund who absolutely burned with the desire to kill the enemy. At times Black had caught the Norwegian with his Colt .45 pistol gripped in hand, and a faraway killer's gaze in his eyes.

Breakfast done, Black ordered his men into action. They hefted their packs and moved onto an open grassy plain, which stretched to the foot of the Svartisen – the Black Glacier. Vast and forbidding, it lay before them like a great, grey glistening slug.

Neither Djupdraet nor Granlund had ever set foot on the Black Glacier, and none amongst them knew if it could be scaled. Yet if they could strike at their target from this direction, they would be able to hit it where it was least defended: the Germans were convinced that the Black Glacier was unassailable, and there were no guards set on the Svartisen.

But as Black and his men made their approach to the glacier, so an old and sleepless woman in Bjærangsjoen was having words with her neighbours: 'I saw a boat on the fjord last night, past midnight.'

The neighbours shook their heads. No matter how much she insisted, they were inclined not to believe her. She went to speak to her more distant neighbours. She repeated the same story. They stared at her with incredulity.

But, slowly, whispers about the twelve strangers in the midnight boat were spreading.

Chapter Two

Black got to his feet and knocked the ashes out of his pipe. Joe Houghton and Granlund had gone ahead to recce a route across the glacier, and they'd just returned with the news that they'd found one. But neither man was pretending it was going to be easy.

Not for the first time, Black found himself thankful for the rigours of their commando training. Over intensive weeks they'd rehearsed assaults under live fire, with machine guns belting out the rounds just above their heads and with explosive charges being thrown at their heels. They'd swum icy rivers in full kit and clawed their way up the most challenging peaks the British Isles has to offer.

No. 2 Commando recruits were required to march 120 miles in 48 hours, snatching sleep in hedgerows and ditches along the way. Anyone who'd failed to make the grade had been sent back to their parent regiment. Knowing that every one of his team had passed such a punishing selection regime put steel in Black's soul.

But even if the climb and the attack went to plan, the chances of escape thereafter seemed slim. Sure, they were equipped with the best escape kit that the boffins at the SOE had to offer. Hidden inside the heel of each man's boot was a tiny silk handkerchief. When doused in water – or peed upon – it would, as if by magic, reveal a map of Norway and Sweden. They even carried a map of Russia, just in case their escape route might take them that far afield.

Mini compasses were sewn into their collars, and each man carried a fat wad of Norwegian kroner, to buy his way out of trouble. They all carried a hacksaw blade – for sawing through a cell's bars – secreted about their persons, plus the iconic commando fighting knife strapped to their calves. That, plus a Colt .45 pistol, completed their complement of hidden weaponry.

It wasn't the escape kit that worried Black; it was the way in which they were supposed to reach safety. En route across the North Sea the *Junon's* commander, Querville, had asked Black if his submarine should wait off the Norwegian coast, so that he could pluck the raiders off again, once their mission was complete.

Reluctantly, Black had had to turn the offer down.

Initially, a Sunderland flying boat was supposed to land in a remote fjord, to whisk the raiders away to safety. The trouble was that the round trip from Scotland and back was right at the limit of the Sunderland's 2,900-kilometre range. Instead it was decided that after the attack they would split into pairs and melt into the darkness, with a long trek ahead of them.

On foot, aided by their escape equipment, they would head east across 160 kilometres of Norwegian wilderness, making for the border with neutral Sweden. Once there, the cover story they'd prepared in advance would come into play.

'We are escaped prisoners of war,' they were to tell the Swedish border officials. 'We managed to overpower the guards on the truck transporting us and escape.'

No papers or documents were to be carried during the escape, so as not to betray the real nature of their mission. Hair was to be longish, with no moustaches to be worn, which was the style then popular in Norway. And while the team would deploy in British battledress, they would only do so for as long as it took to execute the attack. Their packs contained a basic set of civilian clothing, so that they could change and attempt to blend in with the locals.

The escape plan was predicated upon a faith in Black and his men's training, and their intimate knowledge of mountaineering and the wilderness. If any team could traverse the hostile wastes of northern Norway and make it to Sweden, they should be able to. But, as Black knew only too well, the challenges in this were legion. They almost didn't bear thinking about.

With the weight of explosives they were carrying, each man only had enough food for five days. And that begged the question – what were they supposed to eat during their gruelling escape march?

They'd been issued with 500 Benzedrine tablets by MI9 – the military intelligence escape specialists. More commonly known as 'bennies' in the top London nightclubs where the drug was then popular, Benzedrine is a powerful amphetamine. With its euphoric stimulant effect, Benzedrine could keep a man alert for long periods without the need for sleep or sustenance.

The benefits were obvious, even if the use of a 'recreational drug' on a military mission was somewhat controversial. But such were the rigours of the SOE–Commando operations: they were here to wage total war. Each of the Musketoon raiders carried a good forty bennies on his person. Yet it was only possible to fuel a forced march with amphetamines for so long: eventually the body would simply collapse, burned out.

Of equal concern, they carried no skis, and between their target and Sweden lay several vast snowfields. How were those supposed to be crossed? And of the twelve, only Granlund, Djup-draet and Joe Houghton spoke Norwegian, so how were the rest supposed to communicate with the locals, and 'blend in'?

Commander Querville had clearly shared some of Black's reservations. The *Junon* was stocked with fine French wine, and he had proposed a toast to Black and Houghton's mission. Together they had raised their glasses. '*À votre succès,*' Querville had announced. But his grave expression betrayed how in truth he did not expect to see or hear of them again.

Still, there would be time enough to worry about all that once the attack was over. With the exception of Houghton, none of Black's men knew the exact nature of their target, or how they were to go about hitting it. The less they knew at this stage, the less they could reveal to the enemy if captured. In fact, the fine detail of the plan remained unclear even to Black. Only once they had scaled the Black Glacier and had actually set eyes on the target would he be certain how best to destroy it.

At first the climb up the Svartisen proved relatively easy. Their rubber-soled commando boots – great for making silent, stealthy approaches – provided ample grip on rock and ice. But as they gained altitude, the terrain beneath their feet became ever more treacherous.

It was Granlund, at the head of the party, who took the first fall. His pistol in his hand, the tall Norwegian was pushing across a patch of glassy ice when his legs went out from under him. Snatching at a narrow ledge with both hands, Granlund lost his grip on his beloved Colt .45.

It went tumbling down thirty metres or more, coming to rest at the bottom of a deep ravine. Granlund was mortified. The Norwegian's face only brightened when Houghton – the one man amongst them armed with a Sten (a compact sub-machine gun) as well as a Colt .45 – offered Granlund his pistol.

Houghton gave a meaningful nod at the Norwegian's empty holster. 'Best keep it in there, eh?'

They pressed onwards.

Despite the cold of the glacier it proved hot and sweaty work, especially under such heavy loads. One of Black's men paused at the edge of an ice-encrusted lagoon in order to slake his thirst. He needed to reach out past the pack ice to cup clear water in his hands.

As he stretched he lost his footing and crashed through the ice, the weight of his pack dragging him under. In a flash Granlund had darted to the water's edge, reached deep and helped drag the hapless soul up by his shoulder straps.

As he scrambled out of the icy water there was terror in the man's eyes. It had been freezing cold, and he was soaked through and chilled to the bone. But it was the thought of being trapped beneath the ice while weighed down by ninety pounds of explosives that had struck fear into him.

Still they continued climbing.

The glistening crown of the glacier beckoned. But even as it looked to be within their reach, a seemingly insurmountable barrier opened before them: a crevasse slashed through the grey-blue of the ice. It was too wide to vault across, and there seemed no way around it; dark walls of rock rose sheer to either side.

It was now that O'Brien – the chief mountaineer amongst them – came into his own. Each man carried a short length of rope wrapped around his waist. O'Brien took those and attached them end-to-end, knotting one of the free ends around his midriff.

He had spied a narrow ledge snaking along one of the rock

walls that hemmed in the glacier. It looked just about climbable. Face to the dark mass, he edged onto the perilous lip. Below him the crevasse yawned. At times the ledge shrank to less than an inch in width, but O'Brien seemed able to cling to the rock like a spider.

After what seemed like an age he leapt off, landing on the solid ice on the far side. There he took up the slack on the rope, and one after the other he helped the rest across, using the rope to haul their precious rucksacks over.

They turned to survey the final leg of the climb. The crown of the glacier looked solid enough, but beneath crisp snowfall and frozen ice bridges there would be hidden crevasses, just waiting to drag them down into their icy depths.

Breathless, they crested the glacier. Black and his team took a moment to admire the view. It was stunning. The sky was a cloudless blue, and sunlight glinted off the length of the Bjærangsfjord as if reflected by a myriad tiny mirrors. Not a ship – or a submarine, for that matter – blemished the waters. And to left and right ice and snow glittered and gleamed.

Black called a halt. They needed rest, and the man who had fallen into the icy water still needed to dry out. If he tried to press on in his cold, sodden clothes, it could well prove the death of him. They broke out the Primus stove and prepared a brew. It was amazing what hot sweet tea could do to revive energy and spirits.

Seated on their woollen commando hats – 'cap comforters', as they were called – and leaning against their massive backpacks, Black's men ate some food, smoked, and enjoyed the warmth of the sun. But Chudley – the Devonshire man of action – seemed restless and unable to keep still. A dynamo of energy, he was eager to be off.

He got to his feet and quartered their position, his searching gaze always towards the north – the direction of their target. All of a sudden the ice beneath him gave way. There was a muffled cry, followed by a muted splash. Chudley had fallen into a crevasse, plunging some twenty metres into the freezing water below.

Figures rushed to the hidden chasm's edge. 'Are you all right?' Black yelled.

'Yes, sir, I'm okay,' a shaky voice echoed up from the icy deep.

Black turned to his men. 'Let's have your ropes.'

Once they were fastened together, he lowered one end into the crevasse. Chudley – battered and bruised, but miraculously uninjured – was able to grab hold of it and climb up. He emerged soaked to the skin, to be met with sharp words from his commanding officer.

'What in hell did you think you were doing? You've got to be bloody careful. One slip can ruin this job, you know that! If you break a leg or sprain an ankle, what can we do with you and your pack? I don't see any mules around here, do you?'

Chudley, his boots oozing water, took it well enough. He'd messed up, pure and simple. He needed to be more patient and more careful. Curly-haired and smaller than most, Chudley – like Fred Trigg – was a keen boxer and fitness enthusiast. He stripped to his underwear, so he could wring out his clothes and lay them to dry in the sun.

Standing barefoot on his woollen hat, he twisted the water out of his socks, before hooking them onto the end of his fighting knife and holding them over the primus flame. As he moved, his muscles rippled and bulged. The others watched in amusement as Chudley's socks began to steam.

'Kind of cool up here, eh, Bill?' a distinctive voice needled him. It was 'Dusty' Smith, their dour Yorkshireman.

Chudley didn't so much as glance up from his task. 'Is it? I hadn't noticed.'

Smith pressed home his attack. 'Done your exercises this morning, Bill?'

Chudley flexed a bicep. 'I did 'em while you were still asleep.'

'Lovely figure he's got,' another voice chipped in.

'Just look at that chest!'

When Chudley's kit was passably dry, the team shouldered their packs. Their route struck north across a high plateau, which would take them to the brink of a second mighty inlet – the Glomfjord – at the eastern end of which lay their target.

By the approach of dusk Black and his men were inching their way in single file along a rough, narrow trail, which dropped gradually downwards. Below lay a precipitous fall hundreds of metres towards the dark waters of a highland lake – Lake Fykan – and the entire expanse of the downslope was a mass of loose, stony shale.

Great care was required here. One false move could send a rock crashing downward, which would set the whole valley roaring, and it was crucial they made their final approach undetected. If not, the risks entailed in the last-minute change of drop-off point, plus the epic climb that had followed, would all have been for nothing.

It was dark by the time Black called a halt. They could go no further, and the Norwegians had found them shelter of sorts – a gathering of crude stone huts, most likely used by reindeer hunters. Exhausted from the day's exertions, the men crawled into their sleeping bags, and, with a rucksack of explosives for a pillow, they slept through the cold of the Arctic night.

As first light washed over the crude stone huts where Black

and his men had spent the night, the raiders' target became visible. Back at their Scottish training base they had studied aerial surveillance photos of the area. The recently introduced de Havilland Mosquito – the so-called 'Wooden Wonder', a two-engined fighter-bomber of mainly wooden construction – was one of the fastest aircraft in the world at the time.

The Mosquito was able to outrun German fighters, making her perfect for reconnaissance missions. In recent weeks a recce flight had quartered Glomfjord, capturing black and white photos of the target in remarkable detail. Black and Houghton had studied those images intently, but nothing had quite prepared the two men for what lay before them now.

On the far side of Lake Fykan lay Glomfjord, a narrow slash of seawater every bit as dramatic as Bjærangsfjord. Nestled at the near end of the fjord lay an austere, high-walled construction of grey stone, with a peaked tower at the far end. A good thirty metres high, and hundreds long, the castle-like edifice was dwarfed by the scenery. On either side, rock-hewn slopes plummeted, snow-dusted and at times sheer, into the shadowed inlet.

Down one of those slopes ran two giant pipelines – 'penstocks' to those in the know. Those pipes terminated at the rear wall of the many-storeyed building. There they channelled water from a highland lake into three massive turbines, which were sheltered inside the vast and echoing structure. Glomfjord was a hydroelectric power plant, and it had been chosen as one of the highest-priority targets of the war.

It wasn't electricity per se that Black and his men had come here to stop – it was what that power generation made possible. The Glomfjord hydro station was so remote and inaccessible that a tunnel had been blasted through the mountains, leading to the nearest settlement, the village of Glomfjord. But further down the fjord, and linked to the power station by ferry boat, lay a massive factory complex. It was an aluminium smelting facility.

Aluminium was perhaps the single most vital of war metals, its comparative lightness and high strength making it ideal for aircraft manufacture. Roughly a third the weight of steel, an aircraft with an aluminium fuselage could carry more payload over longer distances, with obvious ramifications for Luftwaffe bombings missions. It was also highly corrosion-resistant, meaning less maintenance was required.

Since the Germans had seized Norway they had pounced upon Glomfjord. They'd shipped in 3,000 workers to massively expand the aluminium works, which now churned out 40 tonnes of the precious metal each week.

The new factory complex drank electricity. If the power supply could be cut, the aluminium works would be stymied. If Glomfjord power station could be put out of action, so would the aluminium production – which meant fewer bombers for the Third Reich. But that had been the chief challenge for the Musketoon planners: how were a dozen men on foot supposed to destroy such a gargantuan structure?

Black and Houghton spread before them those documents they'd brought – diagrams of the plant, annotated sketches of the terrain and the air reconnaissance photos. The SOE had at least one local woman working secretly in Glomfjord, risking everything to gather intelligence, and she had gleaned much of what lay before them now.

The two commanders compared the information they had on paper with what they could see of the target through their binoculars right now. They were in no particular hurry. They would need to rest up during the daylight hours, before attacking under cover of darkness.

'Can you see the valve house?' Black asked, as he handed the glasses to his second-in-command.

Houghton focused on the squat structure at the high end of the pipelines. He nodded. 'How long does it take for the valves to shut off the water? About fifteen minutes?'

'Check,' Black confirmed.

Houghton smiled. 'The station'll be hip-deep by then.'

'Check. At least, let's hope so.'

In an emergency, an automatic cut-off system was supposed to stop the water-flow to the pipelines, to prevent damage below.

Black's plan of attack had the men splitting into two parties. One would hit the power plant itself, placing a series of charges around the giant generating turbines. Once those had been detonated, the second party would blow up the pipelines. Ruptured, they would spew water down the hillside, the force of which should unleash an avalanche of rock and debris onto the structure below.

In that way, a dozen men with rucksacks stuffed full of explosives planned to end aluminium production here – at least for the duration of the war.

Once Black and Houghton had decided on the fine detail, they gathered the men. Black briefed them on his plan of attack, and rounded off by stressing the need to minimize German casualties, to prevent the enemy taking reprisals against the locals. Before setting out they would burn their sensitive documentation, having committed everything to memory.

The discussion then centred upon their escape route. One obvious line of egress lay along the pipelines, which climbed almost vertically out of the fjord. At the top lay the lake from which they took their flow, and beyond this were open mountains. It would entail 200 metres of exhausting ascent, but the climb over hard, bare rock would leave little sign of their passing.

The alternative was to follow a track running along the shore of Lake Fykan, directly above the plant, crossing two rivers before climbing into higher ground. It would entail a far less punishing ascent, but the terrain was soft and yielding, and the raiders were bound to leave signs that they had passed that way.

A vote was taken. The second escape route got the majority of support, although Granlund was adamant that the punishing climb up the route of the pipelines remained the better option.

It now only remained to prepare their weaponry and to gather their strength for what was coming. But, as the twelve saboteurs went about cleaning their pistols and double-checking their explosive charges, events were unfolding in the valleys below that threatened to scupper their entire mission.

The old lady in Bjærangsjoen village had told and retold her story of the midnight boat until there was no one left to hear her. Whispers and rumours had spread. Worse still, high above her village a German patrol had stumbled upon signs that a mystery force had trespassed onto the Svartisen – the Black Glacier.

As luck would have it, the day that Black's force had landed by dinghy, Leutnant (Lieutenant) Wilhelm Dehne, of Glomfjord's 10th German Company, had led his troop onto the high ground above the Bjærangsfjord. His was a routine tasking: he had been sent there to draw up a more detailed map of the area.

Late in the afternoon Leutnant Dehne had stopped for a breather, casually scanning the terrain with his field glasses. Suddenly, he had stiffened. He'd caught sight of a group of men crossing the high ground in single file. There was something distinctly military about their movements, but Dehne was too distant to make out their uniforms or their purpose.

Later, he'd halted beside the Black Glacier, where there were signs of recent activity: a mystery 'camp'. He'd picked up a discarded cigarette packet. The design was unfamiliar to him: it showed a black-bearded sailor inset in a life ring. Around the ring were the words: 'Player's Navy Cut'. The uniform of the sailor looked distinctly English, and Dehne was sure that the words were too.

But what was an empty English cigarette packet doing on the Svartisen, he wondered? And was it linked somehow to the mystery force that he had spotted crossing the high ground in the direction of Glomfjord? He showed the crumpled packet to his men. They shrugged, unconcernedly. Maybe it was a Norwegian brand? But Leutnant Dehne remained suspicious. He pocketed the empty cigarette packet.

Once they were done here, he must report this to his superiors.

Chapter Three

It was 20 September 1942 – a Sunday – when Black prepared to lead his force on the attack. They'd been in Norway for four days, the last two of which had entailed a deeply frustrating delay. The previous night Black had been forced to call off the assault owing to unexpected activity on the Glomfjord. A well-lit ship had been moving up the water, making for the power station.

Black and his men had no idea what the craft was doing or who its occupants were, but maintaining the element of surprise was absolutely critical to the success of their mission. Running into a shipload of German troops wasn't part of the plan. Black had been forced to order his men to retrace their steps into the hills.

They hadn't even made the refuge of their camp before the weather had turned. The wind had moaned and biting rain had sheeted down from a suddenly leaden sky, soaking them to the skin and blinding them to their surroundings. And so they'd endured a sodden and freezing twenty-four hours, before tonight's attempt at the target.

Prior to setting out, Black assembled his men. 'We must do it tonight,' he told them. 'Our rations are gone. To wait any longer without food or rest will only weaken us. If for some reason we're held up tonight, we must do it tomorrow in daylight, even if we have to shoot our way through.'

The knowledge that they were going in regardless was

strangely liberating. It blew away the tension and the frustration, which had been building all through that sodden day. All were relieved that, come what may, it would soon be over. They were too wet and cold to face another night's cheerless delay.

The dozen men slipped down from the darkened heights, approaching the cluster of workers' huts that lay on the shores of Lake Fykan. As they went to edge past, a door opened, spilling light across the flat, wind-blasted terrain. The raiders dropped silently to the ground, keeping their faces pressed into the icy earth, as the distinctive form of a German soldier stepped outside.

Only one amongst them readied his weapon. It was Houghton, and his Sten now had the stubby form of a silencer threaded onto the barrel. Their Colt .45 pistols were useless at anything other than close range. It was Houghton's job to take out any would-be challengers noiselessly.

Apparently the German couldn't see or hear anything suspicious. With a final sniff at the sodden chill of the air he turned back to the warmth inside. Houghton lowered the Sten, and moments later a dozen figures flitted past the lighted windows of the hut and were lost in the far shadows.

To the rear of the huts the pipelines ran past the hump of land separating Lake Fykan from Glomfjord itself, which lay several hundred feet downslope. And there, almost directly below Black and his men, in the crook of land lying at the very end of the inlet, was the power station. From their vantage point the throbbing of the turbines reverberated in their ears.

Black crouched, pulling his men close. He eyed O'Brien. 'We'll leave you here,' he whispered.

O'Brien nodded. He'd taken on the role of blowing up the

pipelines, along with Chudley – now fully recovered from his plunge into the crevasse – and his good friend, Curtis, the erstwhile accountant.

'Watch for my signal,' Black added, 'but don't expect it. You know when to start your fuses.'

'Yes, sir.'

Black reminded O'Brien that they would rendezvous at this point once the attack was done, from where they would make their getaway. Without another word he and his team of eight slipped over the lip of land as silent as wraiths and were gone.

O'Brien turned in the opposite direction, and with Chudley and Curtis on his heel he began to climb. They reached a point just below a sharp junction in the pipelines and settled to their task. Here the pipes, when ruptured, would be pointing directly at the power station – like two massive gun barrels.

From their rucksacks they removed their 'daisy-chain' charges, each a string of chunks of Nobel 808 – the saboteur's explosive of choice. Dirty brown in colour and with a distinctive almond-like smell, Nobel 808 could be cut, stretched, jumped on and even shot at, and still it wouldn't explode. But trigger a small charge embedded within it and . . . *kaboom.*

While Chudley stood watch, Curtis and O'Brien worked to thread the first daisy-chain charge under the nearest pipeline, bringing it back around to encircle it. They could feel the pressure within the thrumming steel sarcophagus as the water thundered through at massive speed. Upon detonation, the charge would blow a section of the pipe, which would cause the water to spew out with incredible force, doing untold damage to all that lay in its path.

When he had fixed a charge to encircle both pipes, O'Brien

attached the thirty-minute fuses. Then he and Curtis rejoined Chudley on watch.

'See anything?' O'Brien whispered.

'Nope,' Chudley replied, through a mouthful of chewing gum. 'Nothing at all.'

They crouched together at the side of the pipelines.

'I could do with a pint,' Chudley remarked, rubbing his hands together in the cold. 'I could drain a barrel full.'

O'Brien smiled. 'Yeah. So could I. Two barrels.'

He glanced at his watch. It had just turned midnight. Down below, Black and his men would be getting busy.

Leaving the main body of his force secreted at the base of the steps that ran along the pipelines, Black had executed a stealthy, three-sixty-degree recce of the plant. The building towered above, utterly dark – blacked out, to hide it from Allied bombers – yet reverberating with a hidden force.

On the far side there was an eerie rumbling and gurgling, as the discharge pipes drained the lake water driving the turbines into the dark and swirling fjord. Having satisfied himself there were no guards in the immediate vicinity of their entry point, Black returned to his waiting men.

'Right, come on,' he whispered, jerking a thumb over his shoulder at the ghostly silhouette.

At the far end of the giant building construction work was under way; the Germans were extending the plant to provide extra power for the aluminium factory. The works were sheeted over by a heavy tarpaulin, and Black was certain that would be their best entry point.

One by one he and his men slipped through the canvas sheet,

finding a latticework of scaffolding inside, plus a makeshift wall of heavy wooden boarding. As Houghton stood ready with his Sten, Black's men heaved on one of the boards, forcing an opening just wide enough for the first figure to wriggle through. The others followed, until only Makeham and Abram – the two keenest Scouts amongst them – remained outside, as guards.

Inside, Black and his men darted behind the cover provided by a stack of wooden packing cases. Each was emblazoned with the distinctive form of a Nazi swastika – it was new machinery to be installed in the plant. Peering around, Black could see along the entire length of the turbine hall. It was brilliantly lit, stretching before them a good thirty metres, and towering above like a vast and echoing cathedral.

As if to enhance the church-like feel of the place, along the sea edge ran eight enormous arched windows, and at the far end rose the pinnacled tower. Along the centre of the hall lay the massive forms of three turbines, each a good four times the height of an average man.

The sheer scale of the place was breathtaking, but Black's attention was drawn to the far end, where the tower rose above the hall: behind a long window was the plant's control room. Inside Black could see a group of German soldiers, along with what had to be Norwegian plant workers.

Black slid back into cover. The piercing whine of the turbines seemed to drill into his head. He knew from the briefings that only three or four Germans patrolled the power plant. Normally, one was stationed at a sentry box at the rear, another at the jetty out front, with a third and fourth inside the plant itself.

Black checked his watch. It was turning midnight. A change of shift had to be under way. Sure enough, the party of soldiers in the control room went their separate ways. After descending the spiral staircase to ground level, they headed for the door to the tunnel, which in turn led beneath the mountain to nearby Glomfjord village. If there was any trouble, it was from that direction that reinforcements would come, for the Germans had a garrison of several hundred billeted there.

Black and his men would have to place and detonate their charges before the alarm could be raised and those troops came rushing to investigate. The tunnel was the key, and Black had a plan in mind to ensure that no Germans made it through. He waited until there was just the one figure – the Norwegian plant manager – remaining in the control room, then signalled his men to move.

Using the generators as cover, they darted down the length of the building. The machines were so massive that their bulk shielded the intruders from the plant manager's view. They reached the third turbine, from where the door leading to the spiral staircase was just a few strides away. Above them, the plant manager was still fixated on his panel of switches and dials.

Black led the final dash, flattening himself beside the doorway, his men doing likewise. They were now invisible to the control room, for the instrument panel prevented anyone from getting close to the window and peering vertically downwards. The seven men took a moment to catch their breath. Months of intensive training and planning had led up to this point, and they didn't want to mess up now.

Black eased the door open, sweeping the space inside with his Colt. Finding it deserted, he stole across to the staircase, his men close on his heels. To their left was a small doorway, which

Black knew led to the entrance to the tunnel. It was there that the nearest German sentries would be standing watch.

Silently, they stole up the spiral staircase, Granlund now at their head. He stepped into the control room. The lone form of the manager was hunched over his control panels, seemingly oblivious to the saboteur's presence. But then he must have sensed something.

He turned, spying the wild, unshaven figures now standing before him, each brandishing a heavy-looking pistol. For the briefest of instants – and despite the exhaustive preparations – Granlund was at a loss for words. What exactly was he supposed to say to his fellow countryman – and very possibly a good patriot – suffering, like so many others, under the Nazi occupation?

Finally, he broke the silence. 'Well, we're here,' he announced in Norwegian. 'We are going to blow up the station and the water pipes.'

The seated figure blanched. His mouth opened and closed soundlessly. Finally he managed to splutter: 'Blow up the station . . . But what about us?'

Granlund explained their intention was to tie up the Norwegian plant workers.

The controller gasped. 'You mean to kill us? To drown us?'

'No, no. We need you out of harm's way, that's all. You'll be safe once you're through the tunnel.'

Granlund ordered the man to make a call on the plant's phone system. 'Telephone every Norwegian in the building and tell them to come to this room, right away. Go on, now. Hurry!'

His hands visibly shaking, the controller did as he was ordered. Shortly, three figures – Norwegian workers – entered, to be given a similar talking-to by Granlund. Meanwhile, Houghton and several others dashed back to fetch the explosives.

As Granlund led the shocked Norwegian workers down the staircase, he glanced into the generator hall. Already he could see figures crouched beneath the first of the massive turbines, fixing the charges of Nobel 808 to those places where the machinery was most vulnerable.

Granlund ushered the workers towards the doorway leading to the tunnel. No sooner were they through it than the Norwegian spied a German sentry. Before he could react Granlund opened fire, drilling the guard with several shots from his Colt. But a second grey-uniformed figure, who was standing at the tunnel entrance, turned and sprinted away.

A short distance down the tunnel there was a bend and, before Granlund could react, the sentry had dashed around it. It had been an impossible shot for the Colt in any case, Granlund told himself. But the guard would be sure to raise the alarm. There was an emergency buzzer at the village end, just inside the tunnel entrance, which was linked directly to German headquarters. They needed to put their tunnel-blocking plan into action, and urgently.

Granlund gestured towards where the German guard had fled, exhorting the Norwegian workers to follow as fast as humanly possible. The tunnel would be blown up, he warned, so they needed to run like the wind. With a clatter of boots on concrete, the workers were gone.

Outside the darkened plant the roar of the turbines and the gurgle of the escaping water had served to mask Granlund's gunshots. The German sentry stationed at the wharf and the one at the guard hut had heard nothing untoward. But inside, the tension had ratcheted up several levels.

Once Granlund had warned Black of the German sentry's escape, the Canadian captain had dashed the length of the generator hall, urging the demolition parties to greater speed. On a floor above the power station he discovered a long corridor, with rooms leading off to either side. Inside were more Norwegian workers – some with their families – and even a Swiss engineer.

Doors were dragged open, and the sleep-befuddled occupants ordered to flee down the tunnel. From all directions phones started ringing, as concerned parties in Glomfjord village called to check what on earth was happening. Black ordered the phones ripped from their sockets. The last thing he needed was someone talking, and revealing the diminutive size of his raiding party.

As the last of the figures fled down the tunnel, one dragging a heavy suitcase after her, the distinctive form of Fred Trigg – Londoner and amateur boxer – followed. In his hands he grasped a cylindrical grey device: a smoke canister. When Trigg reckoned he was midway between the plant and the village, he set the canister on its flat base on the tunnel's floor.

Crouching, he pulled the pin and let the retainer clip spring free, at which moment the canister began to pump out a thick greyish-black smoke. On an open field of battle the smokescreen it created would last no more than three minutes. But in the stagnant confines of the tunnel it should linger for hours.

Unable to carry the weight of explosives needed to blow up the underground passageway, as well as the plant and pipelines, this had been judged the next best option. The cloud of acrid smoke, coupled with the fearful reports that would even now be reaching German ears, should put anyone off using the tunnel.

At least that was what Black and his men were banking on.

At the far end of the tunnel the first German soldiers entered.

Warned by cries that 'British saboteurs' were about to blow up the power station, they'd rushed to investigate. But they moved cautiously, and they made it no further than the first, choking clouds of smoke, before hurrying back the way they'd come and punching the alarm button.

In the turbine hall the saboteurs were feverishly busy. Sweating and breathless from exertion, Houghton and his team had threaded a set of charges around each of the pieces of giant machinery.

Fresh from checking that all civilians had been evacuated, Black strode in. 'Get your timer pencils going!' he barked.

Houghton needed no second urging. The 'timer pencil' fuses – each the shape and length of an average pencil, and made from brass with a collapsible copper cap – were designed to give the saboteurs just long enough to finish their work and to make a getaway.

Houghton and his sabotage team placed theirs in pairs, just in case one malfunctioned. They were set to a ten-minute delay – the absolute minimum. Figures hurried down the line of charges, crushing the copper caps to trigger the fuses, before turning for the doorway through which they had made their entry into the plant.

Black ordered everyone but himself up to the rendezvous point at the pipelines. He would round up Abram and Makeham, the two men on watch, and ensure that no Germans made it through the tunnel. In theory, if the enemy rushed the building they still had time rip out the timer pencils and prevent the explosions.

Houghton and his saboteurs were just about to leave when their gaze fell upon the wooden crates of equipment, freshly painted swastikas on their sides. They had a few chunks of Nobel

808 remaining, and they figured they had time. It took just ninety seconds to attach those charges to the crates, after which Houghton led his team in a mad dash towards the heights that reared above.

Black meanwhile had rejoined Abram and Makeham, his two sentries. 'See anything?' he whispered.

'No, sir, not a thing,' came the reply.

Black led them past the end of the building, into the shadows at the base of the mountain. There they watched and waited, eyes on the tunnel and weapons at the ready.

Some 200 metres above them, O'Brien and his team crouched at the pipelines, straining their eyes. If they caught the distinctive flash of a torch beam cutting through the darkness, it would be Black signalling that something had gone wrong with the main sabotage effort. If that happened, O'Brien had orders to blow his charges, no matter what.

He was to do so, even though the resulting avalanche of water and debris would bury his fellow raiders alive.

Chapter Four

In the generator hall the cupric chloride acid ate away at what remained of the delicate timer pencil components. The thinnest wire finally severed, releasing a spring-loaded mechanism that hammered down the timer pencil tube, striking a percussion cap and so triggering the explosion.

It was 12.35 a.m. and the first sign of Black's success was a series of blinding flashes that flared out of the power station and pulsed across the fjord, throwing sea and mountains into momentary stark, jagged-edged relief. As the explosions blew out the massive arched windows in a storm of shattered glass, so the blast wave swept across the fjord and thundered up the mountainsides.

Even at O'Brien's eyrie-like vantage point, the shockwave hit with surprising force. So powerful was it that glass in the windows of the houses that lined the fjord was blown inwards, up to two miles away. And then the roar of the explosion washed over O'Brien, Chudley and Curtis in an awe-inspiring whirlwind of sound.

In his apartment overlooking the fjord, *Oberleutnant* (First Lieutenant) Wilhelm Kelle just happened to be at his window the moment the charges blew. The initial explosion was followed almost instantly by a second, and flames could be seen licking through the generator hall. *Oberleutnant* Kelle knew instantly that something had gone badly wrong at the plant, one that it was his responsibility to protect.

He was unsure if this was some kind of an accident or . . . sabotage. Moments later the air raid siren sited at the aluminium factory began to wail, slowly at first and then with increasing urgency. The rhythmic howl echoed across the fjord's dark waters, serving to alert *Oberleutnant* Kelle that somehow, Glomfjord was under attack.

Crouched next to the pipelines high above the plant, tousle-haired man of action Chudley grinned. He gestured at the power station. 'Ooooo, didn't she glow! Wasn't it lovely!'

The explosions were the signal that O'Brien and his men had been waiting for. They bent to their task, crushing the ends of the timer pencils on their own charges. Black and his sabotage team now had thirty short minutes to make it out of the inlet, before the pipelines blew.

Fuses set, O'Brien turned to his men. 'Come on, if you want to get out of here alive . . .'

There was no easy route to follow. If they strayed downslope, they risked getting caught in the devastation caused by their own handiwork. O'Brien turned east, leading Curtis and Chudley across a rock face slick with running water. They were making for the rendezvous with Black and his men, who even now would be climbing up from the fjord.

As the air raid siren continued to blast out its unearthly, echoing wail, the three parties – Houghton's, O'Brien's and Black's – converged.

'Okay, Joe?' Black hissed. 'Is everyone here?'

'All here,' Houghton confirmed.

Having checked that O'Brien had set his fuses, they made for the rough track that led along the wooded shore of Lake Fykan. Soon, twelve men were moving eastwards at a fast jog, their rubber-soled boots whispering over the uneven, rocky surface. With Granlund in the lead they crossed the first footbridge and powered into the darkness.

It was rough going, but everyone in Black's force knew that speed was of the essence. Relieved of the massive weight of their explosives, they should be able to move fast, and if they could put enough distance between themselves and the German garrison they might well evade capture. They'd have to hole up come daybreak and sneak further away at nightfall, but escape seemed within their grasp.

Behind them, there was a sudden eerie concussion. The blast was muffled by thick woodland, but still the flash of the explosion threw a pulse of harsh light across the high ground to either side. No one doubted that O'Brien's pipeline charges had just blown.

As if to confirm their suspicions, moments later a blinding white flare floated into the dark sky over the power station. Whatever might be happening there, it looked as if a total emergency was being declared.

High above the power plant the two pipelines had been ripped asunder. The initial burst of water exited with such force that it plucked boulders from the ground, threw them high into the air, which landed throwing off sparks visible for several kilometres down the fjord. The massive deluge that followed ripped trees out by the roots, shovelled up gravel and rocks by the truckload, and sent it all plummeting downhill.

The first of the water and heavy debris hit the rear wall of the power plant like a fusillade of cannon fire. As the murderous cascade carved a clearer path down the mountainside, the pressure and rate of flow strengthened. Soon, it was hammering into the rear of the power station with incredible force.

Within minutes a vast heap of debris had piled up against the back wall, the sheer weight threatening to collapse the building. Water surged in through broken windows and doorways, carrying with it a sludge of mud, gravel and detritus. It hit the first of the generators, throwing off clouds of thick steam as it made contact with the mangled metal; where the Nobel 808 charges had exploded, twisted and shattered steel and copper was still glowing hot.

In the aluminium factory further down the fjord, the lights flickered and went out. All machinery ground to a standstill. And as the floodwater surged around the power station, seeking an exit into the fjord, some found its way into the tunnel leading to Glomfjord village, flooding its smoke-filled interior.

At the far end of that tunnel, *Oberleutnant* Kelle had ordered twenty-five German troops to board the *Storegutt*, a small freighter that he had commandeered. The tunnel was out of action, and *Oberleutnant* Kelle was desperate to know the worst. He'd heard reports of British saboteurs at work, and he ordered the freighter's captain to take them across the fjord.

As the *Storegutt* chugged out into the normally pitch-dark inlet, Kelle could see light spilling across the water. Each of the power station's huge blacked-out windows had been blown out. A separate generator house provided back-up electricity, and it had escaped whatever havoc had been wreaked on the main plant, hence the light.

More worrying still, there was a deafening roar coming from the direction of the pipelines above, as if a gigantic express train was thundering down a long and echoing tunnel. It bored into *Oberleutnant* Kelle's ears. He had no idea if the British saboteurs were still at the plant. Were they lurking in cover, waiting to hurl grenades onto the *Storegutt* as soon as she steamed within range?

The freighter nosed cautiously towards the power station's wharf. No British commandos leapt out of the shadows. Instead, one of the German sentries was there to receive the ship, but he seemed to have little idea of what had happened, or where the British saboteurs might have fled to.

Oberleutnant Kelle made a mental note to deal with him later. He split his men into three groups. Two were to search the power station and its grounds. The third was to climb up the pipelines, to see if the saboteurs had fled that way and if they might be cut off.

While Kelle headed for the power station control room, his second-in-command, *Leutnant* Wilhelm Dehne, led his party of men into the generator hall. For a moment *Leutnant* Dehne stood stock still, surveying in shock the scene of devastation. The massive generators had been ripped out of the iron plates that held them to the floor, and gravel, mud and broken plaster were churning around in the floodwaters.

Hardly had Dehne had time to take in the devastation when a salvo of bullets splattered into the water at his feet. He and his men dived for cover behind one of the wrecked turbines, as more shots hammered out. Unbelievably, the fire seemed to be coming from the shattered windows of the power station control room, where his commander was supposed to be with his force.

Leutnant Dehne could only presume that the saboteurs were still in the plant. As he readied his weapon, his mind flipped back to an image from a few days earlier, when he had been surveying the terrain above Bjærangsfjord. He didn't doubt any more that the group of figures in single file that he'd spotted high on the mountains had been the British saboteurs.

Before Dehne could return fire, there was an almighty crack, and the rear wall of the power station caved inwards. The sheer weight of sodden debris piling up behind it had finally become unsupportable. Water thundered in, surging to chest height, and in the force of the flow *Leutnant* Dehne and his men were swept back outside.

The two German commanders, sodden, bruised and enraged, gathered to confer. The bullets fired at *Leutnant* Dehne and his men turned out to have originated from his own side. Some of *Oberleutnant* Kelle's men had mistaken Dehne and his party for British saboteurs sneaking around the plant. *Leutnant* Dehne gave voice to a growing concern: would the British saboteurs try to escape via the same route he now believed they had trekked in – via Lake Fykan?

Oberleutnant Kelle ordered Dehne to take his force in that direction and to find out. A second boat, the *Skarsfjord*, was inbound with more soldiers, so Kelle had troops to spare.

But even as the *Skarsfjord* docked, the power station was plunged into darkness. The floodwaters had found their way into the separate generator house, shutting down the plant's electricity supply. Everything was thrown into dark confusion.

At the rear of the plant, *Leutnant* Dehne was not to be deterred. He led his force on the first leg of the climb towards Lake Fykan. The normal route following the stairway running alongside the pipelines was unusable; it had been transformed into a raging torrent. Instead, he was forced to take them up the rock face to one side.

It was steep and dark and flecked with spray from the water spurting from the ruptured pipes, but still Dehne and his men pushed relentlessly onwards. Below, more grey-uniformed figures slung their rifles on their backs and set hands and feet to the cold rock. The hunt was on.

A way to the east, a breathless Granlund rounded the end of Lake Fykan. He'd been running for a good hour now. Behind him in the darkness Black and his men were strung out in single file. Granlund hit a steep slope where the track started to climb and his pace slackened.

Further east and towering above them lay the dark mass of the Navervann Mountain. If Granlund could navigate them past that, they would be into true wilderness terrain, and the enemy would have little idea in which direction they might have fled. But between their position and open country lay a knife-cut gorge, with a lone suspension bridge running across it.

Granlund needed to lead the saboteurs directly to that bridge, and in the thick darkness he feared that he would miss his way. He spotted a cluster of workmen's cabins. He decided to stop and ask for directions. Once he'd woken from his sleep, one of the Norwegian workers sketched a rough map for Granlund, showing the route to the vital bridge.

As Granlund took the map and thanked him, Joe Houghton and Djupdraet appeared – drawn to the lights now burning in the cabin. But so too were the leading German soldiers. There were two, and somehow they had overtaken Black and the rest of his men. They entered the wooden building, only to come face to face with Djupdraet and Houghton, who were about to leave.

A brutal fight at close quarters ensued. Houghton went to

open fire, but the nearest German managed to knock the Sten's unwieldy silencer aside, and the rounds went wide. As he and Houghton grappled with each other, the second German hurled his bayoneted rifle at Djupdraet, the blade slicing through the Norwegian's stomach.

Djupdraet sank to his knees, but somehow he kept his cool. He grabbed the rifle with both hands and pulled the bloodied blade out. On his feet again he staggered out of the hut into the darkness.

Black was drawn to the commotion. He ducked into the hut, but came under fire from a German rifle. Acting on instinct, he managed to corner the enemy soldier – the one who had bayoneted Djupdraet – behind the hut's stove, and shot him with his Colt.

In the kitchen, Joe Houghton was still grappling with his adversary. Finally he managed to twist the Sten's barrel up enough and he pulled the trigger. The German was blasted away from him, slumping to the ground. Presuming both enemy soldiers to be dead, Black and Houghton backed away from the hut and slipped into the shadows.

Quickly, Black called his men together. It was time to split up, he told them. 'They're after us! Choose yourself a couple of lads and go!' They should make for the Swedish border, Black urged, and with all speed.

In groups of twos and threes the eleven men – Djupdraet was too badly injured to move – melted into the darkness. O'Brien, Trigg and Granlund pushed east, heading for the elusive bridge across the gorge. Others began to head southwards, seeking safety in altitude, struggling through stands of stunted trees.

Fairclough and Yorkshireman Dusty Smith were pushing

through tangled woodland when Smith decided that he had to turn back. He'd been tasked to give morphine to the badly wounded Djupdraet, but in the confusion he had forgotten to do so.

Fairclough waited for Smith to rejoin him, only to hear powerful shots cut through the darkness. Rifle fire. It had to be the enemy, for only they carried such weapons. Remembering Black's orders to get away as fast as possible, Fairclough turned back to the slope and resumed his exhausting climb alone.

Back at sea level, the *Skarsfjord* and *Storegutt* were continuing to ferry German troops to the plant. Scores were sent into the high ground. The gunfire drew them onwards. They converged on the source of the firing, throwing a ring of steel around the base of the mountain up which they believed the British saboteurs had fled. Still more kept arriving. They were ordered to advance through the ring, drawing the noose ever tighter.

It was *Leutnant* Dehne who discovered the injured Djupdraet. The wounded Norwegian was found lying in the darkness, unarmed, and clearly in great pain. Finally, Dehne was face to face with one of the figures he had spotted six days earlier as they had crossed the mountains. The German officer crouched over the wounded man.

'Comrade, don't shoot,' Djupdraet implored, in English.

Dehne bent lower, hooked his arm around the wounded man's shoulder and helped him to the nearest cabin. There he made sure that Djupdraet's injuries were properly dressed, before he turned back to the hunt.

In all the darkness and confusion, Black's force had split in two different directions. While Granlund, O'Brien, Trigg and

Fairclough had fled east, into the shadow of the Navervann, Black and the rest of his men had veered south, up the slopes of the Middago Mountain.

On the Middago's perilous slopes Joe Houghton found himself fighting a desperate rearguard action. The only one of the raiders armed with anything more substantial than a pistol, he squirted off the odd burst from his silenced Sten, only to receive a barrage of rifle fire in return.

The Sten was designed for fighting at close quarters and the Colt .45s were next to useless in such terrain; the British commandos were hopelessly outgunned. Eventually, one of Houghton's pursuers managed to shoot him in the right forearm. His ammunition all but expended, and his trigger arm bleeding profusely, a pain-racked Houghton turned and hurried upslope.

Black and his men climbed ever higher. As they neared the summit the first rays of dawn filtered through the thinning trees. They crested a ridge, only to find themselves on the lip of a shallow crater. Ffity metres across, this was the summit of the Middago Mountain. By now they were all out of ammunition, and still the sound of relentless pursuit echoed from below.

Black surveyed the terrain before them. The crater was mostly bare of vegetation, so there was little cover if they attempted to dash across. He was readying his men to move when the first figures appeared at the crater's edge. Their helmets and rifles were unmistakable, and soon Black could tell that they were surrounded.

Ducking behind some boulders, he ordered his men to dismantle and bury their weapons. Strangely, the Germans still held their fire. Then a voice rang out. Whoever it might be was speaking fine, if heavily accented, English.

'Come out! We don't want to shoot anyone!'

It was *Oberleutnant* Kelle. He repeated the order. Black and his men held their silence. No one moved.

'Come out! You are surrounded. You cannot get away.'

Still no response.

Kelle ordered one of his men to throw a hand grenade. He indicated where he wanted it to fall. It thumped into the open area at the crater's centre, a good distance from the commandos, but the message it sent was clear.

Kelle repeated his order. Finally Captain Black raised himself, hands in the air. One by one the others did the same and were taken prisoner. At gunpoint and bound at the wrists they were herded back down the mountainside. As they reached the final descent, the Canadian captain gazed upon the power station. Water still thundered downslope from the ruptured pipelines, and the rear of the generator hall had been transformed into a mass of sodden boulders and debris.

Momentarily, Black's teeth flashed a smile. *They'd done it. Mission accomplished!*

He wondered why the automatic valves hadn't shut off the water flow. By rights, they should have done so fifteen minutes after the explosions. There was no obvious explanation, but it was immensely gratifying. Black and his men were still smiling as they were led aboard the *Storegutt,* to be shipped across to Glomfjord village.

Once safely incarcerated in the *Ortskommandantur* building, *Oberleutnant* Kelle's headquarters, the commandos' hands were untied. *Leutnant* Dehne was put in charge of searching Black.

Acting on a whim, his memory drifting to the crumpled packet of Player's cigarettes that he had found near the Black Glacier, he offered Black a smoke.

'Have a cigarette. A German cigarette! That's all I have for you.'

Black demurred. He'd far prefer a pull on his trusty pipe.

On *Oberleutnant* Kelle's orders, German soldiers had climbed up to the valve house and ordered the flow to be stopped. The local workers stationed there claimed that the valves were out of order. The German troops had no option but to climb to a higher point where a barrier could be lowered manually. It was only then – and with the reservoir lake drained almost dry – that the flow was finally halted.

By that time, Black and his men had got just an inkling of what fate might hold in store for them. At first, they were questioned firmly but politely by one *Oberst* (Colonel) Franz Henschel, who had flown in directly from regimental headquarters in Fauske, seventy kilometres north of Glomfjord.

Black and each of his men responded to the interrogation in the same manner.

'Did you come by aircraft?'

'Perhaps.'

'By parachute?'

'Maybe.'

'By boat?'

'Not necessarily.'

'Over the mountains?'

'Possibly.'

Nothing was given away.

But then a contingent of SS arrived. The SS officers told *Oberst* Henschel that he was to hand over the captives to them. Henschel refused. For now at least he prevailed. That evening, Black and his six men were loaded aboard a ship, en route for Norway's third city, Trondheim. They were being sent to Akershus Prison, a facility under the control of General Nikolaus von Falkenhorst, Commander-in-Chief of German forces in Norway.

General von Falkenhorst had an interesting résumé. With craggy features and a hawk-faced demeanour, he was both a decorated First World War veteran and something of a favourite of Hitler's. Born a Polish noble, he had changed the family name – Jastrembski – to the Germanic-sounding Falkenhorst – 'falcon's nest' – to better suit his standing as a senior officer in the German military.

In May 1940, when the Führer had ordered that Norway be invaded, von Falkenhorst had been given twenty-four hours to come up with a master plan. The German general had sketched out a scheme of attack based largely upon a Baedeker travel guide that he'd found in a local bookshop, and the invasion of Norway was launched.

Von Falkenhorst was fiercely loyal to the Führer, but he was also a soldier of the old school, and disapproved of the SS and Gestapo's terror tactics. It was far better to fall into his hands, for with von Falkenhorst the Musketoon captives would at least be extended the protections afforded to bona fide prisoners of war.

As the ship carrying them steamed out to sea, so the Musketoon seven had left behind one of their number in Glomfjord: mortally wounded, Djupdraet would not last out the next forty-eight hours. Shortly before passing away he would tell the Norwegian doctor caring for him: 'Some of us must die . . . if Norway is to live.'

They'd also left behind a local German commander, *Ober-leutnant* Kelle, who was mystified as to how the attack could have proven so successful. Surely, eight men could hardly have wreaked such havoc and destruction. There had to be others, and the *Ober-leutnant's* instinct – plus a growing body of evidence – told him that they must have landed somewhere along the Bjærangsfjord.

He sent ships packed with soldiers to scour the length of the fjord. At the same time, he despatched spotter aircraft to fly over the mountains and snowfields to the east, in case the rogue saboteurs had escaped that way.

Come hell or high water, Kelle was determined to find the saboteurs. The power station lay in ruins. His career was hanging by a slender thread. Hunting down the British commandos – every last one of them – was one of the few ways in which he might redeem himself.

Granlund, O'Brien, Trigg and Fairclough – the four raiders still at large – had reached the summit of the Navervann Mountain just prior to dawn. It was freezing cold, and to make matters worse the men fancied a storm was in the air. Without food, they had only Benzedrine tablets with which to fuel their march; unless they could get help – and, crucially, sustenance – they knew that they were finished.

Fairclough shared out the last of the cigarettes. Barely had the four lit up when a pair of German aircraft swooped low across the summit of the Navervann, their engines roaring in the fugitives' ears. The saboteurs dived for cover as the spotter planes turned beyond the peak, and came back for a second run.

The four men – hungry, cold and hunted – were forced to lie low most of that day, as the German aircraft quartered the skies above. Come nightfall they set off eastwards, towards Sweden, and into the teeth of what would soon become a howling blizzard of a storm.

As those brave young men put their shoulders into the biting wind, so in London a grey-haired, balding, fifty-something former Scoutmaster sat hunched over his desk at the SOE's Baker Street headquarters. An alumnus of Scottish public school Glenalmond College – which had transformed him from a sickly infant with swollen glands into the young man who would captain the school rugby team – Major John Skinner Wilson had devised the SOE's entire training programme.

Between 1923 and the outbreak of the war Wilson had been the director of training of the Boy Scouts Association, and the SOE had sought him out in large part due to his Scouting experience. When called for 'special duties' – the euphemism for going into the SOE – Wilson had told the Scouting Association that his new role was 'considered of sufficient importance to justify the Boy Scouts Association in releasing me'. He'd promised that he was not 'deserting the ship', and that he looked forward to a time when 'the clouds roll by . . . and all our energies will be required in the re-establishment of peace and goodwill.'

Wilson had proved admirably suited to his new role at SOE, and in recent months he'd been transferred to their very active Norwegian Section, making Musketoon very much his baby. With his weather-beaten demeanour, prominent nose, balding pate and greying hair, age set him apart from the rank and file at the SOE. By his own admission he often used it to get his own way – others might outrank him, but few were his senior in years or, for that matter, experience.

At Glenalmond, Wilson had earned the somewhat unflattering nickname of 'Tubby'. Nowadays he unarguably did share a stout, bulldog-like profile with the SOE's chief sponsor, Winston Churchill. He'd earned a corresponding reputation for stubbornness and tenacity.

After Glenalmond School, Wilson had joined the then Colonial Police Service in India, where he'd become a specialist in counter-espionage and guerrilla warfare. When not riding elephants or hunting, he'd spent much of his time living with the local Santhal tribes, learning to track animals – and humans – and to hunt with bow and arrow. On one such sojourn he'd been scarred badly on the nose, neck and back by a marauding tiger, one that he'd had to fight off with his bare hands. That episode had earned him a new nickname; to the locals he became 'Baghmara' – the leopard killer.

At school, in India and in the Scouting movement, Wilson had learned to appreciate the camaraderie of like-minded souls. Dry-humoured and implacable to a fault, he cared for his men as if they were his own flesh and blood. He had special reasons to view the Norwegians under his command as 'family'. Wilson traced his lineage back to ancient Norwegian ancestors, and he felt a certain kindred spirit with the Viking warriors he was sending into battle.

As Brigadier Colin McVean Gubbins, then the SOE's operations director, would write, Wilson was 'in day-to-day control of . . . his comrades in Norway, and to him and his staff they looked for guidance, for warning of Gestapo activity, for supplies to enable them to live and to fight – in fact he was their father and mother.'

On 17 September news had reached Wilson of Musketoon's fortunes thus far. A 'Most Secret' report had landed on his desk.

Originating from the *Junon*, it read: 'Black, Houghton and party were landed at 22.30 hrs on September 15th . . . at Point marked X on the map'. The report anticipated that the attack might take place, 'between tomorrow and Sunday'. But several days had passed since then, and he'd had no word of how the mission might have fared.

That was all about to change.

A first message was telegraphed from Norwegian sources, signalling the success of Musketoon. It concluded: 'The attack was carried out . . . with such precision it is believed to be highly improbable that the power station can be put in proper working order again . . . The aluminium works, which have just been greatly enlarged, will also be idle for the duration of the war.'

This was fantastic news and Wilson felt vindicated. Musketoon had done all it had set out to do, which might help silence some of the SOE's more vocal detractors. But the mission's success – it was hailed as being the first of its kind – had been achieved at some considerable cost.

The Germans had calculated that two tonnes of dynamite would have been required to cause the devastation at the power plant. They believed local Norwegians must have provided the explosives, for no one could have carried such a weight over the Black Glacier. Reprisals against the Glomfjord villagers were swift and brutal.

As the story of the raid broke in the Norwegian underground press and was picked up by the wider media, Wilson learned of the probable fate of his men. A Reuters report proved remarkably detailed and accurate. It spoke of Black's force splitting up in an effort to escape the Germans, and of them running out of ammunition. 'Eight are believed to have escaped,' the Reuters report concluded, 'the other six being taken prisoner.'

In fact, eight had been captured and four were on the run.

Wilson waited anxiously for further news, expecting the British press to pick up the scent. Normally, such small-scale clandestine operations were cloaked in utmost secrecy, but with the story of the raid breaking he thought it best to prepare a short communiqué to brief the British media.

It began: 'An operation, small if the numbers taking part in it are considered, but large in its consequences, took place hundreds of miles to the northward, on the coast of Norway.' It went on to detail the perilous approach taken to the plant, and concluded by saying: 'The destruction wrought was in the highest degree effective.'

Effective it most certainly had been, but Musketoon was quick to attract its critics. Few in power liked a shake-up of the 'natural order of things', and the SOE had its share of enemies. The regular military complained that the SOE stole missions that should rightfully fall to them. The Secret Intelligence Service argued that the SOE trod on their toes, especially when it came to running agents in the field.

Musketoon was criticized as being badly planned, rushed and lacking in proper intelligence. Worse still, the team was accused of being successful only 'due to a combination of luck and skill on behalf of the C.O.'

The SOE and Combined Operations Headquarters hit back with a pithy riposte: 'It is not agreed that a party could land on a strange coast; reach a Power Station, blow it up extremely thoroughly, and four of them escape . . . merely by a combination of luck and skill . . . Meticulous preparations were made.'

To hell with their detractors, was Wilson's attitude. For him, Musketoon was proof that Churchill's edict to enforce a 'reign of terror down the enemy coast' was achievable. But lessons would need to be learned: the escape plan had been woefully inadequate; the raiders had been close to exhaustion, even prior to trying to make their getaway; and more training in mountain warfare was necessary, as was better equipment – particularly when it came to rations and weaponry.

Still, Musketoon had succeeded beyond Wilson's wildest dreams.

Indeed, few could foresee the full impact, or the unintended consequences, of this one daring operation. Unbeknown to all at the SOE and their fellow strategists at Combined Operations Headquarters, Black and his men had just played a seminal role in one of the greatest dramas of the entire war: the race to stop Germany acquiring an atom bomb.

To the south of the Glomfjord power station lay a similar, if larger, power plant, which was also the Nazis' single greatest prize in the race for nuclear supremacy. Armed with a nuclear weapon, Hitler would doubtless secure victory: in one fell swoop he would acquire the capacity to cause practically unlimited devastation.

The wildly successful Glomfjord raid would provide a model for how to hit this second – nuclear – target. Yet equally, the fallout from Operation Musketoon would lead to that target being transformed into a veritable fortress, which was something the Allies could ill afford.

For in the autumn of 1942 the Nazis had seized a frightening lead in the race to build the bomb.

Chapter Five

In December 1938 the German physicist, Otto Hahn, aided by his young assistant, Fritz Strassmann, had succeeded in splitting the uranium atom. The process was termed 'fission', and the stunning import of this ground-breaking discovery electrified the scientific community worldwide.

Uranium is the heaviest naturally occurring element. In Denmark, Niels Bohr, the pre-eminent nuclear physicist of the day, described the uranium atom as being like a balloon pumped full of water. When a neutron is fired at the uranium 'balloon' it forms a dumb-bell-like shape – two spheres under great pressure joined by a thin waist. Once the tension becomes too great, the waist snaps and the two are flung apart with unimaginable force.

That is nuclear fission.

The amount of energy released by fission was unprecedented. One scientist suggested that a single cubic metre of uranium ore contained enough energy to lift a cubic kilometre of water twenty-seven kilometres into the air. Or to put it another way, atom-for-atom, nuclear fission promised to be a hundred million times more powerful than any conventional means of energy production.

There were two potential practical applications. One was the generation of unforeseen amounts of power to fuel businesses, homes and even aircraft and ships. The other was to harness the vast amounts of energy released by fission as a new, and terrifying, form of weaponry.

With their exceptional engineering capabilities, coupled with their recent scientific breakthroughs in the field, the Germans were seen as being well advanced in the harnessing of this futuristic source of power. And under Hitler's authoritarian – and expansionist – rule, the Third Reich could command the vast resources required to do so. That at least was the fear.

The great unknown was whether the Germans – whether Hitler and his war ministries – had serious aspirations in the nuclear field. The first hint of an answer would not be long in coming. Two months before Hahn had split the atom, Britain's then prime minister, Neville Chamberlain, had signed the Munich Agreement, which effectively handed over Czechoslovakia to Germany.

Churchill, then languishing in the political doldrums, had warned against this episode of appeasement. At Munich, Britain had faced the choice between 'war and shame'. It had chosen shame. It would get war later, and on far worse terms. In private he lamented: 'We not only betrayed our Czech friends; we gave that guttersnipe new slingshots.'

By 'that guttersnipe' Churchill was of course referring to Adolf Hitler, yet at the time he had little idea what potentially catastrophic power those Czech 'slingshots' might wield.

For years, Churchill had been a voice in the wilderness, railing against German expansionism – warnings that mostly fell on deaf ears. He was jeered in Parliament when he raised the issue of Nazi rearmament. But by March 1939 the German conquest of Czechoslovakia was complete, and with it Hitler had shown his true colours. In short order the German military had seized control over the coveted Czech armaments industry, and, more importantly in terms of the nuclear issue, Hitler had won control over the Joachimsthal mine, then Europe's only source of uranium.

Joachimsthal is an ancient spa town in what was then northern Czechoslovakia. Situated in the Ore Mountains, close to what had been the border with Germany, it had long been a centre of mineral extraction. But in recent years, in addition to the rich quantities of silver, nickel and bismuth, uranium ore had been discovered at Joachimsthal.

Upon seizing Czechoslovakia almost all exports of uranium ceased overnight. The Joachimsthal mine was taken over by Auer Gesellschaft, a specialist German company dealing with rare earths, uranium and other related compounds.

Auer Gesellschaft began industrial-scale production of high-purity uranium at Oranienburg, a town in north-west Germany. In one fell swoop, and with Britain's mute connivance, Hitler – 'that guttersnipe' – had got his hands on the single most important raw material needed to produce nuclear power, or to build the world's first atomic bomb.

The achievement emboldened those German scientists working in the field. On 24 April 1939, Paul Harteck, a top physical chemist, wrote to the Reich War Ministry. He proposed 'the creation of explosives whose effect would exceed by a million times those presently in use'. The country which first developed the atom bomb would have 'a well-nigh irreversible advantage' over all other nations, he proclaimed.

The Reich War Ministry listened closely to what Harteck was saying. Less than six months later, and on the very day that Germany invaded Poland, Harteck was one of a circle of top nuclear experts invited to form the *Uranverein* – the Uranium Club. The men of the *Uranverein* were charged with pursuing the German nuclear project, the *Uranprojekt*, with all due alacrity. Working under the auspices of the *Wehrmacht* – the German armed forces – they were to build an *Uranmaschine* (a nuclear reactor) from which a bomb would follow.

Along with Harteck, Werner Heisenberg was one of the leading German scientists working in the field. At the tender age of thirty-one, Heisenberg, a theoretical physicist, had won the Nobel Prize. But in recent months he had come under repeated attack in *Das Schwarze Korps*, the newspaper of the SS, for being a 'white Jew', and all because he had spoken out about the oppression of Jewish scientists.

With Heisenberg's elevation to the *Uranverein,* he became one of the Reich's untouchables. Operating out of the renowned Kaiser Wilhelm Institute in Berlin, under fellow nuclear scientist Kurt Diebner, Heisenberg began building the Third Reich's first experimental reactor. Heisenberg calculated that he would need a tonne of uranium for his purposes, and the Joachimsthal mines were a ready source of the raw material he required.

It didn't take a wild leap of the imagination, or even a sophisticated grasp of nuclear physics, to envisage what a man like Hitler might be capable of if armed with a nuclear weapon. Churchill feared that Hitler would use it again and again, until every democracy in the West became a fascist state under iron-fisted Nazi rule.

Churchill had long been fascinated by science. This, plus his ability to envisage how the practical application of new discoveries might decide the fortunes of the war, marked him out from other politicians of the day.

As early as 1924 he had speculated about the potential impact of a nuclear weapon. 'Might a bomb no bigger than an orange be found to possess a secret power . . . to blast a township at a stroke?' Churchill knew that vast amounts of energy were locked inside the atom. 'There is no question amongst scientists that this gigantic source of energy exists,' he wrote. 'What is lacking is the match to set the bonfire alight, or it may be the detonator to cause the dynamite to explode.'

In August 1939, Albert Einstein – himself a refugee from the predations of the Nazi regime – had written to US President Roosevelt, alerting him to the nuclear threat. He warned that a 'nuclear chain reaction in a large mass of uranium . . . could be achieved in the near future . . . extremely powerful bombs of a new type may thus be constructed.'

Roosevelt had felt concerned enough to brief Churchill. But what neither leader knew was how advanced Germany's nuclear programme had become. By the time war had been declared the shutters had fallen down on all nuclear research, and it was far too late to try and recruit agents capable of penetrating German laboratories, metal refineries and engineering plants. Britain found herself woefully lacking in credible intelligence about German nuclear activity, and, if anything, America knew even less.

Yet at the same time rumours of Nazi Germany's 'super weapons' stoked fears. The Führer boasted of possessing secret weapons against which no defence was possible. 'Do not deceive yourselves,' Hitler thundered. 'The moment may come when we shall use a weapon which is not yet known, and with which we ourselves could not be attacked.'

British intelligence chiefs tried to assess what Hitler might be referring to. Amongst the weapons which they suspected the *Wehrmacht* was developing were gliding torpedoes and rockets, plus 'the use of atomic energy as a high explosive'. They concluded that Hitler intended to break Britain by aerial bombardment and the use of 'bombs containing a new and secret explosive'.

In such a febrile atmosphere – and in the face of such an intelligence vacuum – concern turned to alarm. In the summer of 1939, Churchill had written to Britain's Secretary of State for Air, raising the issue of nuclear power providing the Germans with 'some sinister, new, secret explosive with which to destroy their enemies'. Churchill had concluded that such concerns were 'without foundation', for it would not be possible to develop such a weapon in the near future.

But what if he was mistaken? By the winter of 1939–40 the argument was turning. Churchill wrote again to the secretary of state for air, this time demanding to know: 'What danger is there, pray, that atomic bombs might fall on London?' The concern embodied in that letter reflected how, in just a few short months, his position had changed.

One of Churchill's key influences at this time was William Stephenson, the quiet Canadian who sought to shore up Britain's fortunes and to stiffen her resolve. With the covert backing of Churchill, Stephenson ran a shadowy intelligence network, and he would become one of Britain's foremost spy chiefs, earning the code-name Intrepid.

But for now Stephenson worried that there were those in Britain who still hoped that a deal might be cut with Hitler – that peace was negotiable. Stephenson, like Churchill, knew other-wise. Both were committed to waging a war in which surrender was unthinkable. Stephenson devoted his vast personal fortune to that struggle, and the principal battleground on which he would fight was the nuclear one.

And that would bring Norway firmly into his – and Church-ill's – sights.

100 kilometres north-west of Norway's capital, Oslo, is the region of Telemark. It is dominated by the high-altitude Hardanger-vidda. Cursed with tempestuous weather, the bare and windswept terrain has an unforgiving, snowbound climate. Europe's largest plateau, it harbours one of Norway's biggest glaciers, and is also known as the region of the Barren Mountains.

Spring meltwaters drain off the plateau into Lake Møs, Nor-way's twelfth largest lake. From there the wild Måna River plunges through the knife-cut chasm of the Vestfjord Valley, a thirty-kilometre rollercoaster of white water and cascading falls. Set a good way down that valley, at Vemork, was what was then the world's largest hydropower station. It was operated by the Norwegian company Norsk Hydro.

As with the Glomfjord power plant, the Vemork hydro station channelled water from a highland lake (Lake Møs) through pipe-lines running down precipitous slopes, to drive turbines. The chief difference between the two concerns was their scale: if Glomfjord was big, Vemork was gargantuan. Eleven steel pipes – as opposed to two – snaked down from the heights, powering turbines that churned out an almost unlimited supply of electricity.

The Vemork plant serviced a very different set of outputs to Glomfjord's aluminium plant: it powered an adjacent hydrogen production factory, which was then the biggest on the planet. From Vemork the hydrogen gas was piped to the nearby town of Rjukan, nestling in the heart of the Vestfjord Valley, where it was used to produce nothing more sinister than agricultural fertilizer.

But in recent years Norsk Hydro had started producing a

second output at Vemork – an obscure and somewhat sinister-sounding substance called 'heavy water'.

Heavy water is extremely rare: it occurs naturally, but only at the concentration of one molecule of heavy water for every forty-one million molecules of normal water. Its more scientific name is deuterium oxide. As with ordinary water, each molecule contains two hydrogen atoms and one oxygen atom. The difference lies in the mass of the hydrogen atoms: in heavy water these are weightier, possessing an extra neutron. To illustrate its weightiness, an ice cube of heavy water will sink when placed in a glass of normal water.

In the years prior to the war, Norsk Hydro had decided to use some of Vemork's excess power to manufacture heavy water – an energy-intensive and time-consuming process. By running a current through vats of normal water, heavy water could be separated out, in a process known as electrolysis.

Norsk Hydro's directors had little idea what the market might be for heavy water. They worked on the assumption that they'd perfect the production process and the customers would follow. In the winter of 1939–40, business was far from booming, so the company was surprised – very – when the first significant demands for heavy water came from Nazi Germany.

From the very first they were suspicious. When the directors asked the Germans what they might need the heavy water for, the response was very vague: 'scientific experimentation'. But Norsk Hydro was in something of a bind. The massive German industrial complex I.G. Farben owned a major stake in the company, and it was ostensibly I.G. Farben that had put in the order.

I.G. Farben would go on to earn untold infamy during the war. Hitler would contract out his chemical weapons programme to I.G. Farben, which manufactured lethal mustard gas, and the even more deadly nerve agents tabun and sarin. Their secret factories would be built by the millions sent to the concentration camps. With these 'slaves' being worked to the brink of death, I.G. Farben also developed a new type of gas – Zyklon B – to be used to exterminate them, in the gas chambers.

And so the evil circle would be complete.

In the spring of 1940 it was I.G. Farben that sought out Norsk Hydro's supplies of heavy water. Their people, working secretly on behalf of the *Uranverein* – the Uranium Club – had demanded an initial shipment of twenty-five kilos. This would be enough to prove a vital element of Heisenberg's research: his reactor required a 'moderator', within which to sandwich layers of uranium.

At its simplest, a moderator fuels the chain reaction of nuclear fission. As the uranium atoms break apart, they shoot out neutrons that in turn split other atoms. Those neutrons are far more likely to cause the atoms to divide if they are – somewhat paradoxically – slowed down. Heavy water has the capacity to curb the neutron's excess energy. As a bonus, a reactor utilizing heavy water could run on naturally occurring uranium, which wouldn't need to be refined.

Heavy water was fast becoming the *Uranverein*'s chosen moderator. In response to I.G. Farben's demands, a reluctant Norsk Hydro agreed to send the first, 25-kilogram shipment, which represented several months' output. Before long, I.G. Farben were back demanding more: they needed 100 kilograms of heavy water, month on month.

By now, the *Uranverein* had allocated heavy water a code name: SH200. Its existence and its role in nuclear research had become a closely guarded military secret for the Reich. Unsurprisingly, no explanation was forthcoming from I.G. Farben as to why they sought such a massively increased supply.

War had already been declared, but this was prior to the German invasion of Norway, which gave Stephenson the chance to slip into the country on a very special mission. The quiet Canadian spent time with the Norsk Hydro managers, intimating just enough about what chilling use the Nazis might have for heavy water to convince them that the exports had to stop.

For now at least, the *Uranverein*'s supply of heavy water had run dry. In truth the Norsk Hydro's management took little convincing: they had no desire to fuel Nazi Germany's quest for an atom bomb. Quite the reverse: it was a horrifying proposition. Stephenson had also talked the company's directors into handing over diagrams of the layout of the plant. If ever Vemork's heavy water production might need to be stopped, those were sure to come in useful.

Back in Britain, Stephenson went about convincing Churchill to use what powers he had at the Admiralty to ensure that no further heavy water found its way into the hands of the *Uranverein*. 'Deny it to the Germans and we stop that line of progress,' he advised Churchill.

The southernmost tip of Norway sits some 800 kilometres to the north of Germany. Between the two nations lies Denmark, plus the Skagerrak Sea. Despite the logistical challenges, Norway had to be squarely in the sights of an increasingly belligerent Nazi Germany, as did its supplies of heavy water.

Churchill's response was twofold. He sent mine-laying ships into Norwegian waters, to mine the routes most likely taken by German vessels shipping SH200 southwards to Germany. Plus he launched Strike Ox, an operation designed to prevent vital supplies for Nazi Germany from leaving Scandinavian shores, 'by methods which will be neither diplomatic nor military'.

Officially, the target of Strike Ox was the Swedish port of Oxelösund, an ice-free harbour from which iron ore was being exported. The ore was rich in phosphorus, which was essential to the German process for making high-grade armour. The supposed aim of Strike Ox was 'leaked' to the Swedish intelligence services. Its head, Walter Lindquist, duly filed a report with German agents, alerting them to British plans to blow up the Oxelösund docks.

In truth, the entire enterprise was a carefully crafted cover. Shipments of plastic explosives were smuggled into Sweden, disguised as modelling clay for a Swedish sculptor. Oxelösund wasn't to be touched. The Nobel 808 was spirited into Sweden with heavy water in mind.

Should Germany seize Norway and the Vemork SH200 plant, the SOE would have to get a force into the area and blow it sky high.

Chapter Six

The code name of the individual perched at the submarine's open hatch was Cheese. Agent Cheese would go on to be one of former Scoutmaster Wilson's star agents. But right now Cheese – one of the first SOE operatives ever inserted into occupied Europe – was preparing to infiltrate the area of the Hardanger Plateau overlooking the Vemork heavy water facility.

That's if he managed to get ashore.

The submarine had already made one abortive attempt to bring him in to land. Early on their third day at sea, Odd Starheim – Cheese's real name – had been called to the periscope, to see if he could pick out his intended landing point amidst the ice-bound peaks and fjords. The vessel had surfaced, only to be pounced upon by a German warship, depth charges tearing apart the waters to either side of her.

They had dived to depth and succeeded in evading the enemy, and there they awaited nightfall. Under cover of darkness the vessel had sneaked in as close as the captain dared before surfacing, and then Starheim's collapsible canoe had been lowered into the heaving blackness of the sea. Unfortunately, the submarine's crew had mistakenly placed Starheim's heavy rucksack in the bow, which drove the canoe down at the front, and the frail vessel had shipped a good deal of water.

Eager to be off, Starheim jumped in and paddled away, only to find that he was getting swamped. He searched, but there was no bailer. Turning for where land had to be, though he could make out precious little amidst the sea spray and the darkness, he paddled for all he was worth. Successive waves swept over the vessel, threatening to capsize her. The ordeal was made all the worse by the fact that Starheim had caught flu during the submarine's crossing: he was feverish, and the water crashing over his flimsy craft chilled him to the bone.

It was January 1941, and he could hardly have chosen a more perilous time of year to attempt such a landing. Ice ringed much of the Norwegian coastline, and he would need to choose his landing point most carefully. As well as his bulging rucksack, Starheim carried with him a leather suitcase, containing one of the SOE's newly developed portable wireless kits for making contact with London.

He couldn't put ashore just anywhere; he needed to make an unobserved arrival. But due to the perilous state of his canoe – now sloshing inches deep in water – his favoured landing spot proved unreachable. Battling bitter seas and freezing winds, Starheim was finally able to reach a remote stretch of coastline on the island of Ulleroy.

Soaked to the skin and miserably cold, he dragged his heavy vessel ashore. With the help of a sympathetic local fishermen he was able to ferry himself and his pack from there to one of the few ice-free stretches of the mainland. Leaving his radio set with the fisherman, and having made arrangements to retrieve it later, he shouldered his pack and headed off on foot.

The long and exhausting trek inland was all the more difficult in that Starheim passed by several houses of people that he knew, but he could halt at none of them – not even the home of his grandparents. He needed to find somewhere remote, where no one would recognize him, before he commenced operations, for he had already earned a degree of infamy in occupied Norway.

Superficially, there was nothing immediately striking about Agent Cheese. He had a shock of wild sandy hair above pronounced brows and a prominent nose. But look a little closer, and it was the firm, steely determination in his eyes that marked him out as something rather extraordinary: he was cool and unflappable, as quiet men sometimes are.

Starheim was the son of a Norwegian ship owner, and an experienced seaman in his own right. He was also a wanted man. Having fought against the Nazi invaders of Norway, Starheim had commandeered a boat, which he christened *The Viking*, and escaped – navigating the long and perilous voyage to Scotland. There he was amongst the first to sign up with the Linge Company, where his exploits had drawn the Germans' attention, making him a marked man.

Starheim's task on returning to Norway was to recruit an intelligence-gathering network, so he could report back to London on all aspects of the German occupation. He was also to arm and train cells of resistance fighters, so they could take action against specific targets if called upon by London to do so. A vital element of Cheese's mission was to penetrate the security around Vemork, in an effort to ascertain exactly what the Germans were doing with the heavy water produced there.

On 9 April 1940 German forces had rolled into neighbouring Denmark. In one of the shortest campaigns of the war, the Danish government capitulated after just six hours. Pockets of Danish fighters had battled heroically, but they were outgunned on all fronts. With Denmark taken, Norway was left open to attack.

The very next day German parachutists had landed at Oslo's main airport, and the Norwegian king and his government were forced to withdraw to a base near the Swedish border. There they had received an ultimatum from the Germans: if they didn't cease their resistance against the German Army and Navy in Norway, the nation's capital, Oslo, would be bombed to ruin.

With Luftwaffe warplanes darkening the skies, the threat was very real. The Norwegian king, decisive and unyielding, issued his riposte: 'No'. The subsequent fighting raged for several weeks, but the German military, under the command of General von Falkenhorst, proved unstoppable. And on the heels of the soldiers had come the scientists – nuclear physicists making a beeline for the Vemork heavy water plant.

In a little over a year the Third Reich had seized control of the two raw materials essential to building a nuclear weapon: uranium, and now heavy water. In theory, there was nothing to stand in the way of their producing the world's first atomic bomb. All they needed was to overcome the scientific challenges, and even in that respect their recent territorial conquests had yielded further advantage.

In the Danish capital, Copenhagen – a city now occupied by German troops – lay the Institute of Theoretical Physics. Its founder was Niels Bohr, who many considered to be the grand-father of atomic research. In 1922 he'd won a Nobel Prize for his work on atomic structure and quantum theory. Amongst other top scientists that Bohr had mentored during the pre-war years was Werner Heisenberg, now the chief mover and shaker at the *Uranverein*.

Bohr's career was distinguished by a seemingly unshakeable passion for sharing scientific knowledge, and a somewhat unworldly belief in pacifism and non-violent resistance. Craftily, the German occupiers allowed Bohr to continue uninterrupted with his work. A string of German scientists called at Bohr's laboratory, breathing good fellowship. Bohr was encouraged to press forward with research that was now quietly under their command.

In Bohr, the 'Germans had the man whose theoretical work was the basis of the bomb', warned Stephenson. 'One of the world's great atomic scientists was lost inside the German fortress ... In a spirit of scientific inquiry Bohr was discussing the atomic bomb with those who wanted to use it to conquer the world.'

In May 1940, just a month after the German invasion of Norway, British intelligence received a disturbing report. The Germans had demanded an increase in heavy water production to 1,500 kilos a year. German scientists made it clear that SH200 was considered 'vitally important for their war effort'. There was worse to come.

On 10 May Germany invaded Belgium, with Holland and France shortly to follow. As their troops overran Olen, a town to the north-west of the country, they seized the largest stocks of uranium in all of Europe. Olen was the headquarters of the Belgian mining firm, Union Minière du Haut Katanga, a company that then controlled the world's richest uranium deposits. The company had its main refinery at Olen, and it was there that German forces had just seized well in excess of one thousand tonnes of uranium ore.

Intelligence on this potentially catastrophic development made for grim reading. A report chronicled how 'several hundred tonnes of crude concentrates had been removed from Belgium'. The destination for that ore was the Auer Gesellschaft refinery at Oranienburg – the same facility that was taking the Czech ore.

Bar a handful of nations – like neutral Spain and Switzerland – Hitler's Germany now controlled the whole of Western Europe, plus all her uranium and heavy water. The Führer's lightning advance yielded one significant boost for Britain: it propelled Winston Churchill to power. In Parliament Neville Chamberlain was confronted by Conservative politician Leo Amery, a long-time opponent of appeasing Hitler. Pointing an accusatory finger, Amery quoted Oliver Cromwell: 'You have sat too long here . . . In the name of God, go!'

In May 1940, just days before German forces swept to the Channel, Churchill was made prime minister. He offered the British people nothing but 'blood, toil, tears and sweat.' With his eleventh-hour ascent to power, science moved to centre stage. The Royal Society, the world's oldest scientific academy, compiled a central register of 7,000 scientists who might contribute to the war effort. Britain's new leader appointed the physicist Frederick Lindemann to be his personal scientific adviser.

The two men were hugely dissimilar, and to many their long and enduring friendship was an enigma. Lindemann was a tall, ascetic, chicken-necked individual, contrasting markedly with Churchill's compact, bulldog-featured, cigar-chomping vibrancy. Teetotal, vegetarian and deeply intellectual, Lindemann would be called to lunch by Churchill with the irreverent cry of 'beet-root time!' Lindemann's sarcasm and cold reserve made him unpopular, but Churchill was fiercely protective, for Lindemann made complex science accessible.

He could 'decipher scientific developments on the far horizons,' Churchill would remark, 'and explain to me in lucid, homely terms what the issues were.' Yet in the spring of 1940, neither man was under any illusions as to how great a march the Germans might have stolen in the race to obtain the atom bomb. Recently, two eminent scientists had penned what became known as the 'Frisch–Peierls Memorandum'. In it, Otto Frisch and Rudolph Peierls – German Jews who had fled to Britain – outlined the scientific basis upon which a 'radioactive super weapon' could be built. The report was groundbreaking, revelatory and frightening in equal measure.

> The energy liberated in the explosion of such a super-bomb is about the same as that produced by . . . 1,000 tonnes of dynamite . . . It will . . . produce a temperature comparable to that in the interior of the sun. The blast from such an explosion would destroy life in a wide area . . . it will probably cover the centre of a big city.

It went on to describe the horrific effects of the radiation such a blast would cause. 'It decays only gradually and even for days after the explosion any person entering the affected area will be killed. Some of this radioactivity will be carried along with the wind . . . several miles downwind this may kill people.

'The super-bomb would be practically irresistible', the report concluded. 'If one works on the assumption that Germany is, or will be, in the possession of this weapon, it must be realized that no shelters are available that would be effective . . . The most effective reply would be a counter-threat with a similar bomb.'

Frisch and Peierls had been working in Germany until the mid 1930s, and so their warning came from the heart of that nation's nuclear endeavour. They predicted that such a weapon might be achievable within a two-year time frame. Lindemann – Churchill's 'beetroot time' scientific adviser – was sceptical about the time scale, but not about the science. He added his voice to Frisch and Peierls' warnings, and Churchill listened.

Stephenson – Intrepid – added urgency to those warnings. Initial research suggested that it would require the labour of 20,000 workers, half a million watts of electricity and $150 million in expenditure to build such a bomb. A totalitarian state run by a dictator who now controlled most of Western Europe could command such resources, and in the concentration camps Hitler had access to millions of slaves.

Churchill was aghast at the thought of such a 'super-bomb' in Nazi hands. It would enable Hitler to conquer continents, making world domination a terrifying reality. No one knew how advanced the German nuclear project might be, but two things were certain: they had stolen a year or more's start on the Allies, plus they had seized control over the key raw materials – the uranium and the heavy water.

On 19 July 1940, Hitler had made Britain what he termed his 'final peace offer', posing as a 'victor speaking in the name of reason'. The response was flung back at him via a broadcast in German on the BBC: 'Let me tell you what we here in Britain think of this appeal . . . Herr Führer and Reichskanzler, we hurl it right back at you. Right back into your evil-smelling teeth.'

Hitler reacted by issuing Directive No. 17 to his commanders: 'Establish the necessary conditions for the final conquest of England.' The Führer added the following, chilling rider: 'I reserve to myself the right to decide on terror tactics . . .'

A large part of Churchill's 'hurling it right back' into Hitler's 'evil-smelling teeth' would be the founding of the SOE. 'How wonderful it would be if the Germans could be made to wonder where they were going to be struck next', Churchill declared, 'instead of forcing us to try to wall in the Island and roof it over'. That July he formed the euphemistically named Ministry for Economic Warfare, a cover organization for the Special Operations Executive.

From the very first, the SOE's remit was to think the unthinkable and to tear up every known rule of warfare. Churchill's first minister of this newly founded outfit was Dr Hugh Dalton, a Labour member of his coalition government. Though hailing from a very different political background, Dalton was as willing as any to consider unconventional means of striking down the enemy.

'We have to organize movements in enemy occupied territory comparable to the Sinn Fein movement in Ireland', he declared. 'We must use many different methods, including industrial and military sabotage ... continuous propaganda, terrorist acts against traitors and German leaders, boycotts and riots ... We need absolute secrecy, a certain fanatical enthusiasm, and willingness to work with people of different nationalities.'

SOE's unremarkable, grey-faced 64 Baker Street headquarters had a brass plaque set into the wall. It announced this to be the 'Inter-Service Research Bureau' – the most innocuous-sounding cover name that Dalton et al. could think of. SOE operators – plain-clothed, and many with little or no military background – slipped down a shady alleyway to gain access. They referred to themselves as hailing from 'the Org', 'the Firm', or perhaps most fittingly, 'the Racket'.

Scores of Special Training Schools (STSs) were established in the country mansions that pepper rural Britain to prepare Churchill's secret army for the dirty war that was coming. Crucially, the SOE's existence was to be kept utterly off the books: its missions were 'secret and independent', and deniable in the extreme.

At first, the military high command was resentful of this new upstart. The SOE's senior positions were invariably filled by those with military backgrounds, but experience in irregular warfare was prized above all. After that, the SOE welcomed bankers, academics, poets, professors, sportsmen, journalists, novelists, film producers and playwrights – civilian amateurs, many of whom had never fired a shot in anger. Even more controversially, it sought out magicians, conjurers, gangsters, safe-breakers, street-fighters and thieves to teach its recruits the new means of waging warfare.

The SOE founded its own gadget department, charged with developing weaponry and other equipment suited to its revolutionary form of fighting. Code-named MD1, it was nicknamed 'Churchill's Toyshop', due to the Prime Minister's boyish enthusiasm for everything it produced. The SOE also had its own propaganda department, the ultra-shady Political Warfare Executive.

At the Thatched Barn, near Borehamwood, there was a Special Training School devoted entirely to camouflage and subterfuge in all its forms. Part of its role was to equip agents with authentic-looking 'local' clothing and personal effects, before they were sent into occupied Europe. Various other stations dealt with the forgery of passports, identity papers and ration books, plus the concealment of innovative weapons in seemingly everyday items.

The SOE operatives would come to revel in their nicknames – Churchill's Secret Army, or the Baker Street Irregulars. But amongst its detractors the SOE earned a very different reputation: it was the 'school for bloody mayhem and murder'. To the top brass, many of whom were veterans of the Great War, the SOE's black arts and guerrilla tactics were 'ungentlemanly' and 'un-soldierly', and out of keeping with the British military's chivalrous tradition.

Churchill, quite simply, did not give a damn. His aim was to 'release the fury of rebellion' in the occupied nations, using all necessary measures. To do so, the SOE would need to surpass the Germans in cunning, surprise, boldness and black endeavour. From the labyrinth of tunnels running beneath Whitehall – resembling dungeons, and known as 'The Hole in the Ground', which now housed Churchill's War Room – he held forth, and directed his secret army.

Lit by flickering candles and lanterns, and with the walls running with damp, an odd-looking system of tubing snaked around the ceilings of the War Room and beyond; within it, canisters containing messages pinged from one ministry to another, propelled by compressed air. And behind Churchill's battered wooden chair sat one of many stacks of shoeboxes: the War Room's filing system.

One was labelled 'B/SOE/1: Formation of Special Operations Executive'. Inside lay a red file outlining the SOE's mandate in the bluntest possible terms. It called for 'a reign of terror conducted by specially trained agents and fortified by espionage and intelligence, so that the lives of German troops in Occupied Europe be made an intense torment.'

With America yet to join the war, Churchill appointed William Stephenson as his secret go-between with Roosevelt. Stephenson's task was to carry crucial Enigma intercepts to the US president, and to build a covert intelligence partnership with the Americans. To that end, he was charged with setting up the SOE's US headquarters, in New York, with himself at its head, thus formalising somewhat his shadow espionage operations.

He was empowered by Churchill to move against Britain's enemies whenever and wherever he saw fit, using covert diplomacy or clandestine warfare, including targeted assassinations. Churchill also sent Stephenson to America with a plain message for President Roosevelt. 'He [Hitler] has a good chance of conquering the world,' Churchill warned. 'All he needs is that a small island capitulate. Tell the President that!'

Stephenson made exhaustive preparations. He assembled intercepts and captured documents that proved beyond doubt the Third Reich's policies of mass murder and enslavement. Orders issued as long ago as 1933 laid down the basis upon which human beings were to be segregated according to Hitler's warped ideals of 'racial purity'. Carefully selected Germans were to sire pure-bred infants – the *Übermensch*, the Aryan 'master race'.

Children deemed worthy of 'Germanization' were to be selected to join this programme. The rest were to be enslaved or left to die. This was no idle conjecture. Stephenson had painstakingly gathered the undeniable proof: the written orders, the propaganda films, the textbooks and the bureaucratic forms via which the human race was to be 'sanitized' with Teutonic thoroughness.

Stephenson was utterly single-minded: he was driven by a

relentless fear of this blind, twisted fanaticism. But most of all he was haunted by the fear that those who espoused such aims might engineer the world's first atomic bomb.

'If Germany conquers Britain,' Stephenson declared, 'the way is clear for the development of this weapon with which Hitler can blackmail the rest of the world . . . Give him respite, and he will make this new weapon of horror.'

It was clear that Britain would have to join the race to build the bomb, but many doubted whether the besieged nation had the time, the resources or the manpower to do so. In the meantime, it would fall to the schoolboy adventurers of the SOE to try to halt Hitler's nuclear programme at source – where the raw materials were being mined, and the heavy water distilled into vats for shipping to the Reich.

Into the heart of this atomic storm had sailed Agent Cheese.

Chapter Seven

Agent Cheese proved prolific. Perhaps too much so. From his secret radio transmitter hidden at a remote Norwegian farmstead his messages winged their way to London. Dozens of them. The intelligence they yielded was revelatory, providing crucial break-throughs in an invisible war.

His radio signal transcripts – many marked in hand-written capitals 'TRANSLATION OF CHEESE TELEGRAM' – came through daily, sometimes several in one day. They proved timely, detailed and accurate.

During the last [two?] weeks 25,000 Germans have arrived in Oslo. The inner harbour at Oslo will be a large naval base . . . Bergen has had orders to billet 20,000 men.

There is 10,000 tons of aero-petrol in several tanks on the most northern Island of STEILENE. At GRANERUD there are 3,000 tons of aero-petrol. No A.A. guns. At FAGERSTRAND there are some 3,000 tons of aero-petrol. This 16,000 tons is the greater part of aero-petrol in Southern Norway.

Battleship V. TIRPITZ and THE PRINZ EUGEN left Bergen at 1300 hours on June 5th, presumably en route to the north. On June 6th 40 warships in the port of Bergen. 75,000 parachute troops have just arrived in Soerland. This points to an attack on England.

The SOE had established its own radio transmitting–receiving station, situated in the quaint village of Grendon Underwood, in Buckinghamshire, where the topography was suited to long-distance communications. From there, Agent Cheese's messages were sent to the SOE's Baker Street headquarters by teleprinter, where they met with both enthusiasm and concern for Cheese's safety:

Your information excellent and we are grateful. Can you inform us whether JU.87 dive-bombers have appeared in Norway and if so where are they? Take utmost care not to compromise yourself.

The dangers of detection were manifest. By the spring of 1941 – several months into Cheese's clandestine activities – the Germans were making intensive efforts to track down the illicit transmitter that was sending intelligence to the enemy from under their very noses. They did so using 'direction-finding' (D/F) equipment, of which they appeared to have established three distinct kinds.

The permanent D/F stations in the region consisted of a series of wooden huts, each with a triangular aerial set atop the roof. When Agent Cheese started transmitting, a D/F station would intercept his signal and attempt to triangulate it with its sister stations. Where the intercept bearings crossed, there would be the clandestine transmitter.

Increasingly, portable stations were also in use. These consisted of a heavy battery, the D/F set itself, plus a tubular aerial three metres high with four branch antennae. It required two men to carry and operate the equipment, and once a transmission had been detected the mobile set could radio an alert to headquarters, sending the Gestapo racing out in the hope of seizing the radio and its operator.

The Gestapo would close in, guided by short-range, lightweight D/F sets. Wearing headphones, the operator carried it strapped to his chest, and brandished a hand-held detector. When the target signal was located, the detector would start to flash in that direction, so leading the Gestapo to the operator's very door.

During the first months of operations, Starheim's actions were characterized by an imperturbable high-spiritedness and good humour. In one episode, the SOE mixed up two experimental air-drop containers with the real thing. The practice containers had been packed with bricks; the real things with food, ammunition and other supplies.

The containerloads of bricks were mistakenly parachuted into southern Norway. The messages that came back from Cheese and his wider network were classics: 'Would like you to know we have plenty of rocks in Norway,' read the first. The second: 'Have received container with secret weapons, but no instructions how to use them. Please send with next drop.'

But on 10 June 1941 the tone of Agent Cheese's communication suddenly changed. No longer was Starheim the cool-headed, fearless master of intelligence. Instead, he sent an alarming message to SOE headquarters:

GESTAPO hunting about for me. [Four words undecipherable] to take bearings of me. They will not get me alive. All for King and Country. Ends.

Cheese's messages rarely contained undecipherable passages – meaning the Morse must have been hurried or scrambled. Cheese sounded distinctly rattled. Former Scoutmaster Wilson – Starheim's handler – replied immediately, urging extreme caution:

> In view GESTAPO search be careful and only send absolutely essential information. Do not fail to listen on scheduled times if safe, even when you have no message.

'Scheduled times' – skeds – referred to the set periods during the day when headquarters were to listen out for Cheese's messages, and vice versa. If an agent missed one of his or her regular slots, that would be the first hint that something had gone wrong. SOE listened out for Cheese's skeds, increasingly fearing the worst.

The Gestapo continued to search for the isolated hamlet where Starheim had set up base. With its rough-hewn floor, crude wooden roof, a single window, plus electrical wiring trailing along the walls, Cheese's headquarters hut was spartan indeed. At a bare wooden desk he hunched over the leather suitcase containing his wireless kit, tapping out his Morse signals. On the desk lay a Luger pistol, shiny with use.

Cheese knew that a D/F station had been set up on a high point just two kilometres away, but still he kept transmitting. While he posed as a simple farm hand, in truth he was orchestrating a network of high-level sources across southern Norway: at the airports, the railway terminus, the docks and, crucially, at the Vemork SH200 plant, there were loyal Norwegians risking their lives to feed intelligence to him.

At first light on 15 June the Gestapo came calling. It was 5 a.m., and luckily Starheim hadn't yet started his early morning sked. As he prepared his equipment a car pulled onto the rough track adjoining his clandestine headquarters. The vehicle had Oslo plates, so it clearly wasn't local. To access the dirt road the five occupants – who were all dressed in dark suits and hats – had to dismantle a fence. This gave Starheim his opportunity.

The much-sought-after Agent Cheese strode across to where the five strangers were standing, telling them that the fence would have to be put back in place once they were done. In the rear of the vehicle he spied a portable D/F set. That, plus their terrible Norwegian, gave them away as Gestapo. They stayed for only as long as it would normally take Starheim to send his messages, and then they were gone.

Starheim knew now how close they were to cornering him. He'd sent over one hundred messages during the last few months. In one, he'd warned of the mighty German battleship, the *Bismarck*, breaking cover from Norwegian waters on what would prove to be her last voyage. British warships had managed to track and to sink her.

That message had led to one British admiral declaring of Starheim: 'Who is this boy? I would serve with him anywhere.'

Agent Cheese clearly needed to go off air. But two days later a courier arrived at the farm with vital intelligence. Starheim felt compelled to communicate this to London, despite the risks. Early on the morning of 18 June he sent several messages, summarizing what he had learned.

The German Army have requested the Swedish State Railways for 200 trains with approximately 3,200 coaches for troop transport . . .

1,000 men are stationed at KLEVENS and are exercising the taking of the Island of Gismeroy using horses. The horses carry machineguns. Similar exercises at other places . . . Constant night manoeuvres . . .

The messages reflected concern that the Germans were preparing for an invasion of Britain, using Norway as a jumping-off point, hence the urgent warning. But Cheese had spent too long on the air. At his very next sked he fired up his set and listened for any messages. He heard what appeared to be the SOE home station calling, repeating that there were no messages for him. Without thinking, Starheim responded, confirming that he had no messages for London either.

It was only when the transmission ended that Cheese realized that he had just replied to what had to be a Gestapo radio operator, entrapping him. London wouldn't call saying it had 'no messages'. What was the point? Knowing how closely he was being hunted, the home station was even less likely to do so right now. Starheim knew that the time had come to flee.

Even as he rushed to hide his radio equipment in a cave deep in the woods, the Gestapo surrounded the hamlet. They brought with them scores of German soldiers. A house-to-house search was begun as the enemy swept the valley. An old woman came rushing from a neighbour's house: three men there had been arrested, she told him. The searchers were closing in.

Starheim realized he would need cover if he was to have any hope of escape. He sent for Sofie Rorvig. The young and pretty Rorvig was his courier, but today she would need to act a very different role. Taking no luggage, so as not to arouse suspicion, Starheim stepped out with Sofie at his side. Arm in arm they strolled through the hamlet – young lovers apparently unconcerned at all that was happening.

Starheim managed to bluff his way past the Gestapo and the German troops as they probed every haystack, barn and isolated outbuilding. He knew that his headquarters hut would be found. He just hoped he'd left nothing incriminating. With Sofie's help he made it to a nearby railway station, but here there were more Germans standing guard. Just before the Oslo train pulled away, he managed to sneak through the barrier and slip aboard.

Starheim decided to lie low for a while in the city. He knew what a close call he'd just had. He'd escaped by the skin of his teeth, and he didn't doubt how aggressively he was being hunted. He had lost his radio equipment and he was effectively on the run: there would be no more messages from Agent Cheese for a good while now.

While Starheim played his deadly game of hide-and-seek with the Gestapo, the situation at the Vemork heavy water plant had become ever more pressing. The last thing the SOE needed right now was Cheese going off air. Recent intelligence from Vemork was hugely worrying. The source was one Jomar Brun, a senior engineer at the plant, and Starheim had been instrumental in its reaching SOE headquarters.

Amongst other things Brun had revealed was the address to which the SH200 supplies were now being sent: 'Forschungsabteilung 1, Hardenbergstrasse 10, Berlin.' This turned out to be the office of none other than physicist Kurt Diebner, the head of the *Uranverein* – the Uranium Club – proof positive of what the heavy water was being used for.

In the spring of that year German officers from the *Wehr-*

wirtschaftstab Norwegen – the War Economy Staff for Norway, the organization tasked with expropriating the nation's natural resources for the benefit of the Reich – had paid a visit. They'd made it clear to Brun that he was being made 'personally responsible' for the heavy water production. Brun, a fierce Norwegian patriot, was forced to perform a high-wire act.

'I must continue my work as usual lest the Germans should conceive any suspicion,' wrote Brun in one intelligence briefing. 'On the other hand I must try to fish out of the Germans everything they might know.' At the same time he had to try to 'delay the production itself' of the SH200, 'and the German plans for increasing it.'

In May 1942 Brun's duplicitous role seemed to grow more challenging still. A string of high-level scientists from the Kaiser Wilhelm Institute came calling, with ambitious plans to increase the output of SH200. Brun was to raise heavy water production to some 3–4 tonnes per year, with more increases to follow.

With his sparse frame, flimsy spectacles and rounded features, Brun was hardly the archetypal hero figure or double agent. But the intelligence he yielded was vital, providing tantalizing clues as to what the German nuclear scientists were up to in the iron fortress of Nazi Europe. In fact the Vemork plant was proving the Allies' single greatest window into the hidden Nazi nuclear project.

In Britain, those few in the know grew increasingly uneasy. That summer Lindemann – Churchill's scientific adviser – delivered a trenchant report to Britain's wartime leader.

'It should be possible for one aeroplane to carry a somewhat elaborate bomb weighing about one ton, which would explode with a violence equal to about 2,000 tons of TNT,' wrote

Lindemann. 'A plant to produce one bomb a week will cost anything up to £5,000,000 . . . whoever possesses such a plant should be able to dictate terms to the rest of the world.

'It would be unforgiveable,' concluded Lindemann, 'if we let the Germans develop a process ahead of us, by means of which they could defeat us in war or reverse the verdict after they had been defeated.'

Churchill concurred: a project to build a British nuclear weapon had to be set in motion, irrespective of the cost.

To that end Churchill formed 'Tube Alloys' – the cover name for the organization charged with catapulting Britain into the atomic race. But with Lindemann offering at best 2–1 odds that such a bomb could be built in time, it was critical that German efforts should be stymied wherever possible, and especially when their nuclear aspirations appeared ever more ambitious.

In a report marked 'Most Secret' British intelligence laid out the new theatre in which the battle for nuclear supremacy was being fought. Entitled 'German Interest in the Belgian Congo', it recorded: 'Since early 1941, at least, the German Secret Service have taken a constant interest in the Belgian Congo.' It described repeated attempts 'to insert agents, some of whom have been of a . . . high calibre, equipped with secret means of communication.'

One such German agent had been caught with a concealed radio set in his possession, plus invisible ink. His mission had been to communicate with fellow agents based in supposedly neutral Spain, sending intelligence onwards to the Reich. The Belgian Congo was the chief location from which Britain – and shortly the USA – would seek to secure supplies of uranium. Unsurprisingly, Germany also had designs on the mineral riches of that country.

At the turn of the year, Jomar Brun – Vemork's fledgling double agent – was called to Berlin. At Kurt Diebner's headquarters he was presented with plans to raise heavy water production exponentially, no matter what the cost. Physicist and ardent Nazi Diebner, flanked by German Army officers, demanded that two new SH200 plants be built, attached to two smaller hydroelectric stations.

Those hydro plants – Såheim and Notodden – lay in the same rugged valley as Vemork. Together, the three plants would produce some 5,000 kilograms of heavy water yearly – the new target set by the Reich. More worrying still, Brun was shown around the laboratories of the Kaiser Wilhelm Institute. There the *Uranverein* scientists unveiled a new process for manufacturing heavy water, one they claimed was five hundred times faster than standard electrolysis.

Brun left Berlin with orders to build a pilot plant at Vemork, utilizing this new process. While in Berlin he'd tried to ascertain what exactly the Germans needed so much SH200 for. The *Uranverein* scientists had tried to claim that it wasn't for the war effort. When Brun had pressed, he'd been warned that 'it was considered as treachery to give such information in wartime'.

Brun's subsequent report to London set nerves on edge. Clearly, the German plans had to be stopped. The question was: how? The narrow, ice-bound chasm that housed the Vemork plant was almost impossible to attack by air. High-level bombing would prove hopelessly inaccurate, and a low-level air strike was out of the question. The Germans had threaded the gorge with metal cables, each with a curtain of thick steel wires hanging beneath. Any low-level sortie would blunder into those.

In January 1942, Professor Peierls – one of the authors of the seminal Frisch–Peierls Memorandum – drew up plans for an innovative means of attack. If a mine could be dropped into the reservoir feeding the Vemork plant, it could blow up the entrance to the pipelines, which would sabotage the turbines in turn. It would need to be a floating type of mine, and to be fitted with a fuse that would only detonate once the mine had reached the grid placed at the entrance to the pipelines.

The grid was there to prevent any detritus from being sucked into the steel pipes and fed onwards into the plant. If the mine exploded there, it would send debris cascading downwards, wrecking the turbines. The problem with such a plan – irrespective of whether such a mine could be built and deployed – was that damaging the turbines did little to destroy the heavy water plant itself.

The only link between the two was power: the turbines provided the electricity to drive the heavy water production process. It might halt output, but only for as long as it took for the turbines to be repaired. More importantly, it would alert the Germans to the fact that Vemork was a target, at which point strenuous efforts would be made to strengthen its defences.

There would very likely only be the one chance to stop the heavy water juggernaut; the SOE would have to get it right first time. What the strategists needed was a better sense of the strengths of Vemork's defences, plus any potential weak spots. That would help them determine what options there were for sabotage. And to get that, Agent Cheese would need to confront his Gestapo pursuers head-on.

By now Odd Starheim – Agent Cheese – was back on the Hardangervidda, and he had been joined by a fellow SOE operative, appropriately code-named Biscuit – fellow Norwegian Andreas

Fasting. Their mission had been upgraded to 'Operation' status and assigned the name Operation Cheese (or Cheesey in some SOE documents), with heavy water as a key target.

'The important Rjukan power plant might be usefully tackled by Cheese's organization,' recorded a 6 January 1942 memo.

Agent Biscuit was a small arms and explosives expert, who would provide local recruits with guerrilla training. A consignment of weapons – including eighty revolvers, ten Bren guns (a light machine gun), a hundred tommy guns, sixty rifles, five hundred hand grenades and a mass of plastic explosives – was to be shipped to Starheim's resistance fighters by the Shetland Bus flotilla. Perhaps a local force – once armed and trained – could take out the all-important SH200 works?

Leaving Biscuit to train the local recruits in the comparative safety of the wilderness, Cheese travelled to Oslo. He needed to make contact with a go-between, one who had promised to introduce him to a key source of intelligence within the Vemork plant. But barely had he reached the city when the Gestapo pounced.

Starheim had billeted himself with Korsvig Rasmussen, a fellow agent. At 10 a.m. on 21 January he was woken by Korsvig's terrified wife. The Gestapo had come, she warned, and Starheim had to hide. But as he slipped into a dressing gown and made his way down a corridor, Agent Cheese was cornered.

The Gestapo had been told there was no one else in the house, so Starheim's presence was immediately suspicious. Half a dozen Gestapo agents seized him. He produced his passport and papers, all in a false name of course, and was subjected to a barrage of questions.

The entire time he was racking his brains for a means to

escape. He couldn't leave that house in Gestapo custody, for as soon as they got him to headquarters and established his real identity, he was done for. Starheim dressed quickly, all under the watchful eyes of his captors. Then he had a flash of inspiration. He'd remembered something odd about the house: the nearest loo had two doors.

Politely and deferentially he asked the Gestapo commander if he could use the toilet. He was given permission to do so, but a Gestapo guard was placed at the door. Once inside Starheim pulled the flush, opened the far door and darted into the adjoining bedroom. With barely a pause Starheim reached for the open window, climbed onto the ledge and jumped.

He was two storeys up and landed on ice, twisting an ankle badly. Regardless, Starheim vaulted over a barbed wire fence and ran for his life. He spotted a delivery van, and in desperation he yanked open the passenger door and jumped in.

'Are you a good and loyal Norwegian?' he cried, his words directed at the startled driver.

'Yes, I'm a real Norwegian all right,' the driver growled.

'Right, drive like hell, 'cause the police are after me!'

Starheim wasn't exaggerating. At the front of Rasmussen's house the Gestapo had a car. At any moment he was expecting to see it come tearing around the corner. The driver asked if it was the Gestapo, and Starheim confirmed that it was.

He smiled grimly, gripping the wheel. 'They'll never get hold of you, I'll see to that!'

The driver set off like the proverbial bat out of hell, making for the eastern part of the city. En route he clipped a motor car, but didn't take his foot off the pedal for even a second. Once he'd navigated the van to his own house, he hustled Starheim inside.

He was to stay there in hiding until they could arrange to get him smuggled out of Oslo.

Eventually, Starheim left the city dressed in the uniform of a Norwegian policeman and carrying a genuine police pass in the name of Harmansen. Thus attired, he was able to sneak out unmolested and return to the comparative safety of his rural resistance network. Using their radio, Starheim put a call through to London, alerting them to his Oslo arrest and subsequent escape.

A decision was taken to extract Agent Cheese: 'Southwest Norway was getting too hot for him,' Wilson remarked. A Shetland Bus trawler packed full of arms was dispatched to a rendezvous along the remote Norwegian coast; it was to deliver its clandestine shipment and collect Starheim. He was to bring with him one other key Norwegian, who was highly sought after by the SOE in connection with the Vemork heavy water plant.

The Shetland Bus vessel the *Olad* tried to make landfall, but it was beaten back by Norway's savage winter coast. 'Mission could not be completed,' read the message the *Olad* radioed to headquarters. 'Could not enter selected Fjord owing to 6/8 mile pack ice off coast. Attacked on return . . . by one German fighter and one Heinkel twin-engined bomber. Only slight superficial damage to boat'.

That last part of the message downplayed the ferocity of the sea battle. One of the *Olad*'s gunners had waited until the German aircraft was within 100 metres of the Q-ship, before 'emptying a full pan of Lewis into her'. The .303 calibre Lewis machine gun typically carried a 47- or 97-round pan magazine, all of which had been unleashed at the German warplane.

Fortunately, the *Olad*'s wheelhouse had been 'strengthened with reinforced concrete' and this had helped to save the vessel, but the Norwegian ice had proved unbeatable.

For the time being, Starheim was trapped.

By now – early 1942 – the *Uranprojekt* had attracted a new and powerful supporter within the Reich – Joseph Goebbels, Hitler's minister of propaganda and one of his most ardent supporters. Hatchet-faced Goebbels had written gleefully in his diary: 'Research in the field of demolishing atoms is so advanced that its results can perhaps be used for waging this war. Here tiny efforts result in such immense destructive effects that one looks forward with horror at the future course of this war.'

Goebbels strutted the world stage singing the praises of the new Nazi 'super weapons' – ones that would signal the rapid demise of Nazi Germany's enemies. America had joined the conflict – she was three months into the war – and thus the enemies of the Reich, and the targets of a nuclear-equipped Germany, included the leading democracies of the free world.

Starheim, meanwhile, felt increasingly hounded. His real identity was known to the Gestapo, as were his physical appearance and his aliases. The injuries he'd sustained leaping from the Oslo window meant that he couldn't make it far on foot. Yet the adverse weather, coupled with increased enemy surveillance flights, made sending a second Shetland Bus ship appear increasingly impracticable.

A hand-scribbled note on a 6 March 1942 memo from John Wilson weighed up the pros and cons of making such an attempt: 'The "Cons" have it . . . We have decided the form of signal to Cheese.'

'Unexpected trouble with boats together with weather conditions makes it impossible for us to send for you at present ...' read the message sent to Starheim. 'If your position becomes impossible make for Stockholm. Regret terribly present circumstances. Keep going.'

Making for Stockholm – neutral Sweden's capital city – was a non-starter as far as Starheim was concerned. His injured foot would never last such a journey. 'And so I waited for the boat that never came,' he lamented, sounding uncharacteristically downbeat and disheartened.

At SOE headquarters, Wilson feared how desperate his star agent was becoming. But there was little he could do about it. SOE agents were sent into the field with no guarantee of a return ticket. That was the harsh reality. Sometimes they had to use their own initiative and resourcefulness to make their own way home. And somehow, he retained every confidence in Agent Cheese.

Starheim decided he couldn't afford to wait for a boat to be sent by London, and so he resurrected a plan that he'd long been toying with. He gathered his team of desperadoes, one of whom would prove to be one of the most important individuals ever brought out of occupied Europe. Starheim knew the SOE wanted this man badly. As he and his men prepared to make a desperate bid for England, he wasn't willing to waste any time trying to clear his proposed actions with London.

SOE agents were challenged to think the unthinkable. So be it.

They were going to hijack a vessel and, like latter-day pirates, sail hell for leather for Britain.

Chapter Eight

Einar Skinnarland had certainly felt better. As he hobbled towards the waiting ship his leg was causing him real discomfort. But the pain was as nothing compared to that of two days ago, when he'd undergone surgery without anaesthetic. It was 14 March 1942, and before him lay his target: the *Galtesund*, a 623-tonne coastal steamer.

With her single dark funnel set amidships, twin masts to fore and aft and graceful white-painted hull with sharply raked stern, the *Galtesund* hailed from a kinder, gentler age. Built by a Danish shipyard in 1905, the 170-foot vessel was designed to carry cargo and passengers on short hauls between Scandinavia's coastal cities. She lay at berth, smoke drifting lazily from her funnel and pooling amidst her rigging, seemingly blissfully unaware of what was about to befall her.

Two days earlier Skinnarland – a resolutely cheerful, flame-haired 24-year-old, whose broad shoulders and hardened physique reflected the physicality of life around Lake Møs, the feeder lake for the Vemork power station – had been flat on his back. He'd dislocated his left knee, just days before he planned to escape from Norway.

The scalpel had gone in, the fluid was drained, the bone was set and the wound stitched up again. Refusing to stay even one night in the hospital, Skinnarland – whose doctor clearly thought him insane – had discharged himself with his knee heavily bandaged and walking stick gripped firmly in hand. If nothing else, it would be good cover for what was coming. Who would ever suspect a man leaning on his crutch of being intent on blatant piracy?

He'd already scrutinized two vessels. One, a steamer called the *King Haakon*, had got trapped in coastal ice. The other, the *Austria*, was not taking passengers. And so it was the *Galtesund* that had fallen into his sights. Posing as bona fide passengers, he and Agent Biscuit were about to join her, to check how much coal she carried – was it enough to reach Britain? – the vulnerability of bridge and engine room, and how many Germans might be aboard.

Skinnarland was relatively new to such work. For centuries the Skinnarland family had lived along the shores of Lake Møs, in country closed to all but skiers for six months of the year. In the shadow of the 5,600-foot Mount Gausta they had worked as fishermen and farmers, following the harsh but regular rhythms of the seasons. And then change had come: Lake Møs had been dammed, pipelines and power plants were blasted out of the rock, and the town of Rjukan was founded to serve Norsk Hydro's industrial needs.

Rjukan came complete with worker dormitories, a railway station, a church, schools, a fire station and police force, as well as a community dance hall. Plus long, harsh winters and an abundance of snow. The eighth child of the Lake Møs dam-keeper, Einar Skinnarland had grown up on skis. He'd skied to school; he'd skied to haul firewood, or to play with his friends; and with his siblings, he'd ski-raced down the slopes of Mount Gausta.

Considered the brightest of the Skinnarland children, Einar had gone to university and studied engineering. He'd just completed his military service when war broke out, and had been in Oslo as Luftwaffe warplanes screamed overhead. He'd fought like so many others in a desperate if noble retreat, before returning home dispirited, only to discover that Rjukan had been one of the last towns in southern Norway to fall.

His brothers had fought in its ill-fated defence. They were exhausted from the action and haunted by the spectre of failure. But the Skinnarland men, whose innate instinct was to endure, recovered their spirits. Einar joined the fledgling resistance, but there were bigger things in store for the Skinnarland's 'golden boy'.

Born and bred in the region, there was no one that Einar Skinnarland didn't seem to have a local connection to. He was also physically tough, resourceful and mentally sharp. In short, he was ideally placed to act as an agent-courier between SOE's assets in the Vemork heavy water facility, and London. Trained as a radio operator, he could form a direct conduit for what had become the most important source of intelligence for the entire Allied war effort.

Skinnarland was told to prepare for a trip to Britain. He was given false papers. Travelling under the name of Einar Hansen, he was to be picked up by the incoming Shetland Bus vessel, along with Odd Starheim. He told his family he was taking his Easter vacation skiing on the Hardanger Plateau, which was remote enough to lose oneself in for several days. Instead, he would travel to Britain where he would receive training for a very special mission.

Raising the stakes still further, Skinnarland would carry with him documents and papers concerning the Vemork works – the latest updates from Jomar Brun, the bespectacled 'double agent' at work in the SH200 plant.

Of course, as matters had transpired, the Shetland Bus pick-up boat had been beaten back by the pack ice. So, over a long and spirited game of chess, Starheim and Skinnarland – along with Agent Biscuit – had hatched their alternative plan: *piracy.*

Walking stick before him, Skinnarland hobbled up the *Galtesund*'s gangplank. He and Agent Biscuit purchased tickets for the short voyage to Flekkefjord, a town on the south-western tip of Norway, and the port at which Starheim intended to join them, should all go well.

The walking stick proved a fine cover. Stumping about the boat, Skinnarland was able to gather the necessary intelligence without arousing undue suspicion: there were twenty-two Norwegian crew members, and no Germans aboard. The captain, a salty old seadog called Knudsen, was unlikely to give up his ship easily, but there was no helping that. As to its fuel supply, the *Galtesund* was carrying some sixty tonnes of coal – more than enough to reach Scottish shores.

When the *Galtesund* docked at Flekkefjord, Skinnarland hobbled off to meet his co-conspirators. He linked up with Starheim and gave him the good news: the ship was there for the taking. Apart from himself, Starheim and Agent Biscuit, there were three other recruits for the coming action: fresh-faced Norwegian sailors, none of whom had had much, if any, military training.

'You'll each get one of these,' Starheim told them, brandishing the Colt .45 revolvers they'd be carrying. 'But whatever you do don't pull the trigger. If there's to be any shooting, we'll take care of it. Leave that to us.'

An hour later Skinnarland was back at the docks, hefting a suitcase stuffed full of pistols. On his lapel he wore a Nasjonal Samling (National Unity) badge, Nasjonal Samling being the

Norwegian fascist party, founded in 1933 by Vidkun Quisling. Following the German invasion Quisling had declared himself prime minister. By the spring of 1942 he was governing Norway in an uneasy alliance with Hitler's chosen appointee – *Reichskommissar* Josef Terboven, who would earn a much-deserved reputation for cruelty and brutality.

With his walking stick and Nazi badge, Skinnarland felt his cover was complete. It was late afternoon, and the *Galtesund* was being loaded with the last of her cargo. Skinnarland made his way to his cabin and broke out his suitcase, checking the revolvers. Some thirty minutes later Agents Cheese and Biscuit joined him, and began their final preparations.

Beneath their feet the twin engines shuddered into life. Above them, the single funnel belched thick black smoke. Slowly, the *Galtesund* nosed her way into the waters of Flekkefjord, where pine-clad slopes swept down to meet the sea's dark embrace. Inside Skinnarland's cabin, Starheim's men synchronized their watches. At 6.20 p.m. exactly, when the vessel should be well away from watching eyes, they would strike.

All were wearing the Nasjonal Samling badges, as if they were good Norwegian fascists. It was a delicious irony for Starheim, as one of the most wanted men in all of Norway, to be masquerading under such cover.

Skinnarland, Starheim and Fasting – Agent Biscuit – left the cabin: they would form the main assault party. Others would head for the engine room and the main passenger cabins. Every man had a revolver tucked into his belt, plus lengths of rope wound around his waist, covered by his jacket.

Skinnarland could feel his pulse racing. He was skittish. Starheim was an old hand at this kind of thing, but Skinnarland himself had seen very little action, and certainly nothing of such a piratical nature. They made their way to the ship's saloon, where they knew the captain would be. Starheim was just about to burst in when Frithjof Halvorsen, the ship's second mate, challenged him.

'Can I see your ticket?' Halvorsen demanded.

For an instant Starheim froze. Intent on their hijack, he hadn't felt that buying a ticket was wholly necessary.

'I'm afraid I arrived too late,' he replied, all innocence. 'I thought I'd pay on board.'

The second mate would brook no delay: Starheim was marched off, leaving Skinnarland and Fasting lurking by the saloon doorway. After what felt like an age, Starheim and the second mate returned, the former with a newly purchased ticket clutched in hand. The second mate entered the saloon, apparently none the wiser as to his passenger's dark intentions.

Moments later, Starheim eased open the door. Fasting slipped in and strolled to the far end of the saloon to cover its second door. Once he was in position, Starheim entered, gun at the ready, a distinctly apprehensive Skinnarland on his shoulder. Before them stood the ship's captain, the second mate, the steward and one other figure, most likely a passenger.

'Hands up!' Starheim barked, as he menaced the four with his pistol.

They stared at him in utter shock and surprise. So discomfited were they that they completely failed to raise their hands.

Starheim repeated the order, more roughly this time. 'Get your hands up!'

Four sets of hands shot above the men's startled heads.

'We're Norwegian navy officers,' Starheim growled, 'and at

this moment my men are seizing your engine room. I am now assuming command of this ship.'

The *Galtesund*'s captain spluttered. His face registered utter disbelief. He began to protest, but Starheim was having none of it. When he tried to fight back, they quickly overpowered him.

'Tie them all up,' Starheim barked at Skinnarland, as he and Fasting kept them covered.

Skinnarland unfastened the lengths of rope from around his waist and bound up the four captives. Leaving Fasting to stand guard, Starheim led the way to the ship's bridge. If they could seize the wheelhouse – the nerve centre of the ship – she would be theirs.

They spied three sailors: the chief mate, the ship's pilot and the man at the wheel. With Starheim leading, they leapt into the wheelhouse, guns at the ready. Seeing the weapons and the fierce expressions, the mate tried to run, as did the man at the wheel. But Skinnarland had by now found his inner steel. Moving remarkably swiftly for a man recovering from knee surgery, he blocked the far exit.

'Get back to your posts,' Starheim barked, gesturing with his pistol. 'And stay at the wheel, if you know what's good for you.'

By now the *Galtesund* had steamed some forty nautical miles north up the coast. She'd just turned eastwards, and was making her way into the next port of call, the narrow-necked inlet of Rekefjord. It was imperative that she didn't dock. Starheim ordered Skinnarland to tie up the ship's mate and take him down below. He didn't quite like the look of the man.

The ship's pilot seemed cool and capable and Starheim decided to take him partly into his confidence. He gave the man a similar speech to the one he'd given the ship's captain.

'Take the ship quietly out to sea,' he ordered.

Under the pilot's direction the *Galtesund* made an about-turn. Once they were free of Rekefjord, Starheim planned to steer a course south-west, full steam ahead for Scotland, the nearest British landfall. But the pilot warned against it. They would be in sight of the German forces based at Egersund, just to the north of where they were now. If the troops there spotted the *Galtesund* steaming west into open waters, they would be bound to raise the alarm.

The pilot suggested they head due south instead, to get them out of sight of the enemy, at which point they could swing west and set a course for Britain. Starheim agreed. Leaving a guard on the bridge, he and Skinnarland made sure the ship's captain was locked in his cabin, before gathering together the *Galtesund*'s other officers and crew.

'We are Norwegian naval men,' Starheim informed them, 'and we're heading sixty to seventy miles due west, to rendezvous with a king's naval ship. If you make any trouble or attempt any sabotage, make no mistake you will be shot. You will muster in the saloon, where you will be kept under constant guard.'

By the 'king' he meant the Norwegian monarch, although this was, of course, a lie. There was no such ship. In truth, the *Galtesund* had some 1,100 kilometres to travel before reaching her intended landfall – the Scottish port of Aberdeen. For much of that voyage she would be alone and unprotected, and utterly vulnerable to attack from the air.

With that in mind, Starheim had timed the hijack very carefully. The sun would set at around 8.30 p.m., barely ninety minutes away, at which point the *Galtesund* would be blanketed in darkness. With sunrise at 4 a.m. the spring nights were painfully short, but at least it would give them a good seven hours in which to make their getaway.

With a top speed of 12 knots, the *Galtesund* should be able to put 215 kilometres between her and her pursuers by daybreak. By then she would be well into the open expanse of the North Sea – a small speck on a vast expanse of ocean – and they would have a real chance of making good their escape. Plus Starheim had an ace up his sleeve. Before boarding the *Galtesund* he'd dictated a radio message, to be sent to the SOE should the hijack prove successful. It read: 'Have captured coastal ship of 600 tons ... We make for Aberdeen. Please give aircraft escort, as we expect attack from German aircraft come morning. Cheese.'

Fortune favoured the SOE pirates. As Starheim set a course south-west for Scotland, so the weather closed in. A squally snowstorm howled out of the darkening heavens, cloaking the vessel in swirling white. Starheim ordered the pilot to head below and to bring up the North Sea chart. He needed to know their exact position.

That done, Starheim went and had words with a very resentful Captain Knudsen. 'I need to know if there is any deviation in the ship's compass.'

The captain glowered, but nonetheless answered. His was a fine vessel and well-kept: the compass was dead true.

Back on the bridge, and with Skinnarland close beside him, Starheim – SOE agent and now pirate commander – set his feet firmly on the deck, as the *Galtesund* shuddered with each passing wave. A fierce gale was blowing from the north-east, so right on his stern. The *Galtesund* was built for coastal work, not for an open ocean crossing in such a storm. He doubted if the ship's lifeboats were particularly seaworthy, but if the adverse weather served to hide them from any marauding German warplanes then, on balance, it was a blessing.

Shortly after nightfall Starheim got word that the ship's captain wanted to speak to him. He made his way to the man's cabin, resolving to make peace with the aged, weather-beaten sea warrior.

'I'm very sorry about the position I've put both yourself and your crew in,' Starheim explained, his voice edged with genuine concern. 'But if you behave well you have my word that you will all be all right.'

The captain appeared sceptical. 'So what's your intention with my ship?'

'I've set a course for Aberdeen. I'd prefer it if the ship's crew and any passengers who wish to leave do so, in the ship's lifeboats.' He glanced momentarily at the storm, gusts of heavy snow beating against the cabin's porthole. 'But—'

'It's impossible to go in the boats,' the captain interjected. 'There's a north-easterly blowing, and they're not the best in any case.'

Starheim reckoned that the captain was talking sense. The gale would drive the lifeboats away from the Norwegian coast into open sea. They might not even weather the storm. There was nothing for it: all aboard would have to endure the passage to Aberdeen . . . and whatever might follow. As a gesture of goodwill Starheim unbound the captain, but he cautioned him to remain in his cabin.

That night the wind shifted direction. It lashed the vessel from the south-east, hitting her sideways. The *Galtesund* rolled and heaved horribly, struggling like a beached whale. Cargo lashed to the deck broke its bonds and tumbled into the hungry sea.

The ship's mate advised Starheim that they needed to reduce her rate of knots. The pirate commander conceded. Speed was of the essence: every turn of the ship's screw carried them nearer to safety.

But there was little point if Starheim drove them all to a watery grave in the depths of the North Sea.

Chapter Nine

With the approach of first light, Starheim and Skinnarland found themselves growing increasingly nervous. There was no sign of the requested RAF escort, and the storm seemed to have blown itself out. Indeed, Starheim had to order a change in course to adjust for the new drift and current. Unless fate somehow intervened, they were going to be sitting ducks.

A dark and insistent worry tugged at his fatigued senses: had their radio message requesting the RAF escort actually been sent? Had the SOE received it? Certainly, there was no sign of any British warplanes.

As luck would have it, the dawn light revealed an utterly magical sight. As the darkness lifted, so a thick bank of low-lying cloud drifted towards the *Galtesund*. Starheim and Skinnarland could barely believe it. The gods seemed to be smiling upon them as neither could have hoped for. The storm-battered vessel steamed into the welcoming fog. Barely had it done so when those on the bridge detected the distant rumble of a warplane. Was it the enemy, or the RAF speeding to their rescue?

Anxious eyes scoured the grey and foggy heavens as the rumble grew to a thunderous roar. A wing tip dipped into view, mist swirling all around it. The sharp black outlines of the Luftwaffe's insignia – a black bar cross against a square block of white – were momentarily visible, before the aircraft flashed past and was gone.

Starheim gave thanks: the fog had saved them.

At 1.15 p.m. a second hidden aircraft droned across the heavens. As it dropped into view, diving out of the fog, Starheim and Skinnarland were overjoyed to spy the distinctive markings of the RAF: red, white and blue circles. *Deliverance.* Starheim ordered the ship's mate to hoist the Norwegian flag. As a second and third RAF warplane joined the first, they ran up the ship's signal flags:

'We are making for Aberdeen and want escort.'

'Congratulations,' the aircrew signalled back to them.

An hour later, an armed trawler steamed into view and signalled to the *Galtesund* to follow. The RAF pilots dipped their wings, waving a final farewell, before roaring into the distance, leaving the trawler to guide them into harbour. The *Galtesund* had to reduce her speed to match the trawler's more stately pace, but at least those aboard felt somewhat safer now.

As the two vessels steered a course for Aberdeen, Starheim's pirates suggested breaking out some of the ship's cargo to celebrate: the *Galtesund* was carrying crates of cigarettes and alcohol. Starheim forbade it – at least until they'd made port. They were a good way out and it was too early to truly drop their guard.

With their reduced speed, it wasn't until 8 a.m. the following morning that those on board heard the sonorous beat of a foghorn reverberating through the sea mist. It marked the position of the lighthouse to the south of Aberdeen. Starheim left it to Captain Knudsen to manoeuvre the ship into dock, where a contingent of military police boarded her.

Starheim told them where the ship had come from, who was aboard, and that there were no known Nazis amongst the ship's crew. He also asked to see Captain Ellman, a Norwegian intelligence officer who was based in Aberdeen. The two men knew each other from previous operations, and he'd feel more comfortable explaining their extraordinary story to him.

'The capture of the ship could not have been accomplished without Biscuit and Skinnarland,' he would write of the operation. 'They were . . . very clever and did their job well. Biscuit has been a very great help to me and is an excellent boy. My impression of Skinnarland is very good.'

As matters transpired, Starheim would have little opportunity to celebrate their safe arrival with one of his co-conspirators. At former Scoutmaster John Wilson's behest, the one-time pirate Skinnarland was whisked away from the port and placed aboard the first overnight train to London. He was wanted urgently at SOE headquarters.

Meanwhile, back in Norway, the *Galtesund*'s disappearance had whipped up a veritable storm. As Starheim had steered her deep into the welcoming fog, so the Germans had put out a story that the coastal steamer had gone to the bottom with all crew and passengers. No one amongst the local seafaring communities believed it.

Word got out that the *Galtesund* had made her way to Scotland, with the six mystery passengers who had boarded her very likely her hijackers. Shortly after, the Germans were forced to admit that a reconnaissance flight had spotted the *Galtesund*, under escort by British warships and steaming towards the Scottish coast. Thankfully, as the seizure appeared to have been a British naval action, no reprisals were taken against the crew's families.

By strange coincidence, the *Galtesund*'s cargo just happened to include some materials of real value to the Reich. Recently, the Germans had finished building ten radio stations dotted along the Norwegian coastline. For two months they had been awaiting the shipment from Germany of specialist equipment to be installed there. Whether by accident or design, that prized cargo was aboard the ship that had fallen into British hands.

In addition to the radio equipment, the *Galtesund* was carrying a newly developed meteorological device. It was Starheim who had smuggled it aboard, for he suspected it would be of interest to British intelligence. They would describe it as 'the instrument which the Germans now attach to meteorological observation balloons . . . Cheese brought it as he wondered if there was anything novel about it from our point of view.'

Apart from alcohol and cigarettes, most of the *Galtesund*'s other cargo consisted of canned food. Wilson's SOE fell on it with glee. 'Not the least important part . . . were the labels on the tins,' he explained, 'which could be copied when sending supplies into Norway.' The SOE's forgery department would make replicas, so when rations were airdropped to agents and resistance groups, it would appear to be a genuine Norwegian foodstuff.

Relieved of her cargo, the 600-tonne *Galtesund* would not lie idle. She was pressed into service with Nortraship – the Norwegian Shipping and Trade Mission – a 1,000-vessel line that operated from London. Made up of the Norwegian merchant fleet outside German-controlled waters, Nortraship was then the world's largest shipping company, and a great boon to Britain's war effort. The pirated *Galtesund* found herself in very good company, as did many of the ship's crew – those who chose to continue serving with her.

In recognition of his role in masterminding the vessel's seizure,

Odd Starheim received the Distinguished Service Order (DSO), at the behest of his SOE taskmasters. They could not have been more delighted at his unsanctioned act of piracy, especially as it had delivered Einar Skinnarland into their eager clutches.

Spiriting Skinnarland to Britain was stage one in a top-secret SOE operation code-named Grouse, the aim of which was to prevent any more heavy water from reaching Germany. Of course, Skinnarland knew precious little about this. Questioned by a security agent upon arrival at the Aberdeen docks, he was surprised to discover that the man knew an awful lot about him, from a 'mutual friend'.

During the long train journey to London that agent briefed Skinnarland about the efforts being made by the Nazis to build a nuclear weapon, and about the vital role of the Vemork plant in this rush towards Armageddon. Upon reaching London Skinnarland was taken to John Wilson's office, set in Chiltern Court, a block of flats situated above the Baker Street tube station, part of the 'rabbit warren' of secretive SOE agencies that peppered the Baker Street area.

It was still very early, but Skinnarland was expected. He was about to get a major surprise. Seated before him he found a familiar figure: Leif Tronstad, a fellow Norwegian who'd spent a good deal of time in and around Skinnarland's home area. More to the point, it was Tronstad who had designed and built the Vemork heavy water plant.

Tronstad had been an eminent professor at Trondheim's Norwegian Institute of Technology, and the dashing 39-year-old had real presence. But nowadays, Skinnarland – himself a former engineering student – admired the Professor for a whole different set of reasons.

Following the German invasion, Tronstad had taken his wife and two young children back to his in-laws' home in rural Norway. As German panzer divisions thrust north of their bridgehead, he'd joined the defence of his homeland. Over three weeks, and aided by the British forces who had landed in the country, Tronstad had fought ferociously to defend the two long valleys that link Oslo to Trondheim.

Pushed relentlessly backwards, when the final order came to surrender Tronstad and his men had buried their arms and ammunition for future use. Publicly, he had returned to his work as a university professor, and as a consultant to Norsk Hydro. Secretly, he had become a leader in the fledgling resistance movement, recruiting amongst his student network to form a cell that became known as Skylark B.

Tronstad earned his own uniquely fitting code name: The Mailman. It referred to his role in sending intelligence on Norway's industries to Britain, revealing how these might boost the Nazi war effort. For a while, Norsk Hydro had been but one of his many areas of interest. But then, in the spring of 1941, London had called, demanding to know everything possible about the Vemork heavy water plant.

The Mailman communicated all that he could: the Germans were determined to raise production massively, but he was unsure as to exactly what they intended to use the SH200 for. Tronstad started liaising closely with Jomar Brun, Vemork's double agent and a former classmate of his. Together they fed back further information to SOE headquarters. But then the Gestapo pounced: Skylark B's radio transmitter was seized, along with the student who operated it.

That student was tortured. He talked. The Skylark B network

began to implode. On 20 September, a warning message was smuggled to Tronstad: 'The Mailman must disappear.' Tronstad had bid a hasty farewell to his beloved wife, Bassa – a childhood sweetheart – plus their two young children, and made himself scarce. Eventually he crossed the border into neutral Sweden and from there made his way to Britain.

Some of this Skinnarland had heard. Some had been guessed at. And now here he was, just seventy-two hours after seizing the *Galtesund*, sitting before The Mailman in a mysterious London office.

Beside Tronstad was a second, much older figure. With his sparse hair, scarred nose, and stout, bullfrog-like appearance, there was something of the war-bitten troll about the man. But beneath the craggy brows Skinnarland saw eyes burning with a peculiar kind of intelligence, and not a small amount of shrewd cunning.

Wilson introduced himself to Skinnarland, and for a while the three did the necessary small talk, before Wilson and Tronstad began firing queries at the newly arrived Norwegian.

'There are two questions we want to put to you. First, do you think you will have been missed by now?'

Skinnarland shook his head. Like many in his home area, he was a keen hunter and fisherman. 'I don't think so. I told everyone I was going into the hills on a hunting trip.'

Wilson exchanged glances with Tronstad. Over the past months the two men had developed a deep and instinctive trust. Wilson commanded the SOE's Norwegian Section, and Tronstad the Norwegian government-in-exile's equivalent organization. Together, they had amassed the most detailed and in-depth intelligence on the Vemork plant.

'We benefited very considerably through the advice and complete cooperation that "The Professor" always gave us,' Wilson would write of his 'dear and close friend'. 'The Professor was a frequent visitor to our private flat at Chiltern Court. There would be a ring at the bell, and immediately the door opened, a shout: "Margaret, have you got anything to eat?"'

Wilson was the son of a Scottish cleric who'd also been the Dean of Edinburgh University. When asked about his knowledge of the UK, he'd written on his SOE recruitment form: 'Have travelled all over Great Britain . . . but give me The Highlands every time.' Wilson had a Scottish wife, and Margaret was their feisty teenage daughter. Tronstad had fostered a deep affection for 'the canny old Scoutmaster', as he called Wilson, plus his family.

Wilson turned to Skinnarland and fired the next question at him – the million-dollar question. 'Are you prepared, with what training we can give you, to parachute back into the Hardangervidda, and before you are missed? We need to learn everything about the situation at Vemork.'

Skinnarland nodded. There was no need to say anything. He was more than ready.

Wilson paused. He eyed Skinnarland, searchingly. 'I'm afraid you're taking on a very tough assignment. There's not an hour to lose . . . Quite frankly we are very worried about what's going on at Norsk Hydro. The Nazis have just demanded 10,000 pounds of heavy water by Christmas. And you'll appreciate what kind of present that might lead to, over London.'

He went on to outline the basics of Operation Grouse. Skinnarland was to return to Norway to establish a totally discrete intelligence operation, in isolation from all other networks. Though he was to be dropped alone, others – a handful of fellow

Norwegian SOE agents – were to follow. Their mission would be to sabotage the Vemork works in a clandestine guerrilla-style operation, and to destroy all supplies of SH200 before they could be shipped to Germany.

Skinnarland's role, as the advance party and the linkman to the Vemork plant, was absolutely vital. They would very likely only get one chance to strike. They had to get it right first time.

'Don't jump into this with your eyes shut,' Wilson warned. 'Parachuting is a tricky business, and we won't have much time to make you an expert.'

Before any attack was launched, Wilson wanted to know everything the Germans might be doing in and around the SH200 plant. Details on security measures and defences were key. If Skinnarland could discover the exact use the Germans were making of the heavy water, so much the better, though Wilson appreciated that this might be tricky. Wilson rounded off the meeting stressing the vital importance of absolute secrecy.

Skinnarland's mission was to be known only to the three men in that room. Much of what he would communicate about Vemork would be too sensitive for radio transmission out of Norway. Instead, it was to be sent via courier to an SOE office in Sweden, and from there by diplomatic bag to London. The couriers – moving by bicycle, train or on foot over challenging terrain – were often young women, for they tended to attract less suspicion.

'Both verbal and written messages were passed,' wrote Wilson, 'the length of the message being governed by the amount of paper a man could swallow in a hurry . . . It might take a courier a week to travel along the tops of ridges and mountains, and so avoid the many controls and patrols in the valleys.'

Those of Skinnarland's messages that proved too bulky to be eaten in a hurry would have to be sent via the postal system, using an ingenious means of concealment. They would be meticulously encoded and sent in 'duff' – or microdotted form. An entire typed page was photographed, reduced to a tiny spot no larger than a pinhead, and scattered throughout an ordinary-looking letter, hidden in the full stops like raisins in a suet (Christmas-type) pudding: 'plum duff' in British Army speak, hence 'sending in duff'. To recover the message a 200-times magnification microscope was required.

Wilson made it clear that Vemork was the SOE's absolute top priority target and their orders were to 'eliminate' it. Time was critically short. Skinnarland had to be dropped back into Norway before anyone realized he was gone. The remainder of his 'Easter holiday' break was all the time they had available to transform this engineer and outdoors man into one of the SOE's most important assets across all of occupied Europe.

Skinnarland's mission agreed upon, Tronstad took him to a local pub, so he could enjoy a few pints of fine British ale. And then . . . training.

The Operation Grouse orders read: 'An organization is to be built up . . . entirely independent of other organizations in Norway . . .' Weapons, radio kit and fellow operators were to be parachuted in to join Skinnarland. A coded radio message would be sent over the BBC to warn him of their impending arrival. Instead of the regular opening line of the evening news – 'This is the news from London' – the announcer would state: 'This is the *latest* news from London.'

Wilson held his Norwegian agents in the very highest regard. 'I knew that any qualified Norwegian I approached would agree to carry it out,' he remarked of Operation Grouse. Wilson's super-agent, Odd Starheim, was sadly out of contention – he was too well known. His role as an undercover operator in Norway was over. Starheim would focus now on offensive, commando-style operations.

Wilson had more or less singlehandedly formulated the SOE's training regime, which was arranged into distinct parts. First came three weeks of simple explosives, pistol-shooting and physical trials, 'mainly to see if the candidate was suitable'. For those deemed up to it, there followed 'a further weeding-out process', based in the Arisaig area of Scotland, consisting of instruction in 'all the latest explosive devices, small arms, unarmed combat and fitness training'. And for those who survived that, there was a third period of specialist training, in the Beaulieu area of the New Forest, learning 'codes, secret writing, psychological warfare' to prepare recruits as agents, wireless operators or saboteurs.

Wilson realized from the start that what the SOE were building was no regular military unit. 'Its discipline had to be largely self-applied. A blind eye had to be turned to certain personal failings and idiosyncrasies. For strict military discipline a policy of mutual confidence and trust had to be substituted.'

He would learn quickly the type of man – and woman – the SOE sought. 'However brave and efficient . . . men were, I began to realize other abilities and qualities were required. The tough gangster of detective fiction was of little use, and in fact likely to be a danger.'

'No normal course of training can determine a man's character,' Wilson would remark. 'It is curious but true that some of the best members of the Linge Company were thought at first not likely to make good agents, and one redoubtable member was almost rejected outright as unsuitable.'

With Einar Skinnarland, Wilson sensed he'd found the right operator, but he had few illusions as to the risks attached to what he was asking of the man. 'Weather is appalling most of the time,' Wilson wrote of the Hardangervidda, Skinnarland's intended drop zone. 'Sudden fogs, unpredictable gales, swift upward air currents . . . with hundreds of dangerous glaciers, marshes, swamps and impassable streams.' Nobody would ever choose to be parachuted into the area.

Skinnarland had less than two weeks to cram in his SOE instruction – including his parachutist's training – something that normally lasted for several months. Wilson would describe this crash course as being 'the quickest turn-around and most vital piece of training we had ever achieved.'

Skinnarland got just two days at the SOE's radio school, followed by three days' parachutist's instruction. His assessor wrote of him: 'He showed great keenness . . . though his training was rushed.' Rushed indeed. After those few days of fevered preparation, Skinnarland was deemed ready.

Wilson's final words of advice to the flame-haired Norwegian were that if ever he found himself in a tight corner or was confronted with a situation not covered by his orders, he was to act as he saw best. As with the hijacking of the *Galtesund*, whatever he did he would have the full support of the SOE.

With those words ringing in his ears Skinnarland prepared to jump, alone and under the cover of darkness.

Chapter Ten

The Armstrong Whitworth Whitley bomber rumbled through the dark skies, her propellers clawing at the cold spring air. It was 28 March 1942 – just two weeks after Starheim's piratical band had spirited away the *Galtesund* from Norwegian waters. The roar of the aircraft's twin Rolls-Royce Merlin engines made conversation all but impossible, not that Einar Skinnarland had anyone to talk to. He was alone in the Whitley's bare hold, which reverberated to the beat of her engines.

The lone aircraft thundered onwards, the dark night her only protector. Armed with a single machine gun in the nose, and four in the tail, the Whitley was highly vulnerable to attack. And with a top speed of a little over 200 mph she was hardly able to outrun the Luftwaffe's night fighters. The aircrew's only hope was to flit through the night skies undetected.

Unbeknown to Skinnarland, this was only the second such SOE mission flown by the RAF into Norway. In the front turret the bomb aimer hunched over his sights, crouched directly below the nose-gunner. Tonight he had no high explosives to drop from the skies. Instead, his task, along with the Whitley's navigator, was to locate Skinnarland's intended drop zone, a point lying to the north of Lake Møs amidst a bewildering patchwork of snow, rock, ice, lake, frozen bog and mountain. The Hardangervidda stretched as far as the eye could see

– Europe's largest plateau, and seemingly a navigator's worst nightmare.

Skinnarland was dressed in his brand new white jumpsuit, the thick padding of which kept him passably warm in the chill of the hold. Beside him lay his backpack, stuffed with his sleeping bag, emergency rations and thermos of tea. Deeper down were spare clothes, his fake papers, 20,000 kroner, and a camera with twenty-odd rolls of film – for spying on the Vemork plant.

Just to the rear of the Whitley's bomb bay lay a large metal tube, packed full of weaponry: 2 Stens, 14 Lugers, 640 rounds of ammo and 20 commando fighting knives – arms for Operation Grouse. In truth, the prospect of combat didn't discomfit Skinnarland greatly. But right now he was scared. It was plummeting through the bomb bay into the howling darkness – such an unnatural thing to do – that struck terror into him.

As Skinnarland steeled himself in the lonely hold, he was painfully aware of how unprepared he was for the coming jump. He kept repeating his trainer's instructions: 'Feet together and launch off gently. Relax every muscle when you hit the silk and when you land. Tuck up your legs and go down on your knees. Get rid of your chute as quickly as you can.'

At a few minutes prior to midnight, the aircraft's dispatcher called him to action stations. There was a high-pitched whine from the hydraulics, and the bomb doors inched open. A sharp inrush of air filled the hold. *Chilling.* Below lay partly frozen lakes, glaciers laced with crevasses, giant boulders and perilous swamps. The dispatcher edged the weapons container further towards the hole in the floor, and as the jump light blinked green he heaved it into the empty night.

Skinnarland crept closer to the slab of howling darkness. He crouched down, and with a feeling like death he dangled his legs over the edge.

'It's just like a lavatory seat,' yelled the dispatcher, 'only I'm the one who pulls the chain!'

It was a brave attempt to take the edge off the tension, but somehow Skinnarland didn't feel like laughing right now. The dispatcher dropped his arm sharply, signalling the moment to jump, but the Norwegian felt utterly frozen. Riveted to the spot. The dispatcher raised and lowered his arm again, with increased urgency. Still Skinnarland didn't move. *Couldn't move.* Stalemate.

The Whitley made several further passes over the drop zone, yet still Skinnarland remained glued to the Whitley's cold steel. Finally, the dispatcher bent to his ear, yelling that they were short on fuel and that he was going to have to abort the drop.

'We're going back,' he cried.

Skinnarland forced out a strangled reply: 'No! I'm jumping!'

It was then that his mind flipped to something very special that he had stuffed deep in his backpack. It was a silver-plated spoon, decorated on its handle with the Houses of Parliament. It was a present for his mother, but if he didn't jump she wouldn't be getting it any time soon.

A few minutes after midnight, and by sheer force of will, Skinnarland made himself move. He shoved off with his hands, and moments later he plummeted into the coal-black abyss. He was hooked up to a static line attached to the Whitley's hold. As he tumbled away from the aircraft the line dragged his chute from its pack.

It blossomed in the darkness above him, the chute's cells filling with air. The canopy went rigid with a sharp crack, like a ship's sail catching a gust of wind. A strong breeze whistled through the dark rigging. This was all very different from parachuting over the balmy calm of an English spring meadow in daylight, but at least now that he had jumped Skinnarland was starting to recover something of his equanimity.

The wind was blowing hard from the north-west, driving him towards a boulder-strewn hillside. He tried to follow his instructor's advice, getting his knees together and bent, and preparing to roll with the impact. Still, he hit the rocky ground hard, his recently injured knee and then his back taking the brunt of the blow. He ended up concertinaed in a heap.

Gingerly, he tried to stand. He felt his backbone pop and fizz painfully. There was nothing he could do about that now. He began to quarter the terrain, searching for the containerload of weaponry. Unsurprisingly it was nowhere to be seen. He'd delayed the jump for a good twenty minutes, as he'd tried to pluck up the courage to go. It could have landed just about anywhere.

He glanced at the nearby Mount Gausta, his childhood playground and ski-run. It was silhouetted faintly in the dull moonlight. He figured he'd landed a good ten miles north of Lake Møs. Not a difficult journey under normal circumstances, but right now he had jolts of pain shooting through his lower back and a knee that was still tender from the recent surgery.

Skinnarland set off through the night, moving painfully slowly. He reached home just as the first rays of dawn illuminated the skies above Lake Møs. Only one person in his family knew where he had been: his brother, Torstein Skinnarland, a fellow member of the resistance. All the others – his mother and father included – greeted him as if he'd just been away for a spot of wilderness vacationing.

Doing his best to avoid any difficult questions about his injured back, he suddenly remembered the Houses of Parliament spoon. How would he explain that? You didn't exactly find such things on the Hardangervidda! He would have to save it for sometime in the future, when his mother might be safely acquainted with his more maverick activities.

Right now his first priority was to secure that containerload of weaponry. Having rested and eaten, he set off on skis to link up with some fellow resistance fighters. Many hands make light work, and he was sure to need as much help as he could muster to track down the errant cargo. If he didn't do so quickly, it would very likely get covered by the next snowfall, and be buried in a drift for the duration of the war.

On the very day that Skinnarland parachuted back into Norway, Wilson compiled a thick dossier of evidence to support an attack on Vemork. In a 'Most Secret' letter to Michael Perrin, a senior scientist at the British chemicals company ICI, now seconded to Tube Alloys, he laid out the stats on heavy water exports to the Reich, showing a six-fold increase since the German occupation began:

April to December 1940:	240 kgs
1941:	300 kgs
1st January to 6th March 1942:	300 kgs

He rounded off his letter thus: 'I see no reason against your using this information for any purpose which is covered by the designation "Most Secret" . . . but perhaps it would be well if you did not disclose the source of the information.' That source was, of course, double agent Jomar Brun.

That same day Wilson scheduled a meeting with Lord Louis Mountbatten, chief of Combined Operations, to discuss their key priority: 'A raid on the Norsk Hydro plant with the object either of putting heavy water production out of action or preferably the . . . abstraction of the highly-concentrated fraction for removal to this country.'

That last part was a new twist entirely.

It was Professor Tronstad who had first proposed that Vemork's SH200 might be stolen away, as opposed to blown up, in an effort to aid the Allies' fledgling nuclear programme. Tronstad's audacious plan – an act of maverick daring every bit the equal to the hijacking of the *Galtesund* – involved a flying boat landing on a stretch of water, possibly Lake Møs, to collect the SH200, which would have been seized by Skinnarland and his Grouse raiders.

Wilson thrilled to the idea of stealing the heavy water from under the noses of the Germans. He had a flair for the unconventional and the unthinkable. At war's outbreak, he'd been appalled to learn that membership of Britain's Civil Defence organization would be limited to those over the age of sixteen.

'An absurd decision,' he had written, as chief of the Scout Movement, and having already offered his Scouts and Rovers as signallers for the war effort. 'Boys of 14 or even 12 could easily, and almost better, act as Messengers.' Spiriting away the Nazis' heavy water was just Wilson's kind of thing.

There was a growing sense of urgency in the air at the SOE's headquarters, and for good reason. Recently, a highly reputable source in Stockholm had reported that 'the Germans are well under way with the manufacture of the uranium bomb of enormous power, which will blast everything . . . Through the power of one bomb a whole town can be levelled.'

Citing a 'Most Secret Source', the Secret Intelligence Service (SIS) had added fuel to the fire, identifying the 'intense interest of the *Abwehr* in German West Africa in general and the Belgian Congo in particular'. The Abwehr was the German equivalent of the SIS, and several of its agents had been caught trying to get into the country, 'in order to carry out espionage'.

From what the SIS could determine, the agents had been sent there to assess Allied troop movements, defensive positions, and to reconnoitre key aerodromes. The Germans were scoping out the possibility of their airborne forces seizing the country, and with it the world's foremost supply of uranium.

To add weight to such concerns, Niels Bohr – the grandfather of atomic physics, now trapped in occupied Denmark – had got a report smuggled back to London, concerning a meeting he had had with his former student, Werner Heisenberg. During their discussions, Heisenberg – the leading light at the *Uranverein* – had admitted that an atomic bomb could be made, and that 'we're working on it'.

Adding impetus to this fearful sense of urgency, Einar Skinnarland was about to deliver his first report. In the third week of April 1942 – less than a month after his return to Norway – Skinnarland made contact with the SOE. In his missive, he revealed that SH200 production had increased yet again, and was slated to rise still further.

The nuclear scientists at Tube Alloys pored over Skinnarland's findings. Like Wilson, they recognized the need to take swift action, and they sent a note to Churchill's War Cabinet. Carefully worded, but crystal clear in its thrust, it reflected their growing conviction that the Germans had to be working on a plutonium-powered nuclear weapon, as opposed to one based around uranium.

'Element 94 [plutonium] would be as good as U-235 for military purposes, and since this element is best prepared in systems involving the use of heavy water . . . an attempt should, if possible, be made to stop the Norsk Hydro production.'

In time, plutonium would become the raw material of choice for an atom bomb. It is easier to make plutonium go 'boom', and cheaper to produce than weapons-grade uranium (U-235). Combining SH200 with plutonium was a sure route to the super-bomb, and the Germans had clearly taken a number of significant steps down that road.

On 29 April the Tube Alloys luminaries penned a telegram to Wilson, entitled 'Heavy Water'. 'The entire production . . . is being taken by the Germans for scientific work of the highest importance. We are exceedingly interested to know to what address the supplies are being dispatched . . . I have been asked if there is any possibility of obtaining this information. Could you help?'

Of course, Wilson already had a sense of this. In June the previous year he'd learned that the SH200 was being shipped to the Berlin office of physicist Kurt Diebner, the head of the *Uranverein*. But that was fully ten months ago. With few, if any, SOE agents inside Germany, and none able to penetrate the Third Reich's nuclear research programme, his best – his only – source of intelligence lay within the Vemork plant.

This was yet another request that would have to be radioed to Skinnarland: *discover where the SH200 is being sent in Germany.*

In correspondence flowing back and forth between SOE, Tube Alloys and their political taskmasters, all sides expressed the pressing need for secrecy. 'This is, of course, an extremely secret matter', a Tube Alloys letter to the War Office stressed. If word should leak out about Operation Grouse it would be a disaster, for such small-scale raids depended above all else on the element of surprise.

In the name of secrecy the Germans had adopted their own codeword for Vemork's precious liquid: SH200. Wilson felt the need for an equivalent. 'Would it not be best to have some code name for this particular subject?' he suggested. A decision was taken: 'Code name Lurgan had been allocated to SOE's interest in deuterium oxide' – deuterium oxide being heavy water's scientific name.

Over the late spring and early summer further reports were filed by Skinnarland, some secreted as microdots hidden inside toothpaste tubes. Wilson's intelligence pipeline had begun to pump information – from Jomar Brun, the inside man; via Skinnarland, the conduit; to Professor Tronstad, the in-house expert and analyst; and on to Wilson himself, the man of action.

Photographs, diagrams and minutely detailed sketches of the Vemork plant – all were reduced to images that could be hidden inside a full stop, and sent to London. Wilson made sure that Churchill was kept abreast of the key developments on heavy water, now referred to as 'Lurgan' in all correspondence. The British prime minister was planning a crucial trip to the USA, and top of his agenda were nuclear weapons.

On 17 June 1942 Churchill boarded a Boeing flying boat for what was possibly the single most important meeting of the war. His final destination would be Hyde Park, in New York, where he and Roosevelt had much to discuss. The four-engine Boeing 318 Clipper was one of the largest aircraft of the time, and it was specifically designed for transatlantic flights. Typically, Churchill was the first head of government to make such a crossing by aircraft, and he had good reasons to take such a risk right now.

As the 150-foot wingspan behemoth crawled into the air above the midnight waters of Stranraer, the issue of the race to build the first atomic bomb lay heavily on Churchill's mind. He knew that Britain alone could never win such a contest with Nazi Germany. He needed America to come on board the nuclear train.

Of course, there was a great deal on his mind during the long flight. In spite of America's entry into the war, all was not going well. In North Africa, General Rommel's panzer divisions pummelled Allied forces; German U-boats hounded the Atlantic convoys shipping vital war materiel from the USA to Britain; the American military had still not fully recovered from the Japanese attack on Pearl Harbor; much of London had been devastated in the Blitz; and Western Europe languished under Hitler's iron fist.

France, Poland, Denmark, Norway, Belgium, Holland, Austria, Greece, Czechoslovakia, Hungary, Romania and Yugoslavia all lay under Nazi Germany's dominion, with fascist Italy as their partners in aggression. But uppermost in Churchill's mind was one burning question: how far ahead of the Allies were the Germans in the nuclear field, and what could be done to stop them?

'We both felt painfully the dangers of doing nothing,' Churchill would later write, the 'we' referring to his good friend Roosevelt. 'We knew what efforts the Germans were making to procure supplies of heavy water – a sinister term, eerie, unnatural, which began to creep into our secret papers. What if the enemy should get the atomic bomb before we did! We could not run the mortal risk of being outstripped in this awful sphere.'

From Frederick Lindemann, his scientific adviser, Churchill

understood that he could, should he so wish, use heavy water as ice cubes to chill his whisky, to water his flower borders at Chartwell, and even give it to his grandchildren to drink. It was as harmless to humans as ordinary water. But combine it with plutonium, and it was another matter entirely.

After a long flight – travelling with the sun seemed to 'slow' the passage of time – involving two luncheons at six-hour intervals, the Clipper arrived in Washington, landing on the Potomac River. The following morning a military aircraft whisked Churchill to Hyde Park, from where he was driven around the Roosevelt family estate by the President.

Intense discussions on the nuclear issue ensued. Both men had been briefed extensively regarding the state of their own nuclear programmes, and the belief – universal amongst the Allies – that Nazi Germany was significantly more advanced. One eminent US scientists had declared recently: 'Nobody can tell . . . whether we shall be ready before German bombs wipe out American cities.'

In truth, if and when Hitler secured a nuclear weapon London doubtless would be his first target. If he could devastate the British capital at a stroke, succeeding where the might of the Luftwaffe had failed, the war would be a giant step closer to being won. In the face of such brute, implacable power Britain would be forced to surrender, and America, deprived of a spring-board from which to launch the liberation of Europe, would be hamstrung.

Both leaders knew of the role played by the SH200 in Vemork. Since a large supply of heavy water was unavailable to the Allies, they had no option but to work with an alternative moder-ator, and graphite was their favoured option. But if Britain and America combined forces, a bomb could be built in the US, while suitable heavy water plants might be constructed in Canada, which had ample hydroelectric potential.

Churchill argued that the two beacons of the free world needed to 'pool our information, work together on equal terms, and share the result, if any, equally between us.' Roosevelt agreed wholeheartedly. The two leaders cut a deal to collaborate. But at the same time they realized the pressing need to sabotage the German nuclear programme at every possible turn.

Somehow, Germany's two-year lead in the nuclear field had to be cut. The Allies needed time and breathing space to pull ahead of the Reich. Crucial to that was heavy water: it was the only raw material being used to make the Nazi bomb that was conceivably within the Allies' reach. It was crucial to cut the supply of SH200: by doing so, they might regain crucial time lost to Germany.

Churchill flew back to London and ordered that the Vemork plant be hit as soon as possible. The great man had spoken, and he had done so with the full weight of the American president behind him. The War Cabinet decreed that 'the very highest priority be allotted to this target'. A 3 July memo raised the prospect of an attack, suggesting: 'It might be a flying boat project.' It was left to Combined Operations HQ's department of Raid Planners to come up with a plan.

Wilson was the foremost proponent of hitting Vemork, but he felt the first twinges of alarm now. In a 'Most Secret' 29 July memo, he reiterated that heavy water was 'regarded as a most highly secret matter'. If a commando-style raid was in the offing, it went against the advice from the experts. Tube Alloys had cautioned against doing anything 'that might attract the enemy's attention to the fact that we are aware of the significance of the Vemork works'.

It was the age-old conundrum. If a raid were launched and failed, the enemy would be forewarned and forearmed. In his 29 July memo Wilson stressed that the SOE had 'a party who could make an attempt to cut the pipeline at VEMORK . . . It is a difficult project, but one worth undertaking.' By 'a party' he meant Skinnarland and his Grouse force – four further SOE operators who were scheduled to join him.

Wilson argued skilfully that Vemork was SOE business and should remain so. Writing of the need to destroy both the existing heavy water and its means of production, he stated: 'The application of this product to H.E. [high explosives] is both Churchill's and Hitler's secret weapon, and bands of scientists are engaged in a race for the final result . . . It is vitally necessary that the greatest secrecy should be preserved, and unfortunately many people appear to have been dabbling in this highly dangerous subject.'

As the summer 1942 heat hit London, Wilson and Tronstad held a crunch meeting with the movers and shakers at Combined Operations and Tube Alloys, to talk through options. Several possible means of attack were mooted:

1. Local sabotage, using those already employed at the plant.
2. Sending in an SOE sabotage party.
3. Sending in a commando force using flying boats for both insertion and extraction.
4. Sending in a 'suicide squad' – one that had no chance of escape.
5. RAF bombing.

Option one was pretty much a non-starter: if it failed, their key intelligence asset – Jomar Brun, the inside man at Vemork –

would be severely compromised. Option five had some merit, in that the suggestion now was to bomb the Norvann dam situated high above the Vemork works. It would doubtless have a cataclysmic impact on the plant below, but would very likely 'prove fatal to the whole population in the valley'. The risk of collateral damage was unacceptably high.

Wilson argued that options three and four were pretty much one and the same thing: a commando force *was* a suicide squad; they would stand little if any chance of escape. Colonel Robert Neville, chief planner at Combined Operations, tended to agree, but still he favoured such an assault. Several dozen commandos could overpower whatever defences the Germans might have in place, and put Vemork out of action for the duration of the war.

Wilson and Tronstad remained convinced that the Grouse force needed to be used, in a small-scale guerrilla-style attack. With Skinnarland on the ground, and four others poised for their insertion, it was the option that made the greatest sense, they argued. A small force of Norwegians would stand by far the best chance of getting into the plant without being noticed, and of making a getaway.

For now at least, Wilson appeared to have got his way. Vemork would remain chiefly an SOE operation, with Skinnarland and party being the means to effect the vital mission. Fortunately, the Operation Grouse team was in the final stages of their intensive training.

And the man that Wilson intended to lead them figured that they were ready to strike.

Chapter Eleven

Jens-Anton Poulsson studied the structure that towered before him – a serried rank of wooden cylinders, eighteen in all, set vertically along one wall of the English stately home. In recent weeks he and his men had been taken to a power station at Fort William, in north-west Scotland, which was powered by the dam on the nearby River Spean.

The Fort William hydro station was seen as being the nearest thing to the Vemork works Britain had to offer, and an ideal place to rehearse the coming attack. They'd also toured the hydrolysis cells at Lever Brothers, then Britain's chief manufacturer of soap, to familiarize themselves with such structures. But nothing beats seeing, and practising, on the real thing. The structure set before Poulsson was as close as he'd ever get to the Vemork heavy water plant, until they blew it sky high or were killed or captured in the process.

This was the culmination of many weeks' training at what the Germans now referred to as the 'International Gangster School'. The SOE's experts had taught Poulsson and his team all there was to know about fighting in the shadows. They'd been shown how to force locks and blow open safes; how to escape from handcuffs; how to cobble together every booby trap imaginable; how to handle TNT, dynamite, gun cotton and Nobel 808; how to fight with rifles, tommy guns, pistols, knives, poison, knock-out drugs and their fists and feet.

They'd practised blasting holes in reinforced concrete and blowing down steel doors; they'd learned how to tap lightly on a tommy gun's trigger, to fire single shots and so conserve ammunition, which on missions such as theirs was bound to be in precious short supply. They'd learned the means of silent death – how to use the commando knife and the garrotte to kill a man before he could utter the barest sound. They'd trained in a life-sized mock-up of a village – learning to unleash fire at pop-up targets that appeared at doors, windows and around corners.

They'd been taught that if it came to a fight, it was often better to 'put a German in hospital. That ties up other Germans. A dead one is buried and out of the way.' They'd been shown the vulnerable points of the body, and reminded that they would almost always have a weapon in their pocket: a nail file; a pin; a fountain pen. So much the better if the pen came from the SOE's gadget department – MD1, Churchill's Toyshop – and was designed to squirt out cyanide. MD1 developed booby-trapped loaves of bread, incendiary cigarettes and exploding mice and rats. An expert at London Zoo had been consulted on what colour to paint explosive animal droppings, to ensure they resembled the genuine article.

And now, at Special Training Station XVII, they were learning how to sabotage a heavy water hydrolysis plant, using a model built to the exact specifications, but entirely out of wood.

The team at STS XVII – based at Brickendonbury Hall, a former country estate requisitioned by the SOE at the start of the war – had been ordered to 'mock-up a 9-cell concentration battery'. Two such mock-ups made an eighteen-piece replica of the apparatus that produced the heavy water.

Creating this model had been something of a challenge, even

for the STS XVII experts. Each of the eighteen hydrolysis cells rose to twice the height of a fully grown man, set a few metres apart from each other. Only one room at the Edwardian mansion was large enough to accommodate such a structure. Fortunately, the boffins, inventors, metalworkers, carpenters, cabinet-makers and other assorted tradespeople employed at STS XVII had proved up to the task.

Using the model, Poulsson and his men were able to practise fixing live charges to the most vulnerable parts of the SH200 apparatus, until they could do so with their eyes closed. Of course, the eighteen cells at Vemork were fashioned out of steel, as opposed to wood, but STS XVII had an answer for that as well. Poulsson and his men had got to blow up a cast-steel turbine, and with wonderful results.

'A hole was blown clean through both the bottom . . . and the top,' recorded a very pleased-sounding Station XVII instructor, in a report entitled 'Operation LURGAN'. Clearly if the charges worked on that turbine's thick steel casing, they were certain to rip Vemork's hydrolysis cells to shreds.

By the time Poulsson and his fellow raiders left Station XVII, they could have navigated their way around the Vemork hydrolysis room blindfolded and with their hands tied behind their backs. Which was just as Wilson wanted it. When it came to the attack, they almost certainly would be operating in close to pitch darkness, they might well be in the midst of a firefight, and they could be injured. He was determined to furnish them with every conceivable advantage.

There would be little point parachuting into Norway as an undercover sabotage force if their clothing or personal effects gave them away. Everything had to appear as if it was genuine, and sourced from behind the iron wall that Hitler had thrown around Europe. Indeed, it was better if every item that the Grouse force stood up in *was* entirely genuine.

A whole SOE department had been established to work to just such an agenda. At immigration desks across the UK and Allied nations, customs agents scrutinized travellers coming from Europe. One or two might be asked to step aside. They wore clothes stitched in European capitals, with European tailors' labels affixed, and they carried pens, pencils and other paraphernalia manufactured in towns now under German occupation.

While those passengers were being questioned, their luggage might quietly disappear. Their attaché cases, stuffed full of 'epistolary paraphernalia' – headed paper, rubber stamps, erasers, and all sourced from Nazi-occupied Europe – would be thoroughly searched. Invariably, the traveller, worried that they might be in trouble, wouldn't notice those few items that had somehow gone missing, or not until it was too late.

Travellers were even followed so that their clothing could be 'liberated' from a laundry or hotel room, to contribute to the SOE's ever-expanding wardrobe. Others at SOE scoured the archives of news organizations and movie companies, seeking that elusive few minutes of film reel that might help an agent better visualize territory now under enemy control.

Such were the exhaustive measures that had gone into preparing Poulsson and his team.

Wilson had chosen Poulsson to lead Operation Grouse for one simple reason: the incredible single-mindedness and tenacity that he had demonstrated in reaching Britain in the first place. If a man was willing to undertake such a desperate journey so that he could join the fight against the enemy, Wilson couldn't conceive of him baulking at a mission such as this.

Born to a wealthy and distinguished family – they owned 10,000 acres on the Hardangervidda, including land around Lake Møs – Poulsson had grown up on the right side of the tracks. In Norsk Hydro's Rjukan town, you either lived in the sun or in the shade, reflecting your wealth and your status. The rich and the powerful owned property on the town's sunlit heights; those at the other end of the scale dwelled in the valley's depths, in near-permanent shadow.

With curly dark hair and a shy manner, Poulsson devoured stories of adventure and heroism as a child. Together with his good friend and classmate, Claus Helberg, he spent much of his youth hunting, fishing, skiing and climbing in the Hardanger-vidda. He loved the outdoors, and grew to have a calm, understated authority over his peers. He'd always known what he wanted to be when he grew up: an officer in the Royal Norwegian Army.

The day the Germans invaded, the twenty-something Poulsson was at officer training school. Within five days his battalion was forced to surrender, with barely a shot fired. It was the saddest day of his life. Still he burned to fight, and he was not to be dis-suaded. In January 1941 he skied across the mountains to the Swedish border. From there he tried to find an aircraft going to Britain, so he could to sign up with the Linge Company, but there were none available.

Impatient, the young Poulsson set off in the only direction left open to him – east across Finland, and onwards into the Soviet Union. From there he'd found his way to Turkey, where he hoped to catch a ship passing through the Mediterranean, and onwards to Britain. But the German and Italian navies menaced the Med, and so Poulsson, the dusty wanderer, was forced to push further south – through Syria, Lebanon and Egypt, where he'd boarded a vessel bound for India.

From India he'd crossed the Arabian Sea to East Africa, travelled down the coast to South Africa, and then caught a ship routed to the West Indies. From Trinidad he flew to Canada, and eventually found passage on a transatlantic convoy bound for Britain. After a nine-month odyssey, he finally reached England in October 1941, on a ship steaming into Liverpool docks.

Recruited into the Linge Company, the six-foot-two and decidedly reticent Poulsson – striking-looking, with his tousled mop of hair and bright blue eyes – wasn't at first glance an obvious leader of men. Indeed, his SOE training officer had concluded of him: 'Much more intelligent than he would first appear . . . Could make a good second-in-command.'

Wilson begged to differ. He had the tall, quiet Norwegian earmarked as Grouse's commander. Anyone capable of such a global voyage must burn to strike back hard against the enemy, and there was no better way to do so than by leading Operation Grouse.

Poulsson, now twenty-four years old, and with a lean, athlete's physique, was never to be found without his pipe. Whether he was stuffing it with tobacco, smoking it or cleaning it, he had made it his constant companion and friend. He had had it stuck in the corner of his mouth when he came calling at the SOE's London headquarters, two months earlier, to meet with Wilson and Tronstad.

As succinctly as he could, Wilson had outlined what they had in mind for him, and the basics of Operation Grouse.

'Interesting,' Poulsson had remarked, as he'd knocked the dead ashes from his pipe into his palm.

If he joined Operation Grouse he would be playing for high stakes. His parents, sisters and his younger brother still lived in Rjukan. If he were captured or otherwise identified as one of the raiders, he didn't doubt what would happen. The Germans had a place for the enemies of the Reich. In a clearing in the forest ten kilometres north of Oslo stood the Grini concentration camp. Formerly a prison, the long, brick-built cell blocks now housed thousands.

Many were sent to Grini; few ever returned. Two sets of barbed wire fences surrounded the camp, complete with guards and watchtowers. If Poulsson were captured, that was where his family was going. Regardless, he hadn't hesitated. He'd sparked up his pipe, puffed away contentedly, and told Wilson and Tronstad that he was their man.

Wilson felt certain that Poulsson was going to make an admirable commander of Operation Grouse. The former Scoutmaster had learned to foster a maverick, bloody-minded independence amongst his agents. Nothing else would get you through the kind of task that Poulsson and his men were about to undertake. That was why he'd left it to the tall, lean-featured Norwegian to assemble his own team.

Poulsson's first choice was obvious: his childhood playmate, Claus Helberg. Poulsson had been given a shotgun for his eleventh birthday, and he and Helberg had practically worn out the barrel during their teenage years on the 'Vidda', as the locals referred to the Hardanger Plateau. But there was never any doubt who was the better hunter. With his innate feeling for movement and terrain, and the ability to act purely on sixth sense and instinct, Helberg had an uncanny way with the wild. He was a born hunter and a natural survivor without equal.

With a wild gleam in his eye, Helberg had a habit of scratching the top of his head while ruminating on his troubles. And trouble did indeed seem to court him. He was renowned for getting into terrible scrapes, and miraculously getting out of them again. He was an innocent-faced but daring improviser. As his friends used to joke: the daring got him into trouble; the innocent-faced improvisation got him out again.

'I've never know a man who could get into and out of trouble so quickly,' Poulsson remarked of his friend.

Helberg had fought against the German invaders and had been taken as a prisoner of war. With typical ingenuity he'd escaped and fled to Sweden, finding his way to the SOE office in Stockholm. He'd volunteered for intelligence work, and returned to Norway as a courier. But during one subsequent run to the Swedish border he'd been arrested, and spent four months in captivity. Finally, he'd managed to get out of Norway and make it to Britain, where he'd signed up with the Linge Company.

Poulsson chose two other Linge Company veterans to join him and Helberg. The first, Arne Kjelstrup, was a short, squat, broad-shouldered powerhouse of a man in his late twenties. Kjelstrup had a bullet lodged in his hip from fighting the Germans. Badly wounded, he'd been taken prisoner, but had escaped at night and headed north to a spot where he and another escapee figured fighting might still be possible.

They'd come across some abandoned Bren guns and ammunition, and set an ambush for the enemy. Firing across a river in the valley bottom, they'd unloaded so much ammunition into a German column that the Brens had overheated and jammed. The two men made themselves scarce, just as the much larger force of enemy troops – having suffered many injured and dead – came after them with a vengeance.

Kjelstrup had fled to Sweden, where he'd joined Poulsson for much of his round-the-world journey to Britain. Needless to say, they had developed strong bonds of friendship and camaraderie during the long months spent in exotic parts.

The fourth Grouse recruit was Knut Haugland. A slender 24-year-old, Haugland had delicate, boyish features set below a wild frizz of blond hair. The son of a Rjukan carpenter, he was already a superlative radio operator prior to the outbreak of war. He'd learned his trade on merchant ships, and following the German invasion he'd found himself on the front line, scrambling through the thick bush to locate the enemy so he could radio their positions to his commanders.

He was forever under attack from machine guns, mortars or enemy warplanes, and he'd learned something a man only realizes when tested under such conditions: for whatever reason, he was almost preternaturally calm when under fire, and especially so when operating his Morse key. Indeed, the worse a situation got, the cooler Haugland seemed to become.

Following the Norwegian surrender, Haugland became a clandestine radio operator with the resistance. But after repeated arrests, he had been forced to flee to Britain. He and Poulsson were fond of stag hunting in the Scottish hills during breaks from training at the Linge Company, and Poulsson had quickly learned that Haugland had what it took to survive in the wild. He was a natural choice as the team's radio operator.

Wilson had every confidence in these men. They'd been tested in mortal combat in Norway, in the most trying of conditions, but they'd also been tested by the SOE, and in ways the men themselves might not even have realized. Wilson was an expert in counter-espionage and psychological warfare, two fields in which he had specialized during his time with the Colonial Police Service in India. Naturally, he'd brought such disciplines into the repertoire of the SOE.

Prospective SOE recruits were first screened at the Royal Victoria 'Patriotic School', in London. There they were made to sign a version of the Official Secrets Act, forbidding them from speaking to anyone about the organization they were aspiring to join. Surprisingly, considering the SOE's desperate need for agents, those doing the screening were ruthless in culling numbers. Only the best were good enough.

There was no set formula for vetting recruits. The Patriotic School 'examiners' preferred to trust their instincts, aided by a number of devious and underhand techniques. The recruits were spied upon at all hours of the day. Even at night they were under secret scrutiny, to check if they talked in their sleep or did anything else that might risk blowing their cover. They were taken out to London bars, and offered as much as they could drink. If anyone started blabbing, or boasting, or became troublesome in his cups, he was an instant reject.

Poulsson, Helberg, Kjelstrup and Haugland had passed such exacting tests. In Wilson's mind, they were as good as it got. They had better be. The list of the men assigned to Operation Grouse was even now sitting on Winston Churchill's desk, along with a mountain of other paperwork. After his meeting with Roosevelt, Churchill had an intense personal interest in their forthcoming mission.

One man was desperate to join the Grouse team: Wilson's good friend Leif Tronstad. Tronstad felt frustrated. He'd come to

Britain so he could fight, but had ended up running intelligence networks and training programmes. When he wasn't in meetings discussing nuclear issues, he was pushing paper around his desk. Meanwhile, many of his close friends were either held captive or dead – victims of the predations of the Gestapo.

Worse still, his family was suffering, and all because of the stand that he had taken. Evicted from their home, his wife was hounded daily for information about what had happened to her husband. Others – Skinnarland, Jomar Brun – were on the ground risking life and limb in a clandestine war to free their country. Yet the nearest Tronstad seemed to get to any action was a little DIY 'commando training' on Hampstead Heath, an area of parkland near his London home.

At thirty-nine, Tronstad was himself a recent graduate of parachute training school. He'd stopped smoking and was exercising as never before. He believed himself ready to accompany the Grouse force into action and pitched the idea to Wilson. The former Scoutmaster demurred. Tronstad was far too valuable in London, serving as the rock to which all Norway's nuclear issues were tethered.

By late summer of 1942 all was set. It only remained for Wilson to give the Grouse team their cover stories and code words. They were each provided with false names, plus forged identity documents and ration cards. Poulsson was a mechanic, Helberg and Haugland were students, and Kjelstrup was a plumber.

Skinnarland would guide them in, placing lights around their intended drop zone. If for whatever reason they missed him, they were to make contact with his brother, Torstein Skinnarland, at the dam on Lake Møs where he worked. They were to use the pass phrase: 'Do you know Auntie Kjersti?' Torstein would reply: 'No, but I know her brother.'

Under Poulsson's leadership, they would link up with Skinnarland and proceed to take an unsuspecting Vemork plant by total surprise, cutting off at source the supply of heavy water. In one fell swoop, the Allies would strike a devastating blow against the Nazis' nuclear ambitions – and not before time. But then came the unforeseen and the totally unexpected.

Operation Musketoon hit the Glomfjord power station like a whirlwind, and the fallout reverberated powerfully across all of the Third Reich.

Chapter Twelve

The Glomfjord power station lay in ruins. The shattered pipe-lines had stopped spurting their deluge, but the damage was already done. No more water would be channelled through the giant turbine hall for the duration of the war, and further along the fjord, the aluminium factory would likewise remain out of action. Seven of the raiders had been taken prisoner, one was dead, and four were on the run.

On 24 September 1942, the ship carrying the Musketoon seven – Captain Graeme Black and his six fellow captives – docked at Trondheim, and they were immediately transferred to Akershus military prison. There they were interrogated once more, but they argued that they had acted as British soldiers and would divulge nothing more about their operation.

For several days the questioning continued, as the German commanders tried to ascertain just how many raiders had attacked Glomfjord, and who had escaped. Black repeated over and over the same phrase, with pointed politeness: 'Very sorry, sir, I can't tell you anything.' So too did Joe Houghton, his second-in-command, and the other captives.

But while the interrogations were ongoing, General von Falk-enhorst, Commander-in-Chief of German forces in Norway, was fighting to keep the captives in his custody, men that he secretly admired for their courageous and daring actions. If he failed, he knew what awaited – they would be drawn into the clutches of the SS.

A week after their arrival at Akershus, von Falkenhorst finally lost that battle. Shortly after dawn a line of trucks drew up at the prison. The German military guards were ordered to handcuff the seven captives. At first they refused, knowing it was illegal to chain prisoners of war. The *Oberleutnant* in charge of the convoy told the guards to do as he'd ordered.

The captives weren't prisoners of war, he snapped. 'They're saboteurs who attacked wearing civilian clothes.'

Of course, this was untrue, but the seven men were chained in any case. They were taken to the docks to be loaded aboard the SS *Donau*, a large cargo ship requisitioned by the German Navy and now used as an armed transport vessel. The *Donau* would become infamous as a 'slave ship', one used to transport Jews to Auschwitz, as she plied the sea lanes between Norway and Germany.

On 7 October, after a long sea voyage followed by a train journey, the Musketoon seven reached the end of the line. Perched on a wooded hill that rises above the town of Colditz, in eastern Germany, is an ancient castle and hunting lodge. Officially known as Oflag IV-C, and to the locals as Colditz Castle, the Allied prisoners of war housed there proudly it called 'the bad boys' camp'. It was to Oflag IV-C that those who'd made repeated escape attempts, or otherwise infuriated their German captors, were sent.

At Colditz, security was paramount. The castle was floodlit at night, and the guards who patrolled the barbed wire fences and watchtowers outnumbered the inmates, who were mostly officers. Prisoners were punished for insulting Germany, for trying to escape – which happened surprisingly often – or for shoving a sentry to deflect his fire away from a fleeing inmate. They enjoyed dropping water, stones and other projectiles onto the guards patrolling far below the high walls, though this could earn them a long spell in solitary confinement.

It was early evening when Black and his men were marched into the outer courtyard of the castle. After being processed, they were locked in an isolated room, out of sight and earshot of the other prisoners. The following morning they were brought out, so they could be photographed. During that procedure two long-time inmates managed to sneak within earshot of the newly arrived men.

'Hello there!' they cried. 'Where are you chaps from?'

'We're commandos from Norway,' came the reply.

'Any messages?' the inmates yelled.

'Get word back where we are.'

That was all that Black and his men could manage before the guards silenced them. Unaware that they had ended up in the most heavily guarded prison in all of Europe, the Musketoon captives decided to escape. That evening, when their jailer came to carry out a head count, they dragged him inside, disarmed and gagged him. But within moments of bursting out of their room the Colditz guards were upon them, weapons at the ready.

As punishment, the raiders were thrown into the solitary confinement cells. But even there, one of the Colditz inmates still managed to sneak a message through to them. In return he was slipped a list of their names. That list would in turn reach the Red Cross, and get passed on to London.

Try as they might, the regular Colditz prisoners couldn't fathom who these mystery captives might be. Why were they

being held in isolation from all the others? Of all the thousands of Allied prisoners, what made these seven so apparently
dangerous? What possible actions might justify such unprecedented treatment?

The answer was known only to those within the highest
echelons of the Reich, and to Hitler himself. The success of
Musketoon – along with previous commando raids, such as
that at Saint-Nazaire – had so enraged the Führer that he had
decided to make a special case of such men. On the day that
Black and his fellow captives arrived at Colditz, he drafted his
infamous *Kommandobefehl* – the 'Commando Order'.

It read:

> Henceforth all enemy troops encountered by German
> troops during so-called commando operations . . . though
> they appear to be soldiers in uniform or demolition groups,
> armed or unarmed, are to be exterminated to the last
> man . . . If such men appear to be about to surrender, no
> quarter should be given to them.

German officers were ordered to 'Report daily the numbers of
saboteurs thus liquidated . . . The number of executions must
appear in the daily communiqué of the *Wehrmacht* to serve as a
warning to potential terrorists.'

The order ended with a chilling warning to any commander
who might have the temerity to oppose it. 'I will summon before
the tribunal of war, all leaders and officers who fail to carry out
these instructions – either by failure to inform their men or by
their disobedience of this order in action.'

Hitler must have known that he was sanctioning war crimes;

the efforts to hide the order's existence were unprecedented. Each copy was stamped: 'This order is intended for commanders only, and must not under any circumstances fall into enemy hands.' It was classified 'Most Secret' and was to be committed to memory, after which all printed copies were to be destroyed.

On 13 October – six days after their arrival at Colditz – the Musketoon seven were moved. Their escorts were now SS, and their destination was the German capital, Berlin. Upon arrival they were taken to the notorious dungeon of the *Reichssicherheitshauptamt* – the Reich Main Security Office – the headquarters of the SS. The *Reichssicherheitshauptamt* was known as a place of terrible suffering, where medieval tortures had been refined to a dark art.

Black and his men spent nine days at the *Reichssicherheitshauptamt*. From there they were moved to Sachsenhausen, a concentration camp on the outskirts of Berlin. They arrived in the late afternoon and were placed in the *Zellenbau*, a prison within a prison. None but a handful of top officials knew of their presence.

That evening, a sheet of paper was posted on the wall of the camp. It listed seven names: Graeme Black, Joseph Houghton, Cyril Abram, Rex Makeham, Miller Smith, Eric Curtis and Bill Chudley. The names were bracketed together, and marked 'SD' – signifying their pending execution.

At dawn on 23 October 1942 – a little over a month after their attack on Glomfjord – they were taken from their cells, and each man was killed with a shot to the back of the head. Their bodies were burned in the camp crematorium.

The Musketoon seven were the first Allied soldiers executed

under Hitler's Commando Order, but the fallout from Musketoon was only just beginning. The SS reported the executions to the German Army, who took swift steps to hide the facts of their deaths. The British government was duly informed that seven prisoners of war had escaped from Colditz. All mail sent to the Musketoon seven was to be returned to sender, marked 'Geflohen' – escaped.

The 'fact' of the raiders' escape was reported to their families in Britain and Canada, and that there was no evidence of their recapture. Understandably, the next of kin hoped that their sons or husbands or brothers were hiding somewhere in occupied Europe. Such a cruel deception would endure until the end of the war.

The four Musketoon raiders still at large – Sverre Granlund, Richard O'Brien, Fred Trigg and Jack Fairclough – managed to escape to Sweden, from where they returned to Britain, but they could shed little light upon the seven captives' plight. The exploits of those four men – battling freezing conditions, storms, German patrols, starvation, exhaustion, the wild terrain, and aided at every turn by brave and loyal Norwegians – earned fulsome praise from Mountbatten himself.

'Congratulations,' Mountbatten told them. 'You've done a great job. It was a complete success.' He showed them an air reconnaissance photo of Glomfjord, taken shortly after the raid. 'The place is a shambles. It will be impossible to replace it for the duration of the war.'

But in occupied Norway, the rendering of Glomfjord into a 'shambles' was having its own, unforeseen repercussions. On the day that the SS Donau had shipped the Musketoon seven out of

Norwegian waters, General von Falkenhorst had paid a visit to the Vemork works. Having inspected the guard force and the defences, the German commander called together the directors, engineers, workers and soldiers concerned with the plant.

Von Falkenhorst spoke to them at length, outlining how just a few days earlier a force of British commandos had blown up a hydroelectric station not dissimilar to this one, at Glomfjord, putting production there at a complete standstill. The German general proceeded to grab one of his listeners in a chokehold, demonstrating how fiercely the British commandos would attack guards. They might arrive at Rjukan by bus or by train, he warned, disguised as ordinary passengers.

They would be equipped with a hidden arsenal of weaponry, including 'automatic weapons with silencers, chloroform, hand grenades, knuckle-dusters'. Von Falkenhorst made clear the great admiration he felt for the commandos and their brave actions, but he warned that Vemork had to be made ready to deter or repulse such an assault. From now on high-ranking German officers would be visiting the plant regularly, overseeing a major revamp of security.

The sure-fire way to prevent such an attack was to block all approaches to the plant. Minefields would be strung around the pipelines, which rose to a great height at the rear of the build-ings, offering the one relatively easy route of ingress. The pipes themselves would be ringed with barbed wire, plus an electrified circuit linked to alarms. If anyone got close to the pipelines, the guard force would have immediate warning.

To the front of the plant the sheer impregnability of the terrain made attack all but impossible: steep cliffs fell away, plunging some 200 metres to the fierce Måna River, which cut through the deep Vestfjord Valley. One single-span suspension bridge forded the gorge, giving access to the plant. It was gated at the far end, and would be guarded and watched around the clock.

As for the plant itself, it would be transformed into a fortress. Searchlights and machine guns would be positioned on the roof, from where they could sweep the entire length of the valley. Booby traps and tripwires would be installed at key points of entry. The guard force would be augmented by thirty-five Alpine troops, some of the Reich's finest, all armed with automatic weapons. A further two hundred troops would be drafted into Rjukan town as a quick reaction force.

Having dealt with Vemork specifically, von Falkenhorst went on to strengthen his defences across Norway as a whole. Around 300,000 further German troops were drafted into the country. Extra guard posts, fortifications and gun emplacements would be installed at key locations. Air patrols would be stepped up, with further night operations. And all lakes in the vicinity of key targets would be blockaded, to prevent the landing of seaplanes carrying commandos.

The nature of von Falkenhorst's orders doubtless reflected what had been learned from the Musketoon captives, under interrogation by the SS at the *Reichssicherheitshauptamt* dungeons. Originally, the saboteurs had been expecting a seaplane to collect them post-attack – hence the blockading of key stretches of water.

Shortly, von Falkenhorst would also draw up plans for the invasion of neutral Sweden, the Musketoon seven's intended route to safety. The hawk-faced general was determined to learn the lessons from the Glomfjord sabotage, to ensure no such attacks were possible in future.

Einar Skinnarland – the Operation Grouse advance party – conveyed news of the Vemork reinforcements to London.

On the 30 October Tronstad sent a report to Wilson, marked 'Most Secret'. It opened: 'LURGAN. I have received . . . information from the other side which does not look at all promising.' It went on to outline the major security measures undertaken at the Vemork plant, as a direct response to the Glomfjord attack.

Wilson felt obliged to draft a letter to Combined Operations, proposing the cancelling of Operation Grouse due to 'an influx of enemy troops, and a great increase in the number and strength of enemy posts, particularly in the immediate neighbourhood of our objective.'

One small-scale raid – Musketoon – seemed to have accidentally backfired upon another, Operation Grouse. It had put the enemy on the alert, and prompted them to beef up their defences, making any attempt to cut off the supply of heavy water that much more daunting. The plan to blow up the Vemork pipelines and inundate the plant with a deluge of debris now seemed unworkable.

News of these developments reached Churchill's ears. The daily list of German signals intercepts that crossed his desk reflected the clampdown across Norway: 'The Norwegian Police have been instructed that meetings of Norwegians and Swedes on the frontier are absolutely forbidden and must be prevented.' There were also orders for a purge of any resistance networks, and especially those with links to possible sabotage operations.

At the same time the threat from Nazi Germany appeared ever more chilling. Over the summer, a report had been drawn up by Tube Alloys asserting that Heisenberg 'was in charge of experimental work on the production of a U235 bomb'. Heisenberg was believed to have half a tonne of heavy water at his disposal, and was 'due to receive a further tonne'.

More worrying still was a stark warning received from US intelligence chiefs. It concluded that 'the Germans had a power plant in operation and that there was a possibility that they might intend to use radio-active fission products as a military weapon in the near future.' Into this nuclear cauldron was about to be added the most worrisome ingredient of all – the V1 'flying bombs' and the V2 rockets, then being developed and tested by Nazi Germany.

At first, the German code name for the V1 – the *Flakzielgerat 76* (flak-aiming apparatus) – helped hide its true nature from the Allies. But then reports began to filter in from agents in occupied Europe of a flying bomb capable of hitting London. The 'V' of V1 stood for *Vergeltungswaffe* – meaning vengeance weapon. That autumn the V1 was tested at Peenemunde, a top-secret military research and development centre in northern Germany.

Shortly thereafter, the massive V2 was launched, reaching a height of 84.5 kilometres – just fifteen and a half kilometres short of the borders of space. The V2 was a decade ahead of its time in terms of both design and engineering. It was the world's first long-range guided ballistic missile. It combined large, liquid-fuelled rocket engines with supersonic aerodynamics, gyroscopic guidance systems and rudders providing 'jet control'.

As the 3 October V2 test flight tore apart the heavens above the Baltic, Walter Dornberger, a key rocket scientist, proclaimed a 'new era . . . of space travel.' Intelligence on the V weapons seeped into Britain. Allied reports spoke of 'liquid air bombs being developed in Germany . . . of terrific destructive power.' William Stephenson – the quiet Canadian, and Churchill's intelligence supremo – noted that these were very possibly *Vergeltungswaffe* rockets carrying nuclear warheads.

At the same time, evidence of the Holocaust – of mass murder on an unprecedented scale – had started to reach the ears of Churchill and Roosevelt. Churchill decried what he called 'this bestial policy of cold-blooded extermination'. The mechanics of mass killing perfected in the Reich were, 'amongst the most terrible events of history'. Churchill's – and Roosevelt's – greatest worry was what Hitler would be capable of, if allowed to harness such evil intent and his rocket technology to a nuclear weapon.

In America, the Manhattan Project – the code name for the joint US–British nuclear weapons programme – was making steady progress. In Canada, work was under way on the P9 Project – the code word for the Allies' first heavy water plant, at Trail, in British Columbia, on the country's western coast. The Trail plant was based on the Vemork design, but it would be two years before it came on stream, and in the meantime the enemy seemed to be surging ahead in the race for nuclear supremacy.

In the dying days of autumn 1942, a telegram was received from the SOE in Stockholm, one emanating from Vemork: 'GER-MANS TO SHIP ENTIRE STOCK OF HEAVY WATER . . . QUANTITY BELIEVED SUFFICIENT TO SATISFY PRESENT DEMANDS FROM BERLIN.'

It created something approaching panic in London; in America, the fears were so real that consideration was given to issuing a public warning of a possible nuclear attack by Germany. It was finally decided that the risk of mass panic outweighed the danger of a Nazi nuclear strike, and a studied silence won the day. But there was a sense of time running out. Stephenson was recalled to London from the US, and the War Cabinet met for an emergency session.

'The Germans were using all heavy water stocks,' commented Stephenson. 'They must be close to a solution.'

Regardless of the strengthened defences at Vemork, the production and shipping of SH200 simply had to be stopped. Despite the odds against them, the decision was made to proceed: the men of Operation Grouse would be sent in. On 18 October 1942 Poulsson led his team into Norway – a plunge into the darkness and the unknown.

As Stephenson would comment: 'The fate of the world seemed to hang on those four young agents.'

Chapter Thirteen

RAF Tempsford was the ghost airport; the aerodrome that never was. Situated in the hamlet of Tempsford, in rural Bedfordshire, few of the locals ever realized that their community harboured one of the best-kept secrets of the war. Down a tiny side road marked 'closed to the public' lay an RAF airbase – that much they knew. In the local pubs they occasionally noticed RAF men enjoying a pint or two. But few realized the cloak-and-dagger work they were engaged in.

To those in the know, it was 'Gibraltar Farm', an RAF airbase designed to appear to any watchers as if it were an old and abandoned farmstead. Opened in the spring of 1942, this was Churchill's secret aerodrome, for it was from here that his Special Duty warriors were inserted into occupied Europe, on the so-called 'moon flights' – they invariably went out during the nights of the full moon, when there was enough light for the pilots to navigate by.

Built over the Tempsford Flats – an area of low-lying, marshy ground – this apparently ramshackle, run-down place had the genuine feel of a deserted farmstead. But only during the hours of daylight. Come nightfall, Hassel's Hall, the nearby manor house that doubled as the officers' mess and sleeping quarters, became a sudden hive of activity, and the local farmhouse, barns and shacks transformed themselves into storerooms, agent reception centres and pre-flight preparation zones.

In many ways, Tempsford was the nerve centre of the resistance network across all of occupied Europe, and it possessed a direct and secure communications link to SOE headquarters in London. From Tempsford weaponry, ammunition, explosives, radio sets, food rations – even carrier pigeons – plus the SOE agents themselves were dispatched across the continent.

The aircrew at Tempsford were all hand-picked – veterans of at least one complete tour with Bomber Command. Their flight missions – known as the 'Tempsford Taxis' – were of necessity lone-wolf undertakings. Moon flights required pinpoint accuracy to locate their distant end points on the ground. The pilots flew with no lights and without fighter escort, and relied upon darkness and low-flying tactics to avoid enemy ground fire and warplanes.

By now Poulsson, Helberg, Kjelstrup and Haugland were all too familiar with RAF Tempsford. Several times they had waited for an aircraft to spirit them into Norway, and at times even been airborne, only for the drop to be cancelled due to inclement weather. Tonight, they were hoping beyond hope that all would go well. At least now the ageing Whitleys had been replaced by more modern and reliable Halifaxes, a four-engine bomber increasingly used for parachutist missions.

There were precious few opportunities to fly agents into occupied Norway. It required darkness to hide the progress of the lone aircraft through enemy airspace, yet it also required enough moonlight for the aircrew to navigate their way across the frozen wilderness. This was the 'moon window', and it lasted for a bare few nights each month.

Tonight Lady Luck seemed to smile upon Poulsson's mission. It was a clear, calm evening and the moon window appeared near perfect. It was just after seven o'clock on 18 October when Wing

Commander Hockey and his Flight Lieutenant, Sutton, lifted the Halifax clear of British soil and set a course for Norway, four hours' flying time away.

As the lone Halifax droned towards the Norwegian coastline, it was now up to the aircrew to match what they could see on the moonlit ground with their maps, and to get the Grouse team over their intended drop zone – a patch of flat, marshy ground that was largely clear of boulders.

The 2,000-metre mountain peaks loomed to left and right, their heights glistening bluish-white in the ghostly light, the plunging snow and ice fields both bewitching and beguiling. Innumerable frozen lakes threw up their glassy reflections at the passing aircraft. From three kilometres of altitude, the Hardan-gervidda was an awe-inspiring sight – 5,600 square kilometres of barren and largely uninhabited territory.

Lying at 1,000 metres above sea level, the weather across this frozen moonscape of glittering snow and rock was famously unpredictable. Terrible ice storms could blow up in an instant, only to be followed by an unseasonable thaw. Blizzards could white out the surroundings for days. There was little food, shelter or means of creating warmth, for the windswept plateau was largely bare of woodland. Stands of birch trees fringed the lower lakes. Above that there was nothing.

It was hardly surprising that few chose to make their home here. Apart from the odd hunter's shack, built upon the shores of a lake, there was little sign of human habitation. No roads crossed the Vidda. No railroads intersected it. The Barren Mountain plateau stretched north and east from the Vemork plant a good 100 miles, making it the ideal place in which to hide – that's if Poulsson and his men could survive there.

They would have to, and for as long as it would take to get the mission done, or – as unthinkable as it might seem – they would fail. Post-Musketoon, and with Vemork's defences being daily strengthened, the chances of failure had to be that much higher; so high in fact, that those in command in London had decreed that Grouse's mission objectives would have to change.

With such a strength of guards as now existed at fortress Vemork, Poulsson and his men would act as the advance party for a far larger force – one boasting sufficient firepower to rout the plant's defenders. Even now, a group of British soldiers was being put through a crash training course, with that very task in mind.

Prior to departure, Wilson had summoned Poulsson to London to brief him on his new mission. They were to recce an area where a sizeable number of soldiers could be dropped – either by parachute, flying boat, or possibly even glider. They were to steer that force to the ground, setting out lights on the drop zone and using a special radio beacon to guide them in. And, crucially, they were to lead that force directly to the target.

The new mission was code-named Operation Freshman, and it was supposed to be an in-and-out, hit-and-run affair. Wilson had asked Poulsson to suggest an area where he thought the force of British soldiers might land. There was only one place that seemed suitable: the Skoland Marshes, a slice of land on the remote eastern flank of Lake Møs. A stretch of flat terrain devoid of boulders, it was only thirteen kilometres to the north-east of Vemork. The Skoland Marshes would put them near enough to make such a lightning strike possible.

Wilson had made no mention of how the British raiders were supposed to make their getaway once the attack was done, and

Poulsson didn't ask. He got the distinct impression that their chances of surviving the mission were not considered high.

As the Halifax thundered onwards high above the Vidda, Poulsson reflected upon Wilson's last words, spoken to him just prior to their departure.

'This mission is exceedingly important,' the former Scout-master had told him, his voice ringing with an unusual intensity. 'The Germans must be prevented from getting their hands on large quantities of heavy water.' He'd fixed Poulsson with a look that demanded absolute attention. 'They use it for experiments, which, if they succeed . . . could wipe London off the map.'

Wilson had told him all that he was able to, Poulsson figured; all that he was permitted to, security-wise. He'd given him a window into his world, one in which he was privy to intelligence of frightening import. But was there really any such explosive that could be so powerful? To wipe out an entire city? Poulsson didn't know, but he'd promised Wilson that they would get the job done.

The excitement of returning to Norway was tempered by the thought of the coming jump. From 3,000 metres the Vidda looked so much flatter than Poulsson remembered it from his childhood hunting trips. If it were really this featureless, there would only be the lakes – still not fully frozen – to worry about, as they drifted down towards their landing.

Poulsson ran his eye along the aircraft's hold. Thankfully the Halifax – designed as a heavy bomber – had ample space for all that they were bringing with them. Eight bulging containers lay adjacent to the bomb doors. He and his men would go out first, after which the pilot would make a second run, so that the containers could be shoved out after them. Those eight steel cylinders were crammed full of all that they would need on the Vidda: tents, sleeping bags, survival gear, weaponry and ammo, and, crucially – food.

All of a sudden the aircraft's wings began to judder as Wing Commander Hockey put the Halifax into a steep descent. They were going down to jump altitude. At 300 metres Hockey levelled off, and from this altitude Poulsson could see the true nature of the Vidda. To left and right lay an undulating pattern of ridges, each dusted with fields of glistening snow, and interspersed with sullen, grey, rock-strewn valleys.

There didn't appear to be a flat stretch of terrain anywhere. The jump light flashed red: the warning signal to make ready.

'Action stations,' Sergeant Hill, the dispatcher, ordered, in a voice that brooked no dissent.

Poulsson and his team needed to jump as swiftly as possible, to ensure they fell as one 'stick'. If not, and with the Halifax travelling at sixty metres per second, they could end up scattered across the Vidda. A ten-second delay between jumpers translated into a 600-metre separation on the ground.

No sooner had Poulsson squatted at the open bomb bay, legs dangling into the aircraft's roaring slipstream, than he saw the jump light flash green for go. He snatched a momentary glance below – at a blur of rock and snow and ice flashing past – before the dispatcher yelled at him.

'Number one – go!'

The Grouse team – who, unlike Skinnarland, had enjoyed the full SOE parachutist's training course – jumped; Poulsson first, followed closely by Haugland, Kjelstrup and lastly, Helberg. Poulsson had been a bag of nerves as he forced himself to go, but as his static line dragged his silk parachute out of its pack and it snapped into shape above him, he felt a renewed sense of contentment.

Only a few seconds now, and his feet would be on home soil.

The last man in the stick, Helberg – the born hunter and trouble-seeker amongst them – glanced skywards. Beyond his chute the Halifax was making a second pass, and a string of containers plummeted through the moonlight, which glistened along the bomber's steel belly.

All the jumpers were out. So too were the containers, which floated earthwards in a neat formation. There was just the one problem. The terrain below didn't look a lot like their intended drop zone.

The four men drifted towards a mountainside strewn with boulders and smaller stones – the kind of terrain that breaks legs and sprains ankles, even on a daylight jump. There was no obvious place to land.

The Halifax droned into the distance, its aircrew intent on flying a diversionary mission. They would drop several thousand propaganda leaflets around the outskirts of Stavanger, Norway's third city, to make it seem as if their flight had been a propaganda exercise, providing cover for the parachutists' insertion.

Luckily there was little crosswind over the Vidda. Choosing the clearest patches of terrain possible, Poulsson and his men felt their boots thump into the hard, frozen surface. They had trained relentlessly for this mission, and they had hardened themselves well. All four survived the landing, as did their containers. Even the radio equipment seemed to be unharmed.

After a year or more in Britain, the harsh, cold, empty vastness of the Vidda took the breath away. Helberg had landed up to his waist in a snowdrift. As he surveyed the unending expanse of the moonlit plateau, he felt as if he were alone in the world. The sensation was all the more bizarre because for him – as with Poulsson and Haugland – his childhood home lay just a few dozen kilometres away, complete with parents, grandparents and siblings.

They would need to camp in the frozen desert of the Vidda, knowing that home was just a short ski away, but never being able to go there or to make contact with their loved ones. Snow caught in the breeze and drifted, like wind-blown sand. Helberg cupped some in his gloved hand, and let it trickle through his fingers.

He stretched back and admired the dome of the heavens, glistening clear above him. The soft heather and gentle mists of the Scottish moors seemed a distant world now. In a way, Britain had become like home for him and the others in the team. But now they were back in their real homeland, and there were few who knew how to survive on the Vidda as they did.

It was too late to collect together all their containers, and the men needed rest. They gathered the bare necessities – food, sleeping bags, paraffin stove – and huddled behind a massive boulder for shelter. They knew from long experience that cold, dry snow was one of the best insulators. Let it drift around your sleeping bag, and it would help keep you toasty.

With his back to the boulder, Poulsson pulled out his trusty pipe and palmed some tobacco into it. He struck a match, put it to the bowl and sucked away contentedly. Oddly, it was a calming sight for them all; a slice of normality amidst the wild otherness of the Vidda.

'It's time I told you as much as I know,' Poulsson began, his voice a quiet purr above the rustle of the wind. 'We're here on a vital assignment – to help destroy the heavy water factory at

Vemork.' He puffed away, exhaling a dense cloud of aromatic smoke, before explaining the basics of Operation Freshman. 'We're to find a good landing site, and guide the troops from there to Vemork.'

A few brief words were exchanged, and it was agreed that the Skoland Marshes were the place to start looking.

'The operation is to be carried out in the next moon period,' Poulsson continued. 'We have four weeks to reconnoitre the plant, get information on the German guards and check out the landing site. But first thing tomorrow, we have to get our supplies together. The dispatcher got us out pretty quickly, but I don't know about the containers. Some must be miles from here.'

As Poulsson bade his men goodnight, one worry preyed upon his mind. If snow fell during the hours of darkness it might cover the containers, making them impossible to find. The skies were crystal clear right now, but that didn't signify much. On the Vidda, the weather could switch in the blink of an eyelid.

It was 19 October 1942, and Poulsson didn't relish what lay before them: life on the Vidda at the start of winter. For the next several months this would become a forbidding, snow-blasted wasteland inhabited only by the odd grouse, Arctic fox and the wandering reindeer herds. Humans entered the Vidda in winter at their peril. But Poulsson and his men were going to have to live here.

Come first light the weather was still good: calm and clear. The four men began to quarter the terrain, seeking out their supplies. Their task was made all the more difficult in that their skis – vital for moving across such terrain – were packed in one of the errant containers. It took two days wading through thick snow before all of them had been located, and it was sod's law that the skis were in the last container found.

By now they'd managed to work out where Wing Commander Hockey had dropped them: they were in an area called Songdalen, a good ten kilometres west of where they had intended to land. It was no wonder that Einar Skinnarland was nowhere to be seen. They had some thirty kilometres to travel before they reached their intended destination, a remote hunter's hut set just to the north of Vemork.

Normally, such a distance would be easy for these men, especially when moving on skis. The problem was that they were carrying 700 pounds of weaponry and equipment, plus food rations for a month. They decided to cache the 'non-essential' supplies, burying them under the snow in a place they could return to later, but this still left them with crushing loads.

To make matters more frustrating, somehow no paraffin fuel had been packed for their Primus stove. While they would have preferred to head directly over the mountains, heat was vital for warming food and bodies, and for drying out wet clothes at the end of a long day's march. They would have to stick to the valleys now, where the birch trees grew, from which they could gather firewood as they went.

Haugland tried to make radio contact with London. It was never easy from the Vidda, for the precipitous terrain had a habit of blanketing radio signals. He failed to raise any response from SOE headquarters. Perhaps it was their surroundings, but a part of him worried that the radio equipment had been damaged during the drop. If it had, and it proved impossible to fix, they would have no way of making contact with SOE headquarters. And without that radio link their mission would be rendered nigh on impossible.

'Tried in vain to make radio contact with London,' Poulsson

would write of their present situation. 'We had no paraffin for our Primus stove, and had to ignore good mountain routes, where there was no wood to be found ... We set out on our heavy march. I hoped that our food, with the strictest rationing, would be sufficient for thirty days. We had been told to make no outside contact except in the gravest emergency.'

At least the weather looked set fair. Skis clipped on, the four men set off on the next leg of their journey, but the going proved painfully slow. 'At high altitude and in bitter cold, no man can be expected to carry a load weighing more than thirty kilos,' Poulsson noted. 'The ground was bad and rugged; the snow heavy and deep. Men who left the ski tracks sank up to their knees.'

The rivers that flow through this part of the Vidda have deceptively poetic names: the Well of All Water; the Singing One; the Deep One; the One that Cuts off All Travel. In truth, the altitude of the plateau – a kilometre above sea level – renders it hugely exposed. Savage winds sweep in without warning, and the temperature can plummet to thirty degrees below zero. In the worst of the snowstorms, it's impossible to see your hand in front of your face.

Shortly after the four young men had set out the weather turned. The skies darkened, a biting wind howled down from the heights and a violent snowstorm exploded out of the heavens. Such conditions can chill a man to the bone, sap his strength and kill him within hours. The secret to enduring on the Vidda was knowledge built up over countless generations; to survive here, you had to know how to survive.

Bowed under their loads and pushing into the driving storm, Poulsson and his men knew what they had to do: they needed to find shelter. They headed for the Haugedalen Valley, where Poulsson and Helberg knew there was a good, stout hut. But search as they might they couldn't seem to find it. It made little sense. They knew this was the correct spot. The hut should be right here. But somehow it wasn't.

Unbeknown to Poulsson and Helberg, the owner had recently dismantled the wooden cabin and moved it to a more convenient spot. Such were the dangers of being absent from the Vidda, if only for a few short years. This had become a matter of life and death now. Winter had come early to the Vidda, and it had arrived with a vengeance. They needed shelter urgently.

With that in mind, they pressed onwards into the teeth of the storm in a desperate race for survival.

Chapter Fourteen

While Poulsson and his men battled the monstrous storm, Wilson was wrestling with his own demons. He had one ear tuned to his Operation Grouse team, newly inserted into the Vidda. From the Halifax aircrew he'd received a report of their successful arrival: 'Load dropped from 700 to 1,000 feet flying due south ... Men jumped well and without hesitation ... 12 chutes seen to open and all men to land ...'

But since then, silence. It was disconcerting.

He had his other ear tuned to Operation Freshman. The powers that be were trying to thrash out the final details of the mission and, frankly, Wilson didn't like what he was hearing. In his view Freshman was ill-conceived in its present form, and he didn't rate its chances.

Worse still, if the operation failed it risked alerting the enemy to a pending attack on Vemork. If that happened, it would spell disaster. There was little doubt how General von Falkenhorst would react: it would be the Musketoon effect, but quadrupled.

It wasn't the assault force itself that worried Wilson: they were well capable of the job. It was the means of their insertion into the Vidda. The scribbled notes of an October meeting at Combined Operations HQ listed the basics of the Freshman plan of attack. First, a truck was to be hijacked at the Lake Møs dam, adjacent to their landing zone. From there, the soldiers would drive hell for leather to Vemork.

'Lorry with our men could drive up and do in sentry,' the notes proposed, referring to the guards on the bridge that gave access to the Vemork plant. Having gained entry that way, the force would blow up certain targeted buildings, which should 'explode and wreck whole installation and kill whole valley . . . Turn off tap closing pipeline . . . warn families to fly.'

The handwritten notes recorded that 'access is barred on south side by impossible precipices'. In other words, no one was about to descend into the Vestfjord Valley and scale the 600-foot rock-face that led up to the plant, which was why a 'lorry or bus [was] strongly recommended' as the means to gain access, via the suspension bridge.

In theory, all of this was fine. But the proposed means of insertion – using a pair of Horsa gliders, towed by Halifax aircraft all the way from Scotland – had Wilson seriously worried.

The Airspeed AS.51 Horsa was named after the legendary fifth-century British warrior-leader of the same name. It measured sixty-seven feet from nose to tail, and was constructed from a solid timber frame with a curved outer skin of plywood. It was considered a sturdy and nimble aircraft, at least for a glider. The bare cockpit seated two, and the Horsa could carry a payload of four tonnes – a jeep, or a field gun, for example – plus there were foldable seats to accommodate troops.

But glider-borne missions were notoriously hazardous in the best of conditions, and Norway didn't exactly offer those. Gliders needed flat landing ground – near impossible to find, and especially on the Hardangervidda. Putting down on a frozen lake was considered, but it was just as quickly discounted: as the Horsa careered forwards it would bulldoze up its own wall of rock-hard ice, the weight of the aircraft finally breaking through the lake's frozen surface.

To make matters worse the weather over Norway was proving atrocious, as the Grouse party had discovered. The gliders might take off in perfect conditions in Britain, only to fly into a hellish storm, especially over the Vidda.

Being a glider pilot was one of the most dangerous roles in the entire British armed forces, but this mission was truly off the scale. Combined Operations ran the Freshman plan past Wilson and Tronstad. They formulated a detailed response, one that typically didn't pull any punches.

'Of all countries, Norway is the least suitable for glider operations. Its landing grounds are few; its mountains thickly clustered, precipitous and angry.' The success of the mission demanded fine conditions over the Vidda, where 'in winter the weather is seldom favourable and hardly ever predictable . . . The plateau is noted for sudden up-and-down air currents powerful enough to make a bucking bronco of a Horsa glider.'

'The landing-site would be difficult to identify if clouds obscured the moon, or if, more likely at that altitude, there was low cloud cover . . . The night landing of a fragile craft in an area known for its fissures and ridges, huge boulders and outcrops of rock would be extremely hazardous.'

An official report on Freshman would echo such concerns. 'Even in the planning stage, it was realized that the operation was exceptionally dangerous. Of all countries, Norway is the least suitable for glider operations . . . To a pilot . . . the mountains seem to rear up, claw at his wing-tip and sink back almost with a snarl as he passes . . . Weather conditions in the Autumn of 1942 were vile.'

The fact that Operation Freshman got the green light, regardless, reflected how desperate the Allies were to strike back at the Nazi's nuclear programme. Vemork had to be destroyed at all costs.

Wilson would describe Freshman as one of his 'biggest headaches' in the entire war. Obdurate and plainspoken to the last, he decried what he feared would prove to be a disaster. 'Against all outside advice, including mine, Combined Operations had decided to dispatch a force of 30 Special Service . . . troops, in two gliders towed by aircraft.'

He was not alone in expressing such concerns. 'I do not consider the use of gliders is either necessary or desirable,' the chief of the air staff wrote of Freshman. 'We have not enough experience of long-distance towing at night, and the operation apparently can be done by parachute.' He added a hand-written note: 'Use of gliders seems mad to me . . .'

In his view – and Wilson's – the Freshman force should follow in Grouse's footsteps, and parachute in. The counter-argument – that gliders would get the force onto the ground as one concentrated unit, thus enabling them to launch a fast and concerted attack – didn't add up. It only made any sense if the soldiers survived the glider-borne insertion, and the fear was that they had precious little chance of doing that.

Wilson also questioned how the force was supposed to escape once the attack had taken place. They would need to cross several hundred miles of wilderness in the midst of winter, hounded by the enemy all the way. The men would have to 'fight their way to Sweden', with little chance of making it. They were back to sending in a 'suicide squad', with little real prospect of any of them getting out alive.

Regardless, by late October 1942 Freshman had been green-lit as a glider-borne operation and training was in full swing. The operational plan involved each Halifax towing a glider packed with troops to a position above the Hardangervidda – a landing zone marked by team Grouse on the ground. There the tow lines would be let go, the Horsa gliders would drift down to the marshes that edge Lake Møs, landing on the skids that ran beneath their fuselage.

The Horsas would be packed with explosives, weaponry and . . . folding bicycles. A mountain road led from Lake Møs to Vemork. Upon landing, the thirty troops would unfold the bicycles, mount up and pedal like hell for the target, which from Lake Møs was largely downhill. They'd reach Vemork in darkness, the bicycles giving them the added advantage of silence and surprise.

All telephone lines into the plant would be cut. In case they encountered electrified wiring, the team were to carry 'Gloves – rubber: for 500 volts'. They'd sneak across the suspension bridge, kill the guards using silenced Sten guns, and blow up the plant and any existing stocks of heavy water. That done, they were to split into small groups and escape to Sweden. Any injured were to be given a morphine injection and left behind, for flight would be impossible if laden down with wounded.

Crucially, the plan relied upon a new and untested piece of equipment, the Rebecca/Eureka homing beacon system, which was designed to 'steer' an aircraft onto target. More accurately known as the 'Rebecca/Eureka transponding radar', it consisted of an airborne receiver and antenna system – the 'Rebecca' – fitted to an aircraft, which picked up a radio signal transmitting from the ground-based 'Eureka' unit.

The Rebecca calculated the range and position of the Eureka, based upon the timings and direction of the return signal. It was accurate up to eighty kilometres in good weather, and even under cloud or thick fog it was still detectable from up to several kilometres away. The Grouse team had flown in with the Eureka, which in theory they should be able to use to steer the aircraft in, no matter what the weather on the ground.

Overall command of Operation Freshman – something of a poisoned chalice – fell to Lieutenant Colonel Henneker of the Royal Engineers Airborne Division. In recruiting a team for the forthcoming mission, he faced what appeared to be an impossible task. He was to ask for volunteers for hazardous duties, without being able to tell them any details of the mission, including the country they were deploying to.

The entire operation was cloaked in such secrecy that he could reveal only this much: it would be a mission deep behind enemy lines. Any volunteers with compelling reasons not to go, such as having young children or a pregnant wife, would be allowed to withdraw at any time, and without any repercussions.

It was 19 October 1942, the same day that the Grouse team had parachuted onto the Vidda, when Henneker addressed his potential recruits. They gathered at Bulford military camp, set on Salisbury Plain in the midst of the Wiltshire countryside. In a cold and bare Nissen hut, Henneker stood before the men of two Royal Engineer units – the 9th and 216th Field Companies – to appeal for volunteers.

Henneker – his craggy face hardened by his experiences fighting a desperate battle against the advancing Germans during the fall of France – told the men that they were all 'keen as mustard' to see some action, that he knew. But the forthcoming mission was no ordinary undertaking. It was extremely dangerous. Its outcome might determine the fortunes of the war: if they failed, the Germans might seize victory within six months.

It says much for the calibre of these men that every single one amongst them stepped forward. The oldest, at thirty-one, was Ernest Bailey, just back from leave in his native Hampshire. The youngest was Gerland Williams, of Doncaster, who'd just celebrated his eighteenth birthday with one pint of beer too many. A third was Bill Bray, a former truck driver whose wife was due to give birth in three months' time.

Henneker was right: these young men – former plumbers, cobblers, carpenters and mechanics – hungered to hit back against the enemy. None wanted to turn down a chance – however mysterious, however daring – to do so.

Henneker was immensely proud of his men. He wanted nothing more than to see them accomplish the mission. But one thing troubled him: the insertion. This would be the first operational use of gliders in the war. Henneker wasn't interested in firsts. He didn't want his men to be 'fresh men', as the mission name implied. He wanted them to get in, to get the job done, and to get out again alive.

A cover story had to be provided, to explain why these men would now disappear for weeks of punishing and intensive training. They were supposedly taking part in 'The Washington Competition', an endurance contest held against their American equivalent unit, hence the name.

Royal Engineers – more commonly known as 'Sappers' – had been chosen for Operation Freshman because this was first and foremost a demolitions job, one of the Sappers' specialist skills. An official planning report on Freshman gave a sense of the scale of the task before them.

Describing the Vemork electrolysis plant, it recorded: 'This, the world's largest, is housed in an eight-storey building . . . The building is of ferro concrete, 45 metres high and strengthened internally with ferro concrete beams and supporting pillars.'

There were thousands of tonnes of steel and reinforced concrete to blow up at Vemork. Highly regarded by the wider British military, these combat engineers were more than capable of fighting their way into the plant and setting the explosives to wreak havoc.

To prepare for what lay ahead, the Sappers were put through a commando-style training course, involving forced marches under 80-pound loads. They were dropped in the midnight darkness of Snowdonia, surviving on what they carried on their backs, as they made their way to a prearranged rendezvous using only map and compass.

At the summit of one peak former truck driver Bill Bray collapsed from exhaustion. His companions picked him up, dusted him down and split his load between them. Anyone who didn't last the course was off the mission, and they didn't want to lose him.

One of those who helped carry Bray's load was Wallis Jackson, a well-built 21-year-old, with three sisters back in his native Leeds. A natural at handling explosives, Jackson had a surprisingly soft side to his character. He was in the habit of penning letters to his mother and sisters, full of affection, and hope for the fortunes of the war.

But there was nothing he could write home about the forthcoming mission. Even had he known anything about it, they were forbidden to breathe a word. The Sappers moved on to the Highlands of Scotland to rehearse mock raids and assaults, and at every turn any who failed were mercilessly weeded out. Only the best would be good enough for Freshman.

Despite such rigorous training, the specialists at MI9 – the secret wartime escape and evasion agency – didn't rate the Sappers' chances of survival any more than did Wilson. Major de Bruyne, an MI9 escape expert, pointed out the dangers of their escape plan – fighting a running battle over 300 kilometres in hostile terrain. He feared that none would make it back alive.

MI9 produced a set of Norwegian-looking clothes for each man, to boost their chances of survival. They were to get them worn in and comfortable prior to the assault. The Sappers were to go in wearing full British battledress, so the Germans would be left in no doubt as to who had hit the plant. This was crucial, to prevent local reprisals. But as soon as possible thereafter they were to change into their civilian clothing, and to escape posing as locals.

A hand-scribbled note from MI9 listed the escape and evasion 'Necessities'. These included 'files to cut padlocks for boats'. Lakes would need to be crossed, and if a boat was borrowed by an escapee a few kroner were to be left in it, as a 'thank you'. And, of course, high on the list was a generous supply of Benzedrine, to fuel their escape march.

Key phrases in Norwegian were taught to the Freshman volunteers. These included: '*Jeg har vært ute og kjøpt litt proviant til mor*' (I've just been out buying stores for mother); '*Leve Norge og Heil Quisling*' (Long live Norway and hail Quisling); '*Unnskyld men jeg ma hurtigst til tannlegen*' (Sorry, but I must get to the dentist as quickly as possible). That last phrase was 'to be spoken with stone or cork in mouth'.

Paper and envelopes embossed with the words 'Reich

Commissioner for the Occupied Norwegian Territories', were to be carried. A note was to be stuck onto each of the glider's windscreens, with the words 'DO NOT TOUCH!' written on it in Norwegian. Hopefully, the locals would conclude that the aircraft were German, and so delay reporting their presence to the occupying authorities.

En route to the plant and during the attack, members of the assault force were to identify themselves as friendly to each other by whistling 'Hurrah for the CRE', the de facto anthem of their parent regiment, the Corps of Royal Engineers. A martial tune sung with gusto by Sappers the world over, it ends with the immortal lines:

> Ma-ninga sabenza, here's another off.
> Oolum-da cried Matabele, oolum-da, away we go,
> Ah, ah, ah, ah, ah, ah ah.
> Shush . . . Whoow!

At the eleventh hour, Lieutenant Colonel Henneker asked for permission to join the mission, and to lead his men in the field. It was refused. He was needed back at headquarters to coordinate what was in any case a complex undertaking, involving several different arms of the British military.

On 18 November Mountbatten wrote to Churchill, laying out the final plan for Freshman. 'Thirty-six all ranks of the Airborne Division will be flown in two gliders to destroy the Power Station, electrical plant and stocks of "heavy water" . . . The Germans have about 1 ton of "heavy water" . . . When they have 5 tons they will be able to start production of a new form of explosive a thousand times more potent than any in use today . . . '

Churchill replied: 'Approved. Ask Lord Cherwell to report to me on the technical aspect. He is already my advisor on the main question. W.S.C.'

The die was cast.

There was one unforeseen problem, as far as Wilson was concerned: right at this moment he had no reception party to guide the Freshman force in. For days now he'd not heard a squeak out of Grouse.

Poulsson and his men had dropped into the Hardangervidda, seemingly to disappear without trace.

Chapter Fifteen

The four Norwegians had weathered the storm. Or at least, the *first* storm. Others had followed. And those were interspersed with periods of unseasonal warmth, in which the going became horribly wet. There seemed to be no happy medium on the Vidda: it was either a freezing, biting blizzard, or a soggy thaw. Clumps of snow stuck to their skis like chewing gum. Mostly they only had candle wax to lubricate the undersides, and it proved next to useless.

Poulsson had put them on a daily ration of a quarter of a slab of pemmican, four crackers, a smear of butter, a slice of cheese and a square of chocolate, plus a handful of oats. They were burning far more calories than they were eating, as they attempted to haul their supplies to the hut above the Skoland Marshes, their intended destination. Hunger gnawed at their stomachs.

To make matters worse they were forced to move in relay. Much of their equipment just couldn't be left behind at the landing zone. They were carrying the one radio, the battery to power it (which alone weighed thirty pounds), the Eureka homing beacon, a hand-operated generator, weapons, survival kit and food. It was impossible to move all of that in one journey. So they would advance, dump what they were carrying, and retrace their steps for a second or third load.

It was backbreaking; soul-destroying.

Then they got lucky. On the third day of their leaden march they came across an abandoned farmhouse. They devoured the frozen meat and some old flour discovered in the kitchen. But, better still, they found an ancient-looking wood and canvas sledge. Upon examining it more closely Poulsson could barely believe it: his father had given him it as a child. Somehow, it had ended up here.

It was as if Providence had saved them in their hour of greatest need. This was deliverance. No longer would they need to move in relay. Over the next six days they pushed steadily onwards, their loads split between their packs and a heavily laden sledge. It was still tough going, but at last they were making real headway.

At one point Poulsson – leading – crashed through the skin of a half-frozen lake. Kjelstrup, lying prone on the thin ice, had to reach out a pole to their leader to help drag him free. Poulsson was soaked to the skin, and there was no easy way to dry out on the Vidda. They pushed onwards, the heavy sledge being dragged behind them and Poulsson feeling chilled to the bone.

Lips blistered. Exposed skin cracked and wept painfully. The four men were constantly wet and cold, and never able to get properly dry. Their feet, plodding through the damp snow of the valleys and across semi-frozen lakes, were permanently sodden. Even the wood of their skis became waterlogged, making each step a trial of endurance. Their leather boots began to fall apart. Each morning they would have to stitch them up with needle and thread. With wild beards, sunken eyes and emaciated looks, they began to resemble a band of desperadoes.

Wherever they found one, they made the Vidda's hunting cabins their base for the night. In several Haugland had discovered fishing rods. These he expropriated and strapped to the sledge – donations for the war effort. One evening, thirteen days into their march, he cobbled together a mast for his radio using fishing rods bound end to end, so he could raise his antennae to a greater height. That should increase his chances of making contact with London.

They'd paused at another hunting hut, in the Reinar Valley. Here Poulsson had scribbled in his small diary: 'We are fairly done in.' Haugland was determined that now was the time for team Grouse to break radio silence. It would raise their spirits considerably, and they sure needed that right now.

For Haugland, learning to operate a radio and to send in Morse code had been like trying to learn to touch-type. At first he'd been all thumbs – making clumsy and snail-like progress. But with time he became a virtuoso. At war's outbreak he'd been serving as the radio operator on a 3,000-tonne merchant ship. He'd tuned in – spellbound, horrified – to distant SOS signals, as ships were sunk in fierce sea battles, while all he could do was listen.

Later, at the SOE's Special Training Station 52 – its school for wireless operator agents – he'd been the star pupil. He could punch out Morse faster than most, and cipher codes with great aplomb. He could build a wireless set from the barest assortment of spare parts. In fact, his teachers had decided that *he* should be instructing *them*. Now, thirteen days into Operation Grouse, Haugland still had not made radio contact with London.

It irked him greatly.

At dawn – one of the best times of day for raising a signal – he fired up the shortwave system. Just as soon as he started tapping away at his key, he seemed to get reception. London was hearing him, after all. But just as quickly, the radio went dead. Haugland could see what had happened. Somehow, the huge and weighty battery that should have lasted a month had died – perhaps the intense cold of the Vidda had done for it. He tried charging the battery with the hand-held generator, but no joy. There was no way around it: the battery was kaput.

The mood in the hut was grim. In a little over two weeks the moon window would open, and the Freshman force was scheduled to fly in. But without a working radio they could provide zero intelligence to Wilson: no update on Vemork's defences; no assessment of the Skoland Marshes as a landing zone; no weather reports; and, crucially, no reception party for when the Sappers dropped in.

It was now that Helberg stepped forward. Lake Møs was less than a dozen kilometres away. He would push ahead and track down the Skinnarlands – either Einar or Torstein – and seek help. If a replacement battery could be found, they could still rescue the mission.

As the lone skier set out, Poulsson scribbled in his diary: 'Helberg proved the old saying: "A man who is a man goes on till he can do no more and then goes twice as far."'

Hours later Helberg reached the Lake Møs dam and tracked down Torstein Skinnarland, who worked there. Torstein had been warned by his brother to expect friendly company. He confirmed to Helberg that his brother had some stores – including a precious battery – hidden away on the Vidda, in preparation for the Grouse team's arrival.

They parted, agreeing to link up once the Skinnarland brothers had got the battery – plus some extra food supplies – sorted. On his way back to the hut, Helberg met up with the rest of the Grouse party. The temperature had dropped and there had been a fresh fall of snow. The going was easier, and they decided to press onwards.

Early on 5 November – sixteen days after they'd dropped into the Vidda – Poulsson and his men reached their intended destination, the small Sandvatn hut, above the Skoland Marshes. It lay in a remote bowl of snow-blown land, with few high peaks in the immediate area. It was the kind of place four men could remain undetected, and the open terrain should be good for making radio contact.

Despite the improved weather, they were utterly spent. Grey-faced, emaciated, their clothing hanging in tatters, their boots in ruins, they slept the sleep of the dead, relieved that they had at least made it thus far. Even Poulsson's childhood sledge had found the journey too much: en route the wood had begun to warp and crack under the strain.

The following morning a hungry Poulsson and Kjelstrup set out on skis to recce the marshy terrain around the shores of Lake Møs – the would-be glider landing zone. By now, the four men were pretty much out of rations. Helberg set forth alone for the Møs Dam, to check if the replacement battery was ready, and to scavenge food. Haugland stayed at their Sandvatn 'home', to set about building a new and improved radio antenna.

First he lashed together two fishing-rod radio masts – each like the frame of a tepee – and between them he strung a length of insulated copper wire. Next he threaded the radio's signal cable out through one corner of the hut window and attached it to the copper wire, which hung between the two towers like a washing line. If anything could raise a signal to London, this should.

All he needed now was a source of power: the elusive battery.

In London, Wilson was feeling distinctly edgy: more than two weeks and still not a word from Grouse. Only silence. Dwell on the issue, and the possibilities were endless. Radio problems: that was the most likely. The weather: atrocious over the Vidda, by all reports. The enemy: perhaps Poulsson and his men had been betrayed by a 'quisling', as local Nazi sympathizers were known, and caught.

If that were the case, it didn't bear thinking about. The SS and Gestapo had ways to make just about any man talk. They all did, eventually. If any of the Grouse team had been taken alive before they could swallow their fast-acting cyanide capsules, Operation Freshman would be blown.

At times like these, Wilson had a way of calming the inner storm. When confronted with what he termed a 'ticklish situation', he would take himself back to his schooldays at Glenalmond. In his mind's eye he would hear the comforting, musical rumble of the Almond River – his bedroom was on the north side of the school, overlooking the water – as it gushed under graceful boughs and around polished boulders. It served to centre him.

'This gave me the strength and the will to carry out whatever was required,' Wilson remarked. And if the sounds of the Almond didn't do the trick, he'd transport himself into the nearby glen, where the gentle rustle of the leaves served to soothe troubled thoughts. Over the past two weeks he'd been spending a lot of time at Glenalmond, at least in his inner thoughts.

Just a few days earlier Wilson had received a long report from Einar Skinnarland, detailing the most recent defences put in place at Vemork and the local weather conditions. 'There is at present a German guard of about forty men and auxiliaries . . . twenty-five are ordinary Austrian soldiers, and about fifteen German sappers . . . Vemork is barred by barbed wire and possibly land mines . . . Personnel of the guard equipped with standard rifles and hand grenades ... Snow on mountains and most of the mountain lakes are frozen over.'

This was useful, but Wilson needed a direct and instantaneous radio link. He needed bang-up-to-date intelligence on Vemork's defences, and in much greater detail. Skinnarland's intel came by courier, so it was days and sometimes weeks old. Most crucially, he needed a team to whom he could radio through a warning that the Freshman force was in the air, and to ready the landing zone.

Yet there was still no word from Grouse. Despite the Glenalmond effect, the situation was nerve-racking. On 8 November Wilson sent an encrypted telegram to the SOE office in Stockholm. He needed a message sent by courier to Einar Skinnarland, asking him to seek out the Grouse team and determine their fortunes.

'We have been unable ... to establish proper wireless communications with party and for urgent and important operational reasons we must, repeat must, be in touch with them at the earliest possible opportunity.'

Wilson didn't know how quickly the message could be got through to Skinnarland, and a reply fed back to London. It was inconceivable to green-light Freshman without having a team on the ground to guide the force in. If Grouse had failed, then Freshman would have to be abandoned, at least until Wilson could raise and insert a replacement team. And, with the best will in the world, there just wasn't the time.

A month ago the Tube Alloys experts had warned of the seemingly unthinkable – that Britain should prepare for a Nazi attack employing 'fission products', the by-products of a working nuclear reactor engineered into a crude radiation bomb.

'Precautions should be taken to avoid a surprise attack. This could be done by the regular operation of suitable methods of detection ... routine tests should be carried out in large towns ... Special precautions to preserve secrecy would have to be taken.'

Fresh intelligence from Vemork fuelled such concerns. That autumn Kurt Diebner, the chief of the *Uranverein*, had paid a personal visit to Norsk Hydro. He'd made it clear that 'all necessary measures' were to be taken to ensure that the rate of heavy water production was boosted. Work was well under way to introduce a new type of 'catalytic exchange' technology, designed to massively boost production.

One of the scientists working at Vemork was an Austrian, Dr Hans Suess. Having discovered that he was secretly anti-Nazi, Jomar Brun – Vemork's inside man – lured Dr Suess into a series of candid conversations, asking exactly what lay behind the Germans' urgent demands for heavy water? Dr Suess's reply was revealing: the *Uranverein* needed five tonnes of SH200 as the moderator in their 'uranium machine'.

Time was fast running out. In fact, this was a ticking time bomb. The Allies were anticipating a nuclear attack on their cities. Britain – the SOE – had to act, and fast. What in the name of God had happened to Grouse?

In the Sandvatn hut, Haugland hoped very much that their fortunes were turning. At nightfall on 9 November 1942 – three weeks after their insertion onto the Vidda – he made his final preparations. He glanced out of the hut window. In the faint moonlight his fishing-rod radio towers glistened eerily. Before him on the hut's crude wooden table lay a replacement battery, courtesy of the 'magician' – Einar Skinnarland.

But would it work? Would the radio power up properly and the message get through? Only one way to tell.

On a notepad Haugland had scribbled a seemingly random series of letters: his cipher message. The SOE taught its wireless operators to use the 'poem code'. Both sender and receiver had before them the same poem. Certain words were selected from the verses, and these would be used to formulate the code. All the receiver needed to know was which the chosen words were, and they would be communicated by an indicator group of letters set at the start of the message.

At first, radio operators tended to pick easily remembered verses: Shakespeare was an obvious choice. But such classics proved too obvious to the Germans, who were intercepting messages and trying to break the code. The Grouse team would settle upon a far harder poem to crack: a piece of verse popular only in Norway, and written in Norwegian. 'Fjellsangen' was actually the 'anthem' of Gjest Bårdsen, one of the most notorious outlaws, jailbreakers, and, subsequently, authors, in Norwegian history.

In 1939 a hugely popular biopic had been made in Norway telling Bårdsen's life story. 'Fjellsangen' was its theme song. For Poulsson, Helberg, Kjelstrup and Haugland – four fugitive raiders, hiding out in the snowbound wastes of the Vidda – it was a peculiarly apposite choice for their poem code. In English Fjellsangen translates as 'The Mountain Song'.

Haugland reached for his Morse key. Behind him stood his three fellow SOE operators, watching him like hawks. Haugland noticed that oddly for him – a man who'd proved cool under fire so many times – his hand was shaking. He powered up the radio. It came to life, no problem. He tapped out his identity call sign, and listened.

Almost instantly, a series of bleeps pulsed through his head-phones, telling him that he had contact with the SOE home station, at Grendon Underwood. Behind him, his three fellow mountain men practically danced with joy. Smiling faintly, Haug-land bent further over his cipher pad as his hand began its delicate dance with the Morse key.

'Happy landing in spite of stones everywhere,' he tapped. 'Sorry to keep you waiting for message. Snowstorm, fog forced us to go down valleys. Four feet snow impossible with heavy equip-ment . . . Had to hurry on for reaching target area in time.'

His second message outlined what they had learned about Vemork: 'Important news: after Glomfjord sabotage German sen-tries sent to industrial centres . . . Forty-four Germans arrived area of Rjukan . . . German engineer troops just finished the tunnel along the water pipelines . . . Later message about what we need get from glider.'

Grouse had arrived. They were in place and on the air.

The following morning they struck doubly lucky. Haugland and Helberg came across a sheep that had got trapped amidst some rocks. They killed it and brought it home for the pot. Poulsson, who fancied himself something of a cook, boiled the head over the wood-fired stove, adding some tinned peas and whatever else he could lay his hands on. The others were staring at his back, salivating. They even set a cloth on the table.

Outside the wind howled, driving gusts of snow against the window. Yet another storm had hit the Vidda, but no one inside the Sandvatn hut seemed to mind. All thoughts were focused on the coming feast. The single candle lighting the hut flickered as the wind beat against the walls. Poulsson turned from the stove, stew pot gripped in hand. He took a step towards the table, tripped on a reindeer skin rug on the floor, and the precious meal went flying.

With barely a moment's hesitation the four got onto hands and knees and spooned up the stew from the floorboards. When they had finished eating only a few gnawed bones remained. Kjelstrup had complained continuously about having 'hair in my soup', which had the rest in fits of laughter.

Poulsson recorded in his diary: 'The chaps were not too amused.' Regardless, they went to bed that night with blissfully full stomachs.

In an excited-looking scrawl on the transcription of Haugland's radio message, Wilson had written: 'Ask for full list of extra equipment needed.' It made sense to fly in any supplies requested by team Grouse with the Freshman force, and as soon as possible.

From Haugland's radio messages, it was clear that Vemork was being further reinforced and strengthened against an attack.

If London could get the gliders in, the time to strike was now.

Chapter Sixteen

Things were not going quite to plan at RAF Skitten, a flat, wind-blown, treeless slab of moorland set beside the North Sea.

RAF Wick, on the north-east tip of Scotland, is about as close as you can get to Norway without setting off to fly or sail there. The neighbouring Skitten aerodrome – a collection of desolate huts, forming the satellite airfield to Wick – had the advantage of being more remote and private, and screened from watching eyes.

It was 17 November 1942, and the thirty-odd Sappers had flown up to Skitten to prepare for their leap into the unknown. But the lead Halifax tug – A for Apple – had become unserviceable due to a leaky oil seal. A for Apple's aircrew, led by Group Captain Tom Cooper, were forced to turn around, travel south in a spare aircraft and then by train and car, returning to RAF Netheravon, where 38 Squadron – the unit tasked to fly Freshman – was based.

The following day two Halifaxes – one the replacement aircraft – were in the air again, flying a 'nickeling' (test) flight from Skitten towards the target. This time B for Baker was forced to turn back with a cracked radiator and a partially seized engine, but at least the lead aircrew made it to a point where they figured they'd got sight of the Skoland Marshes landing zone. As a bonus they'd run into no obvious flak, searchlights or enemy fighters.

It was just after dawn when the two aircraft touched down once more at Skitten. Over a breakfast of bacon and eggs in the base canteen, Group Captain Cooper and Lieutenant Colonel Henneker – who'd been riding shotgun in one of the Halifaxes – exchanged notes. Henneker had insisted on being on the nickeling flight, so he could get a closer look at what his Sappers were heading into. He didn't much like what he had seen.

From 3,000 metres the ridges and valleys of the Hardangervidda had lined up to the far horizon in bands of 'dark and light', like a tiger's stripes. In anything but perfect weather the terrain would be hugely confusing. It all looked pretty much the same. And that meant they would be relying upon the Rebecca-Eureka homing system to guide them in, which worried Henneker and Group Captain Cooper greatly.

The group captain and his men had had precious little time to train for the coming mission. Unaccustomed to flying four-engine Halifaxes, they'd had just a few short weeks to convert to the new aircraft. Not only that, but the Halifaxes had been delivered with none of the vital homing devices installed. The 38 Squadron ground crew had been forced to fit the Rebecca-Eureka units themselves.

'The difficulties of carrying out the operation were tremendous,' Group Captain Cooper would write of Freshman. 'It demanded exceptional weather conditions for . . . a glider tow by night far longer than had ever previously been attempted . . . even in daylight; a glider landing in very difficult country . . . crew of very limited experience who had had only a small amount of training . . .'

The only available photos of the landing zone had been taken from a Norwegian tourist guidebook. Likewise, mapping left a great deal to be desired. Norwegian skiing charts had been made available, but different versions gave differing shapes to the lakes of the Vidda, which were essential navigational markers.

Of even greater concern, the generators powering the Rebecca units proved to have a habit of burning out their wiring, which made the Rebeccas malfunction. On this mission more than any, Cooper realized that 'location of the landing area would be extremely difficult unless "Rebecca" could be used'. In short, Group Captain Cooper feared they were setting themselves up for a fall.

He'd stressed the willingness of 38 Squadron to fly the mission, 'in the knowledge that a small team of handpicked men can . . . accomplish things far beyond those contemplated in normal operations'. Yet at the same time he'd appealed for more time to prepare. He'd been turned down.

'It is too late to stop, and we must hope for the best,' his commander had told him.

One other thing troubled Cooper greatly. The Horsa gliders would be attached to the tugs by ropes of plaited hemp – a tough plant fibre – which also carried a cable intercom strung between the aircraft. But what would happen, the Group Captain wondered, if the ropes froze solid? They were flying a November mission three kilometres above Arctic Norway. It would be colder than the devil's heart up there. If the ropes iced up would they lose their flexibility, and become brittle and prone to breakage? There was just no way of knowing.

Only Grouse had provided the rarest of upbeat moments. Radio reports from Haugland had conditions for once holding cold and clear over the Vidda. Snow blanketed the Skoland Marshes, but it had been packed level and firm by the wind.

'Landing place . . . cannot be seen by Germans,' Haugland signalled. 'Nice flat ground without trees or stones approximately 700 yards in length'. It should make for a decent strip, but the snowfall meant that bicycling to the target was a non-starter. 'Impossible for the party to cycle. Depth of snow on landing place is 30 centimetres. On road about 10 centimetres and very hard.'

Due to the wintry conditions, the folding bikes would have to be left behind, but Haugland was certain that a stiff march would get the Sappers to their target. 'Whole march even under difficult snow conditions not more than five hours.'

Crucially, Grouse had secured eyes-on intelligence. They'd found a vantage point from which they were able to spy on the SH200 plant. 'A German guard patrols the suspension bridge . . . On the Vemork side there is a sentry box . . . . At the door into the factory one German sentry . . . The suspension bridge is easy to hold if . . . reinforcements arrive from Rjukan.'

Grouse had confirmed that the heavy water plant was there for the taking, in spite of the fallout from Operation Musketoon, but only if the thirty-odd Sappers could be got onto the ground safely.

Apart from Freshman personnel, Skitten had been hermetically sealed and security was vice-tight. The gliders were pulled into good cover, where they were invisible to any traffic that might pass, not that there was a great deal. The assault force wore standard Sappers' badges on their uniforms, and no airborne flashes or caps, so as not to prompt any difficult questions. Everything possible had been done to prevent the men from 'talking carelessly'.

All mail and telephone calls were curtailed, at least until the aircraft were in the air. That hadn't stopped former trucker Bill

Bray penning a letter to his pregnant wife. 'A few lines in haste to let you know I am off on a raid. I can't say where, but don't worry too much darling if you don't hear for a couple of weeks . . . I shall be back for Christmas so get that chicken ordered up . . . bye-bye and God bless you. From your ever loving hubby, Billy.'

Wallis Jackson – who had helped carry an exhausted Bray's kit over the Welsh mountains – didn't have a sweetheart to write home to. Indeed, his mother was still doing his washing. Still, he managed to dash off a few short lines, the pace of things seeming to indicate that departure was imminent. 'Mamie. If you send my laundry and letters here it will be okay. Looking forward to my next leave. Bags of love, Wallie.'

Shortly before Cooper and Henneker's nickeling flight, Wilson had got a deputy to fly the final Freshman orders north to Skitten. They were to be carried into the field by the mission commanders either in paper form or committed to memory. And then, on the frozen Skoland Marshes, the Sappers would be given their final briefing prior to the attack.

Wilson's man eventually got to hand those orders to one of Lieutenant Colonel Henneker's deputies, and he reported back to Wilson what he'd learned. Henneker's men seemed 'very confident of pulling off the job, if they got to the right place . . . I asked how he intended to destroy his gliders, and he told me they had no orders to do so. He agreed that this was rather odd.' It would be far better to rig them with explosives to deny them to the enemy.

Then to the point of greatest concern: how had the Horsa gliders performed? Henneker's man had said they were fine over Salisbury Plain, but that they'd 'never used them over mountains and expected a rough passage'. Plus one of the Halifax pilots had

reported having, 'a bad trip up towing a glider over the Highlands, when owing to air currents he found himself dropping 500
feet a minute at full climb!'

To Wilson this was all very alarming. The glider side of the
operation was looking increasingly ill-starred. But only one thing
could put a stop to Freshman now, and that was the weather. That
month's moon window was almost upon them.

Haugland's next radio message pretty much decided things.
'Last three nights light and the sky absolutely clear. Temperature
about minus five Celsius. Strong wind from the north has quiet-
ened down. Tonight beautiful weather. Ends.'

Dawn on 19 November proved grey, drizzly and dreary at
Skitten – a typical day for this part of Scotland in winter. But in
light of Haugland's upbeat message and weather report, Cooper
and Henneker decided Freshman was a go: the operation would
proceed that evening, just after nightfall.

Amongst the specialist advisers at Skitten was a Norwegian
meteorologist, Lieutenant Colonel Sverre Petterssen. Petterssen
spent the entire morning poring over charts and weather reports.
In spite of Grouse's update, he was worried about strong westerly
winds that were blowing up over the North Sea. At lunchtime he
issued his own advice: they should delay for two days, when an
'outbreak of Arctic air' should bring cold, clear, settled conditions.

Henneker and Wilson paused for reflection. How should they
play this? They had to balance the urgency – the period of the
moon window would close fast – with the likelihood of success. Eventually, they decided the weather was 'sufficiently good
enough for an attempt to be made . . . the odds against another
opportunity during the moon period were considerable.'

On being told of their decision, Wilson sent a final message through to Grouse. 'Signal earliest possible whether attack had been successful ... It is important to know this. Good luck to you all.'

At Skitten the cold fog and rain persisted throughout the day. Along with the other Sappers, Wallis and Bray munched on sandwiches and chain-smoked to kill time. There was a little banter, just the odd wisecrack – the put-on bravado of courageous men waiting to fly deep behind enemy lines on a mission that would, one way or the other, change the course of the war.

Shortly before zero hour Lieutenant Colonel Henneker gathered his force for a final briefing. He surveyed the party before him – two officers and thirty other ranks, brave Sappers all – and told them the basics of their mission, which was going ahead that evening.

They were headed for Norway, where they were to blow up a power station and a 'hydrogen plant', after which they were to escape on foot to Sweden. If captured, they were to reveal their 'name and number only, and refuse to give any other information'. They were warned not to make 'any mention of having had local assistance' – a veiled reference to the four men waiting to guide them in.

The two gliderloads of Sappers were commanded by Lieutenants Alexander Allen and David Methven. Each officer knew that should the other party not make the landing, he was to lead his own force forward to execute the attack. 'Whatever happens,' Henneker stressed, 'someone must arrive at the objective to do the job. Detection is no excuse for halting.'

His briefing done, he wished his men Godspeed and good luck. In his heart at least he would be going with them.

The Sappers gathered their kit and weaponry – each carried a

Sten – and stepped out into the dusk drizzle. They'd been issued with silk 'escape maps', which were in fact a ruse. They showed a false route dotted in blue, and were to be scattered around the scene of the attack, in the hope of throwing off their pursuers.

Group Captain Cooper and his aircrew mounted up Halifax A for Apple. B for Baker was piloted by a 26-year-old Royal Canadian Air Force pilot, Arthur Parkinson. Behind them, two lines of men – fresh-faced; most in their late teens or early twenties and barely out of their school uniform – boarded the Horsas. The ground crew closed the hinged tail entries of the gliders, and the Sappers were boxed into their wooden coffins.

They burned to get the airborne leg of the mission over and done with, but instead faced a frustrating delay. For some reason, those on the tow aircraft couldn't seem to get the intercoms with the gliders to function. No matter what they tried, it proved impossible for Halifax to speak to Horsa. Finally, a decision was taken to get airborne regardless, and to use signal lights to communicate between glider and tug.

At 6.45 p.m. the two Halifaxes clawed into the dark and soggy overcast, each with its four Bristol Hercules radial engines straining mightily, as it dragged behind a 7,045-kilo dead weight on a 360-foot hemp line. From the runway at Skitten, Henneker gazed skywards, until the four aircraft and the four dozen men they carried disappeared into the low and ragged cloud.

He turned away and headed for his operations room to await news of their fortunes. Radio was his only link now: to the Halifax aircrew, who should signal news of the gliders' successful release over the drop zone; to the Grouse party on the ground, who should call through confirmation of Freshman's successful landing.

Above left and right: Have tommy gun; will fight. In the spring of 1940 Churchill called for Special Duty volunteers to 'develop a reign of terror down the enemy coast'. Thankfully, they flocked to his cause. Britain's wartime leader backed an unrelenting training regime, combining the best of air, sea and land forces. On the wild and unforgiving Scottish moors, far from prying eyes, commandos prepared to take on the Nazi war machine … and hunt down Hitler's nuclear threat.

The Free French submarine, the *Junon*. Chosen for her close resemblance to a German U-boat, her mission was to sneak some of the first commandos onto enemy-occupied shores, intent on blowing their target to smithereens.

Above: The Glomfjord power station, nestling at the foot of the mighty Navervann Mountain – the objective of the dozen commandos undertaking the daring raid, codenamed Operation Musketoon.

Above: Captain Graeme 'Gay' Black MC, Canadian volunteer with the commandos and Musketoon's superlative commander.

Above: Captain Joseph 'Joe' Houghton, Black's second-in-command. A former public schoolboy and sometime joker, he had a core of inner steel.

Above: Private Eric Curtis, a bespectacled former accountant and just one of Musketoon's unlikely – and unsung – heroes.

Above: Job done. The Glomfjord power station was inundated with floodwater and buried under tonnes of rubble. After the commandos' dramatic sabotage, it – and the critical Nazi war effort it powered – was ruined.

The team of the SOE's last-ditch operation to stop the Nazi nuclear project, meeting HM King Haakon VII of Norway. *From left to right:* Knut 'Bonzo' Haukelid, Operation Gunnerside commander Joachim Ronneberg, Operation Grouse commander Jens Anton Poulsson, and Kasper Idland.

This page: The Vemork heavy water plant at night. Its defences were fearsome: minefields, anti-aircraft emplacements, machine gun nests, razor wire, electrified fences, booby-traps, guard dogs, searchlights, barrage balloons and scores of German guards. Yet the Special Duty raiders would need to breach them, if Nazi Germany's nuclear project was to be stopped.

Above: Viking warrior. Agent Cheese – Norwegian Odd Starheim – one of the SOE's first and finest behind-enemy-lines operators. Hunted by the Gestapo, he would mastermind the daring hijack of the *Galtesund* (*below*). A latter-day pirate, Cheese would bring to Britain vital intelligence – the *Galtesund's* human cargo – boosting the hunt for Hitler's nuclear weapons.

No holds barred. Brigadier Colin McVean Gubbins, the Special Operation Executive's chief and doyenne of unconventional/guerrilla warfare.

Baghmara – the leopard killer. Former Scoutmaster Major John Skinner Wilson had wrestled tigers and Hindu holy men in India; he proved equally unyielding when heading up the SOE's hunt for Hitler's nuclear weapons programme.

A rogue's gallery. From left to right: Vidkun Quisling, leader of the Norwegian Nazi party; Heinrich Himmler, Reichsfuhrer of the SS; Josef Terboven, Nazi Germany's infamous governor in Norway; General Nikolaus von Falkenhorst, commander-in-chief of German armed forces in Norway.

This page: Against all odds the SOE's desperate sabotage operation succeeded, and where all else had failed. But it would take a bombing raid by USAAF warplanes to convince Hitler to move the surviving stocks of heavy water to the comparative safety of Germany. It was needed in their nuclear pile, to breed plutonium – the raw material for the Nazi bomb.

The SF *Hydro*, the ferry tasked to carry the drums of heavy water towards Germany. It would take an act of bravery beyond measure for the SOE raiders to sink the vessel, laying Hitler's nuclear ambitions finally to rest.

The German atomic pile (reactor) was hidden in a cave beneath a church in the town of Haigerloch. When US and British forces overran it in April 1945, they had orders to salvage it or blow it up, to deny the Russians.

The Skitten radio room sent a short message to both SOE and Combined Operations headquarters: *Freshman was in the air.* Now, the wait.

In the cockpit of A for Apple the pilot set an initial course south-east, in an effort to get above the thick overcast. It extended to 1,500 metres, and the tugs would need to thread a course through holes in the cloud cover to reach clearer skies. The Halifax laboured ever higher, eventually breaking free of the shadowed mass. Tug and glider turned towards the north-east and set a course for Norway.

Some three hours later A for Apple's navigator had by skilful dead reckoning brought them above Egersund, the German base that Odd Starheim and his pirates had given a wide berth, as they'd steamed away from Norway's coast in the hijacked *Galtesund*. This was the exact point at which the aircrew had planned to cross into Norwegian airspace – no small feat of navigation, after flying 1,100 kilometres across the North Sea.

All eyes scoured the surroundings. It was a truly beautiful night. The moon was bright, the clouds light and fluffy, and visibility very good. In fact, these were near perfect conditions for making such a drop. Over the intercom the tail gunner joked that the 'fluffy white clouds' were more than likely mountain peaks, waiting to rip the Halifax's belly asunder.

Many a true word is spoken in jest.

Having cleared the first mountain range, A for Apple set a course for Vemork, 300 kilometres north-east of their present position. By following a distinctive chain of lakes, they planned to find their way directly to the release point, whereupon they would cut the glider free. But as A for Apple thundered onwards, the mood in the cockpit suddenly darkened.

Smoke fingered up from a spool of electrical wiring. The generator was overheating. Seconds later the wiring burned out and the Rebecca unit went kaput. This was exactly what Group Captain Cooper had feared: a repeat of the problems they'd experienced during training. He'd warned about it. He'd begged for more time. None had been given. Now this.

With only their maps to guide them, the crew of the lead tug – with glider in tow – zigzagged across the hostile skies. Below them the dark valleys were mercifully clear of fog, the skies above mostly clear of cloud. But still the frozen silhouette of Lake Møs – like a roughly drawn 'Y' lying on its head – eluded them. They kept searching, a needle and thread twisting this way and that through the dark heavens.

To their rear, B for Baker was faring little better. Out over the North Sea their Eureka had also started to malfunction.

Finally, Cooper and his crew got an accurate fix on their position: they were within twenty miles of the landing zone. If they couldn't complete the drop it was touch and go as to whether they had enough fuel to tow the glider back to Scotland, but where was the welcome that the ground party had supposedly set out for them?

To one side of the Skoland Marshes Poulsson strained his ears. He *wasn't* mistaken. He *could* hear a faint droning in the skies above. He felt his pulse quicken. Freshman was in-bound.

Beside him Haugland was crouched over the Eureka set, earphones clamped to his head. In the past hour the breeze had freshened, but the conditions were still good enough to get the gliders in. Haugland glanced up, his eyes burning with anticipation.

'I can hear it!' he cried, above the whine of the wind. 'They're coming now!'

In response, Poulsson pushed off hard with his ski poles. He headed downslope to where Kjelstrup and Helberg were waiting.

'Up with the lights!' Poulsson yelled. 'Up with the lights!'

The two men dashed to it, and moments later an L-shape of red lights burst into life in the snow. Poulsson skied to the apex of the 'L'– L for London – and switched on his torch. With the beam lancing skywards, he flicked his hand across it rhythmically: on-off, on-off, on-off. Above the wind he could hear the low grumble of an aircraft approaching from the south-west.

'I can hear it!' Poulsson yelled. 'I can hear it!'

The noise grew to a loud rumble as the Halifax drew overhead. It was now that it should release the glider. Four sets of eyes scanned the night, as they waited for the boxy form of the Horsa to come whispering out of the heavens. But their wait – and their labour on the Skoland Marshes – went unrewarded. No glider came.

Not to worry, Poulsson reasoned. The Halifax would make a second pass. Sure enough, several minutes later, the night sky reverberated once more to the beat of aero engines. Again the sound drew closer, and there was a repeat of the fevered activity at the landing zone. But again no glider materialized from the ether.

What, the four men wondered, could have gone wrong? The tow aircraft had flown right over the drop zone. How could they have failed to see the lights on the ground?

High in the skies above the Vidda, Group Captain Cooper made the only decision left open to him: he ordered his navigator to set the straightest course for Scotland. He figured they had a little less fuel remaining than was needed to make landfall. But they should be able to tow the glider to within fifty kilometres of the Scottish coast, at which point it would be able to ditch in the sea.

Hopefully the wooden-framed Horsa should stay afloat for long enough for the Sappers, and the two pilots flying her, to be rescued.

By now A for Apple had quartered the skies above the Vidda, and still found no lights marking the landing zone. Thin cloud had blown in, and maybe that had obscured them. Either way, the Halifax had lost height in doing so. As she turned towards the south-west, a dense bank of cloud loomed ahead, rising to 4,000 metres. A for Apple was heading right for it. She was now at 2,700 metres with the glider right behind her. Towing such a heavy load, the Halifax had to go to full take-off revs to climb, which burned up the fuel.

Gradually, painfully, A for Apple – and the Horsa behind her – gained altitude. She topped 3,000 metres. At 3,300 she hit the first clouds. By the time she lumbered out of the cloud tops at 3,600 it was 11 p.m., and she'd been airborne for over four hours. But in climbing through the overcast Cooper could tell that his aircraft had collected ice. He could see it glistening on the propellers and spinning off into the moonlight like shards of broken glass.

More worryingly still, the glider – plus its tow rope – felt like a lead weight behind them. The Horsa was icing up. The temperature outside the aircraft would be minus ten degrees Celsius, far lower with the wind chill factor. Cooper feared that the tug and its tow were fighting a losing battle with the ice. He ordered A for Apple to full throttle, but the Halifax just couldn't seem to maintain altitude. Instead, with a sickening sense of inevitability, she started to lose forward momentum and drift back into the opaque and freezing mass.

As they sank into the icy clutches, only one course of action lay open to Cooper: he'd have to descend as rapidly as he could, in an effort to pop out the base of the clouds. The lower they went the warmer the air would become, and hopefully the ice would fall away from both aircraft. But, of course, below them lurked jagged-edged peaks, some rearing as high as 1,800 metres.

Cooper gave the order, and as he did so he knew he was taking the lives of his aircrew, and of those in the glider, in his hands. The pair of iced-up aircraft dropped through the clouds. All lights were switched on, as those in the Halifax's cockpit strained their eyes for any obstructions that might loom out of the murk. At 2,000 metres A for Apple hit the thickest cloud yet, and the first of the turbulence.

Within moments it felt as if the heavy bomber were a leaf being thrown around in a violent storm. Slam! The Halifax hit the first air pocket and she seemed to shudder from end to end. Slam! She careered into a second. Slam! And then, as she hit the third, bucking like a wild pony, it happened. What Cooper had so feared had come to pass. To their rear, the ice-encrusted tow rope snapped in two.

A for Apple's glider had cut loose, and was spinning into the dark storm.

Chapter Seventeen

It was midnight at RAF Wick, where Henneker had established the Freshman ops room. A dense fog of cigarette smoke hung heavy in the air. So too did the tension. The first hint of bad luck and trouble had come in five minutes ago, and it had thrown the place into utter chaos.

Out of the blue a radio message had been received from A for Apple: 'Glider released in sea.' *In the sea?* Henneker could only imagine that the lead tug had been trying to return to base when something had gone terribly wrong.

He tried to scramble aircraft for a search and rescue operation. None were available. Unbeknown to him, this was largely a blessing. Group Captain Cooper's message had been a deliberate deception, designed to alert Wick to the dire situation without betraying the errant glider's location. If the Germans were listening in – and they were bound to be – it made sense to try to obfuscate where the Horsa had broken free.

The situation grew more and more confusing. A garbled message was received from B for Baker, asking for a bearing on Wick. It looked as if both tug aircraft were trying to make it back to base. But what of the gliders and the men they carried?

Then . . . nothing. No further contact could be made with either of the aircraft. Ashen-faced, Henneker could know few of the details of what had happened, but he feared the worst.

At two kilometres of altitude, the ice-encrusted Horsa had broken away from A for Apple without any warning. For the previous few minutes the heavy glider had been thrown about like a toy in a giant's hands. The grooves in the aircraft's corrugated metal floor were there to prevent vomit from making it slippery underfoot. But as the Horsa had bucked and twisted and writhed in the grip of the savage turbulence, the Sappers had turned sick with fear.

The Horsa felt like a snowflake in the grip of a blizzard. Then a sharp crack had been heard from forward, as if from a giant gun, and the aircraft had plummeted into freefall. The wooden-walled Horsa went into a violent spin. In the cockpit the pilots, seated side by side, wrestled with all their strength at the controls. To their rear the Sappers gripped their fold-down seats for the hellish bare-knuckle ride into the unknown.

As the Horsa plummeted, from all sides the mountain winds cried out in shrieks and howls. The thin wooden fuselage answered, creaking and groaning horribly as it threatened to tear itself to pieces. The Sappers might be strapped in, but much of their equipment wasn't. It tumbled around the enclosed space, cannoning off the plywood ribs of the hold and beating out a terrible funeral rhythm.

With the cloud and the darkness thickening, the pilots tried to steer blind for where they guessed the ground had to be. But they were riding a runaway express train, and the cliff was fast approaching. At around 600 metres they tore out of the base of the cloud, and got a glimpse of their surroundings, which were wreathed in fog. Snow, rock and ice flashed past the cockpit at a dizzying speed.

'Ditching stations!' they cried.

The fifteen Sappers and their one officer just had time to link arms, before the glider ploughed into the mountainside. The glass nose cone crumpled like tinfoil, and the pilots were killed at once. As the Horsa careered onwards, tearing itself to pieces on rocks and boulders, its wings were torn asunder.

When the wreck of the aircraft finally came to a halt, the fuselage had been ripped open in several places, and a trail of kit and equipment had been vomited across the frozen wilderness behind her. The miracle was that some of those who'd suffered that hell ride to earth had survived.

If anything, B for Baker had suffered a blacker fate. Having likewise quartered the Vidda for the landing zone, tug and glider had finally been forced to turn for home – into the same freezing cloud mass as had claimed the first glider. In terrible visibility and icing up, B for Baker had been forced to descend to a lower altitude.

Just as the Halifax crossed the Norwegian coastline she had clipped the hidden peak of the 1,700-foot Haestad Mountain, smashing herself to fiery ruin on the far side. So cataclysmic was the resulting explosion that it was visible from the other Halifax, although they hadn't at first known that it was their sister aeroplane. The crash had appeared as a bright flash that illuminated the cockpit of A for Apple with a ghostly orange light.

None of the aircrew of B for Baker survived. To their rear the Horsa had broken free of its tow. The wooden-hulled aircraft had swept across a thickly wooded valley, where the pilots had attempted an emergency landing. The fir trees had cushioned the blow for the Sappers, but not for those to the fore of the glider. Broken boughs had smashed into the cockpit, killing both pilots instantly.

The Horsa came to rest with its nose sheared off and its fuse-lage badly mangled, but the brave actions of the pilots had at least saved the lives of many in the rear. There were a number of injuries, but incredibly only one of the Sappers had died.

As the wind shook the wreckage, and thick flurries of snow blasted through the Horsa's shattered entrails, their commander, Lieutenant Alexander Allen, wondered where on earth they had come to rest, and what in the name of God he was supposed to do now.

Three hours later A for Apple made landfall in Scotland. Having lost its glider, the Halifax had ample fuel to make it home. Group Captain Cooper told Henneker as much as he was able: that their glider could never have made it to the intended landing zone. When it had broken free it was dozens of kilometres away from the Skoland Marshes; it had no hope of getting there.

'The tow finally parted,' Cooper explained. 'There was nothing we could do for the poor devils spiralling down into the snow.'

At dawn the first search aircraft got airborne, although Henneker held out few hopes. B for Baker must have gone down. The Halifax hadn't the fuel to stay airborne for such a length of time. There was of course a vague possibility that B for Baker had made it to the landing zone and released its glider successfully before coming to grief. For now, that was all the Freshman commander had to cling to.

Those hopes were shattered with Haugland's first radio message. 'Light and Eureka O.K. at agreed time. Weather changed at 1900 hours to wind and in parts low cloud cover. Plane heard in Eureka about 2040 hours . . . Later during course of an hour loud engine hum. Eureka battery running for four hours.'

The Grouse team had waited on the landing zone as arranged. They had heard aircraft overhead and had appeared to get a positive Eureka reading, but no gliders had appeared. Both Horsas had to be lost somewhere as yet to be identified.

Henneker paced the runway alone and lost in an inner darkness. What were the chances of the wooden-hulled aircraft having made a safe landing? In Norway? In a storm-swept night? In uncharted, wild country? They had to be pretty near zero. In which case, were there any survivors? If there were, had any been taken captive? And if they had, what hopes were there that they would not be made to talk?

Those men had set out with pure hearts and with the bravest of intentions. Volunteers all. Yet in the back of Henneker's mind there lurked the darkest worry of all: Freshman had failed, which meant that the Nazi nuclear monster had not been slain.

Henneker sought scant comfort in the thought that any Sappers captured would be made prisoners of war. The German Army should treat them humanely. They were a professional and respected military force, after all. But that wasn't the key point right now. It was this: who now would take on the monster that was Vemork? Who now could conceive of a mission that might succeed, after Freshman's failure and all that it doubtless signified?

Fortunately, there was one man, a scar-faced former Scoutmaster who'd once earned the nickname 'Baghmara': the leopard killer.

Once, in India, Wilson had been called to a remote settlement to deal with some apparently minor dispute. He'd arrived in the village to find a major riot about to break out. Not for the first time in India it all boiled down to religion: a Muslim boy had come and washed in the well from which the Hindu villagers drew their water.

A hugely obese Babu – a respected elder and Hindu holy man – was leading the charge, whipping the crowd into a frenzy. Wilson ordered the man to be quiet while he tried to sort things out. The Babu had refused. 'I'm afraid I lost my temper with him,' Wilson recalled. He grabbed the immense Babu, upended him and threw him into the nearby water tank.

Now you've torn it, Wilson told himself. *That'll finish you.*

The holy man had bobbed to the surface, his head covered in a magnificent crown of green waterweed. At the very sight of it the villagers had burst into laughter. The murderous atmosphere dissipated. In one fell swoop the troubled situation had been defused. Wilson helped the Babu out, and the two men apologized to each other. From time to time thereafter they would run into each other, and they would joke about that first unforgettable meeting.

Sometimes, Wilson told himself, you just had to take the bull – or the Babu if it came to it – by the horns.

As soon as he'd heard that morning's dire news from Henneker he'd called Tronstad. The two men sat in his Chiltern Court office contemplating the very worst. It was early on 19 November 1942 and Freshman had proved an unmitigated disaster.

Somewhere in the Norwegian wilds two gliders packed with Sappers, explosives and other specialist demolitions kit had crash-landed. Of the thirty-two men aboard, some would surely have survived. And a living man – even if badly injured – could be questioned. Wilson and the Professor had to work on the assumption that the Germans would discover everything.

This was potentially catastrophic as far as stopping Hitler's nuclear programme was concerned. No one could foresee the full consequences on the ground, but one thing was for certain: Vemork was about to be transformed into a veritable fortress. And that, as far as Wilson saw things, meant there was absolutely no time to lose.

He didn't hesitate for long. Without a word to his superiors he picked up the phone and called the officer responsible for Freshman at Combined Operations. Having expressed his sympathies for their loss, he broached what he had in mind.

'Our latest information and deductions tell us that the job can be done by a small party of Norwegians,' Wilson explained. 'All expert skiers. All with detailed local knowledge. Would you be happy for us to take over all responsibility?'

There was an audible sigh of relief on the far end of the line. 'Thank God. Please do.'

The SOE had just been handed all responsibility for the heavy water sabotage.

Still without any formal clearance from on high, Wilson dialled a second number. He spoke to Colonel Charles Hampton, who ran the SOE's Norwegian training school at Glenmore, in the Cairngorms. He asked the colonel to release one Joachim Ronneberg – presently an instructor at the school – from all other duties. Ronneberg was to select five men, all good skiers, for 'a particularly dangerous enterprise'.

Wilson promised to send someone by the night train to Scotland to brief Ronneberg. Meanwhile, he had a little business to deal with: getting all this cleared on high. His calls made, Wilson wandered across to the office of Brigadier Colin McVean Gubbins, the SOE's Director of Operations. Of course Gubbins knew about the Freshman debacle, as did so many of the Baker Street Irregulars that grim morning.

'I've been in touch with Combined Operations,' Wilson announced. 'I've expressed our sympathies.' A weighty pause. 'And I've taken over the job as a wholly SOE enterprise.'

The normally imperturbable Gubbins visibly blanched. 'But you can't do that! It's too difficult.'

It was time to play the age card. Gubbins was forty-six, Wilson fifty-four, and with his tiger-scarred features and balding pate he looked all his years and more. His face adopted a mien of seasoned gravitas, his voice resonating with experience as he set about talking Gubbins around.

'I've already done it. I've appointed a mission leader, at Glenmore, and he's selecting the others who'll be required. I'm positive we can do the job. It will be done.'

For some unfathomable reason Wilson felt certain that the seemingly impossible *was* possible, if only the right men could be got in to do this in the right way. And Brigadier Gubbins also had reasons to believe. He had a particular affection for Norway and its people. He'd fought there in the spring of 1940, and had a huge respect for the Norwegians as guerrilla fighters. Plus he'd sponsored Wilson's appointment as the chief of his Norwegian section, having every faith in the man.

But if they failed in such a high-stakes enterprise as this, it might well sound the death knell for the SOE, which had powerful detractors. More importantly, it might well result in nuclear supremacy – and ultimately victory – for the wrong side: Hitler's Germany. Against all that he was being asked to bet on a grizzled former Scoutmaster and a handful of Norwegian raiders mounted on skis.

It says much for Gubbins's inspirational leadership that he let Wilson have his head, in spite of the odds. But Wilson wasn't being given total free rein: Gubbins made it clear that from now on he was to be kept informed at every juncture.

With Wilson gone, Gubbins bent at his desk. He scribbled a note for his secretary to type. It was addressed to Mountbatten, head of Combined Operations. 'We might now be able to attempt the operation ourselves on a smaller, but, we hope, effective scale,' he wrote, as he struggled to find a diplomatic way of saying that SOE was taking over where they had failed. From the point of view of the scientists, he added, they could brook no delay.

Wilson, meanwhile, was drafting his own urgent communiqué – this one for Grouse. 'Your work has been done magnificently. Change in weather meant gliders had to be released over 100 KM from target. Operation cancelled for this moon period. We are planning to effect it with our own men next moon. Have you any suggestion? Eureka should be hidden most carefully for future use.'

Haugland's reply typified the seemingly unbreakable spirit of the small team working in utter isolation on the Vidda. 'Is the operation still to be carried out by Englishmen? . . . Skiers would be advantageous. If it would assist the operation we would gladly take active part.'

The following morning Wilson's darkest fears were largely confirmed. The Germans had sent out a report by radio, which had been picked up by the BBC. '19–20th November two British bombers, each towing a glider, flew over southern Norway. One of the bombers and both gliders were forced to land. The sabotage squads brought by them were engaged in combat and finished off to the very last man.'

The detail in the message convinced Wilson that much of it had to be true. *One British bomber and two gliders*: just as he had feared, the three missing aircraft had gone down. Whether all aboard had been killed 'in combat', as claimed, was a moot point. In a sense, he'd prefer it if they had. Dead men can't talk. But he doubted if it was true. It was more than likely disinformation. Right now, some of the Freshman Sappers were very likely in German hands.

Churchill was informed. It was far from being the first such setback that Britain had suffered during the war, but the stakes with this, the single most important sabotage effort of the entire conflict, could not be higher. Typically, Britain's wartime leader remained unruffled. He scribbled a poignant one-word comment in reply: 'Alas.'

Having taken on the responsibility of hitting Vemork almost singlehandedly, Wilson worked around the clock. In a 'Most Secret' communiqué he laid out exactly what the ramifications were of that morning's German radio broadcast and with remarkable foresight and clarity.

'Almost everything depends on whether: A. Any of the force have been captured alive; B. Documentary evidence is available disclosing the target; C. The enemy's deductions lead them to the vulnerable point.'

The 'vulnerable point' was the four SOE agents presently holed up in the Sandvatn hut, above Lake Møs.

'Grouse's position is of primary importance,' wrote Wilson. 'The party must be safeguarded both for its own sake and on account of its future usefulness.' Wilson proposed that Haugland be sent a warning message, outlining in full the content of the German broadcast, so they could take all possible precautions.

Wilson's warning was duly sent. It ended thus: 'It is vitally necessary that you should preserve your safety ... It is almost equally important that we should have earliest possible information in regard to increases of enemy troops in neighbourhood of target.' Wilson asked the Grouse team to work with Einar Skinnarland to gather that intelligence, whereupon they should disappear.

'Keep up your hearts,' he urged. 'We will do the job yet.'

On receipt of his message, the four men hunkered down at the Sandvatn hut had few illusions as to what was going to happen. The Germans were bound to send up a hue and cry as never before. It would soon be time to slip even deeper into the wintry wastes of the Vidda to lose their pursuers.

'We will withdraw from the area in next few days,' read Haugland's reply to Wilson. 'Wireless communication will still be partly maintained.'

In truth, the four men had been deeply shocked to learn the fate of the Freshman Sappers. 'London's radio message about the glider disaster was a hard blow,' wrote Poulsson. 'It was sad and bitter, especially as the weather in our part of the country improved . . .'

In the shock of the moment, Haugland had made a rare and potentially deadly error in his radio message. Wilson sent him an urgent warning by return, ordering him to burn all his codes. 'In the stress of the moment on the 21st you transposed your message No. 1 once only. This may make it possible for the enemy to break your code.' Wilson advised them to get out of the area without delay and to disappear.

Haugland's reply sounded harried: 'Primus code burnt . . . going into the mountains today.' With that, he, Poulsson, Kjelstrup and Helberg upped sticks and left the Sandvatn hut. They headed north on skis, making for the remote and frozen heart of the Vidda. They had an idea where they might hide up and ride out the coming storm.

They left only just in time. Messages would be sporadic now, but one reached Wilson indicating that Haugland was shutting down all communications: 'Working conditions difficult. German ski patrols searching huts and farms . . . Radio D/F station established at Møsdammen. Only contact now Grouse One.'

Von Falkenhorst had found out about Operation Freshman, and in great detail. The German counter-actions had begun, including placing a radio detection station on the Møs dam itself, adjacent to the Skoland Marshes. And the Vidda's snowbound hunting shacks and farms were being scoured by German troops equipped with skis.

With Poulsson and his men in full flight, Wilson's attempt to force through a new attack on Vemork appeared increasingly doomed. Running from a vengeful enemy, Grouse had handed over to the one man who could keep London briefed: Einar Skinnarland – 'Grouse One'. But even now, the Gestapo were closing in on Skinnarland and his family.

Wilson was not to be deterred. By 23 November 1942 – just three days after the Freshman debacle – he'd secured Brigadier Gubbins's go-ahead for the new mission to destroy the Vemork heavy water plant, plus the War Cabinet's blessing. Operation Gunnerside – named after a remote Scottish hunting lodge with which Wilson was familiar – was a go.

The stakes with Gunnerside could not have been higher, as William Stephenson – Intrepid – made clear to US president Roosevelt. 'If the Germans capture the . . . team alive, they may well deduce that such a suicidal attack has been launched only because the Allies have now proved an atom bomb is a practical proposition.'

With Gunnerside, no longer would they attempt to blow the entire Vemork plant to pieces. With only a small band of raiders to hand, Wilson's aims were far more focused.

'Object: To destroy the essential plant necessary to prevent output of LURGAN . . .' A force of 6–8 men would 'attack the essential cells in the basement of the manufacturing plant' – those that produced the final, concentrated SH200.

With no time to lose, Wilson's force would go in during the very next moon window.

Chapter Eighteen

Joachim Ronneberg was one of those rare beasts: a soft-spoken, modest individual, but also a born leader of men. He'd proved a natural at the kind of dark arts that the Linge Company commando school specialized in. At age twenty-two and with no prior military experience he'd completed his training, only to be made the Company's newest instructor.

New recruits couldn't believe that one so young was in charge of teaching them. Then they got to know him. Ronneberg was not a man most would choose to cross lightly.

'Ronneberg was one of the most outstanding men we had,' commented Colonel Charles Hampton, his boss at the SOE'S Glenmore training school. 'He was well-balanced, unflappable, very, very intelligent and tremendously tough.'

Six foot three and steely-eyed, Ronneberg had escaped to Britain like so many of his compatriots on a fishing boat. He'd carried with him a strong sense of right and wrong – the moral compass that had compelled him to leave Norway and join the fight against Nazi Germany.

He was clear on what he had come to Britain for: 'We felt that there was no sacrifice too great to get the Germans out . . . People must realise that peace and freedom have to be fought for every day.'

Ronneberg had been in Britain for eighteen months, and he'd

started to view the island nation as his new, and much-loved, home. 'I will never forget the welcome that the British showed us,' Ronneberg would remark. 'We never felt like guests in Britain, more like partners in the same cause . . . I always felt I had two homelands: one where I was born and one where I lived during the war.'

Joachim Ronneberg was just the kind of man that Wilson was looking for. The SOE needed 'men of character who were prepared to adapt themselves and their views – even their orders at times – to other people and other considerations . . . Common sense and adaptability are the two main virtues required in anyone who is to work underground, assuming a deep and broad sense of loyalty, which is the basic essential.'

Ronneberg hailed from Alesund, on Norway's rugged north-western coast. Growing up and working in the family fishing business, he was a natural over the mountains. There was a side of him that was intensely physical and thrilled to danger. At the SOE's training school he'd proven particularly gifted at handling explosives and executing mock raids.

When Ronneberg travelled to London to be briefed by Wilson, he still knew practically nothing about Operation Gunnerside. All his commander at Glenmore had been able to tell him was that he was to choose five men to take on a mission about which he could give no further details.

Ronneberg towered a good eight inches over Wilson, but very quickly the two men found that they were seeing eye-to-eye. Wilson had once told the Linge Company recruits that he had 'Viking blood', though it had thinned over the years, just like his hair. In Ronneberg he figured he'd found the real thing.

'So, where are we off to?' Ronneberg asked, diving right in.

When he spoke, he seemed to do so with all of his body, his powerful shoulders and arms moving in rhythm to the beat of the words. It was as if a top athlete was limbering up for some incredible feat of human endurance. Wilson didn't doubt what Ronneberg would be capable of, if only he could get him and his men in on the ground.

'To Vemork,' came the equally direct answer. 'To blow up the plant there.'

Wilson proceeded to brief Ronneberg on the specifics of Operation Gunnerside. Then he took a very unusual step – one that reflected the high respect that he afforded the Norwegian, in spite of his youth. He explained about the Operation Freshman debacle, going well beyond Ronneberg's need-to-know.

Wilson concluded with this: 'One plane crashed, and one returned to base. Both the gliders are missing, and according to reports we have received the prisoners from at least one of the gliders were shot by the Germans, although they were all in uniform.'

That last bit of news – fresh in – had come as a real shock to those who had overseen Operation Freshman.

At first, Lieutenant Colonel Henneker had insisted that his men should be listed as missing in action. The families – including the wife of Bill Bray, who was due to give birth in just a few weeks' time – were told that 'it was by no means certain that the raiding party are killed, captured or wounded'. Some might still be at large. Their relatives were advised to 'be patient and say nothing'.

But then reports had filtered in from the SOE office in Sweden, based upon reliable sources in Norway, confirming that three British aircraft had been forced down by bad weather. One had suffered a cataclysmic crash, with all aboard killed. A glider had crash-landed with several survivors. Those men had been rounded up, taken to a German camp and executed by firing squad that same day.

A second glider had also crash-landed. Some of the survivors at least had been taken in for questioning. Others were apparently shot. The situation was confused, but one thing did seem certain: Henneker's conviction that the Germans would behave in a humane fashion towards the Freshman captives had been sorely misplaced.

Wilson held little back from Ronneberg. He pointed to the fate of the Musketoon captives before Freshman, who were also feared to have been murdered. Indeed, reports received from Stockholm suggested that all British forces sent to carry out acts of sabotage were to be 'shot out of hand, whether in uniform or not'.

Wilson warned Ronneberg that he and his men would likely suffer a similar fate, should they be taken prisoner. And their chances of capture were high. Post-Freshman, any element of surprise was almost certainly gone: the German defenders at Vemork would be alert to any attack.

'You have a fifty-fifty chance of doing the job, and only a fair chance of escaping,' Tronstad explained, bleakly.

Ronneberg and his men were to be given suicide capsules, so if capture did threaten they could kill themselves. Wilson's stark orders left little to the imagination on that front. 'Two "L" pills of potassium cyanide are to be carried by each man. Any man about to be taken prisoner will take his own life.'

Wilson moved on to the one positive aspect of Operation Gunnerside: he had conjured up a cunning plan. Ronneberg's force would hit the plant on Christmas Eve, the one day of the year when he figured the guards at Vemork might be inclined to drop their vigilance.

'The raid has to be carried out before the Germans can build up their defences still more,' Wilson concluded. 'And that means there's no time to lose.'

Ronneberg and his men were to fly in on 17 December – giving themselves a week to link up with Grouse, acclimatize, and familiarize themselves with the target. To hit that timescale they had just three short weeks to prepare.

Ronneberg seemed utterly unfazed by what Wilson had told him. He replied that he was ready. 'We didn't think about whether it was dangerous or not,' Ronneberg would remark. 'The most important decision you made during the whole war was the day you decided to leave Norway to report for duty. You concentrated on the job and not on the risks.'

He'd already chosen his team, going for 'strong, physically fit men with a good sense of humour who would smile their way through the most demanding of situations.' They were suited to a mission that would demand stamina, guts, determination, snow craft and survival skills in equal measure.

Ronneberg had chosen as his deputy one of the most battle-hardened men in the entire Linge Company: Knut Haukelid. Haukelid was twenty-nine years of age, comparatively old for a Linge Company recruit. He had a twin sister, Sigrid, who was a rare beauty. Discovered by a Hollywood producer, she had become a famous actress known as the 'siren of the fjords'.

Sigrid shared her twin brother's fervent anti-Nazi views, but not his looks: there was nothing immediately striking about Haukelid. Five foot ten, he had a massive chest and muscled shoulders beneath wavy blond hair. It was the eyes that had it. In the blink of an eyelid Haukelid's piercing blue gaze could switch from joker to hunter to lone survivor, as the need arose.

Knut and Sigrid Haukelid had been born in the USA. Their father – a civil engineer – had emigrated in 1905, seeking work. But a year after the twins were born, the family moved back to Norway, where their father established an engineering business. From the very start, Knut – dyslexic, but intellectually gifted – hated school. He found the droning teachers boring, and the slight stutter he suffered as a child only served to tighten the classroom screw.

He rebelled, turning to pranks. Once he released a live snake in class, earning yet another detention. The one place where he truly seemed to come alive was the wild. His parents owned a lodge on the Vidda, and young Knut would spend every spare hour there, hunting, fishing, camping and skiing with his grandfather, Knut Sr. During evenings around the campfire Knut Sr. would regale him with tales of old: of wood trolls, dwarves and elves ruling the wild.

Knut Jr. loved those stories. He believed in the trolls especially. The only thing he seemed to be more attached to was his child-hood teddy bear, Bonzo. That name – 'Bonzo' – would become both his childhood nickname and his code name within the SOE.

In his teenage years Bonzo devoured novels by the American authors Steinbeck and Hemingway, whose universal themes of love, war, loss and injustice spoke to him powerfully. Something of a lost soul or searcher, he travelled to America in his late teens, seeking to 'find himself' in the nation so compellingly portrayed in Steinbeck's and Hemingway's prose.

He took a job labouring on a rural farmstead. He loved the out-door, physical life. But he rebelled against the farmer's puritanical ways. One evening at dinner he offered to say grace. He proceeded to sing a song in Norwegian not remotely connected to God. Once he was done, he tucked in with gusto, relishing the sheer irreverence of the moment.

When Haukelid returned to Norway he remained something of a rebel without a cause, but that cause was coming. Still a wanderer, he travelled to Berlin to study. One night he was confronted by a drunken Nazi Party zealot, spouting vile prejudice and invective. Haukelid flattened the man with one punch.

He returned to Norway, but the Nazis' blind hatred followed him there. When the Germans invaded, Haukelid volunteered to fight. He was given a rifle and thirty rounds of ammunition – it was all the Norwegian Army officer could spare from their paltry supplies.

'There are plenty of Germans at Klekken village,' the officer advised Haukelid and his fellow volunteers.

They commandeered a truck and set out, fighting hard for several days, but the Germans brought in armour and Haukelid found himself on the retreat. As he left the area, he saw entire villages in flames. The German troops were torching any settlement where they encountered resistance. It was a brutal warning: *fight, and we will burn you out of your homes.*

'We swore that we would never give in,' Haukelid would later write of this time, 'not even if the Germans won the war.'

Haukelid and his fellows retreated to the back country, where their local knowledge should lend them an advantage. They were pursued through the sweeping valley of Valdres, in central southern Norway. With no air cover and no anti-tank weaponry, Haukelid and his brothers in arms were reduced to sniping at German armour with their small calibre Krag rifles.

At the head of the valley lay the thickly forested Tonsaasen gorge. From the high ground and in thick forest cover Haukelid and his fellows hurled Molotov cocktails – glass bottles filled with petrol, and plugged with burning rags. They managed to torch twelve of the monster tanks. Trapped, the German soldiers panicked, retreating a good twenty miles down the valley.

Haukelid and his fellow fighters seized prisoners and much weaponry. 'But the Germans seemed to have unlimited forces,' Haukelid would write of this time. 'At last we were with our backs to the snow-covered high mountains.'

Haukelid and some others escaped. They decided to head for Oslo. En route they took a ferry across the Mjosa Lake. On-board they discovered a man wearing the uniform of the Hird, Quisling's Nazi guards. When the ferry reached the middle of the lake, Haukelid approached the man. 'Heil Hitler,' he announced, offering a handshake. The Hird man reached out, and Haukelid and his fellows lifted him over the rail and into the water. Only his cap was left floating.

The captain of the ferry came aft to investigate. When he found out what had happened, he remarked: 'Excellent. Full speed ahead!'

Haukelid still had faith in the ancient creatures of the wild. He believed the trolls would never let his country be ruled by the Germans. But there was worse to come. After he escaped to Britain, his house was ransacked and his wife and mother were arrested by the Gestapo. His hatred of the enemy deepened, becoming deeply personal.

By now Haukelid was at the SOE's so-called 'gangster school', a name that he concluded was 'undoubtedly right'. The motto of the gangster school was: *never give the enemy half a chance.*

It was drilled into trainees day and night. Haukelid was taught to fight hard, fast and dirty: 'If you've got the enemy down, kick him to death.'

Haukelid didn't so much as flinch. 'We, who came from a small oppressed country, gladly resorted to every method which could injure the enemy, for the underdog cannot afford to carry on war according to the rules of the stronger party.'

None other than Brigadier Colin McVean Gubbins would write of Haukelid:

> Knut is first and foremost a hunter, a man who knows and loves the wild, who is a part of it, whose every sense is observant; next he is a philosopher, a man who has seen all sides of life . . . and has come by his own experiences to a sense of values reminiscent of the Greek philosophers.
>
> Thirdly, and lastly, he is a man of action who faces directly any situation that comes to him, with the confidence that there must be a solution . . . and that he will find it. Warm-hearted, cool-headed – there is no better combination in peace or war.

Ronneberg had one worry about Haukelid: he was a through-and-through rebel, willing to break the rules simply for the hell of it. He was also several years older than Ronneberg and far more experienced in guerrilla warfare. The Gunnerside leader wondered how a rebellious Bonzo would take to being under his command. Only time would tell.

Haukelid concluded of his SOE gangster school training: 'It is incredible what a man can do with a handful of explosives placed at the right place at the right time – he can halt an army or

devastate the machinery on which a whole community depends.'
With Operation Gunnerside, Bonzo was about to be called upon
to do just that.

Only now, the fortunes of the entire world would turn around
the forthcoming mission.

Chapter Nineteen

Birger Stromsheim was Ronneberg's next choice for his team. With his broad face and curly blond hair, Stromsheim – at thirty-one, the grandfather of the group – was as honest as the day is long. His SOE file concluded that he was level-headed and 'reliable as a rock'.

After 'grandfather' Stromsheim came Fredrik Kayser, a thin beanpole of a man who was another veteran of the war in Norway. He'd been shot at, suffered frostbite and put an axe through his own leg by accident, none of which had dampened his good humour or stopped him from fighting. He was unyielding and relentlessly cheerful under pressure, ideal qualities for what was coming.

After 'cheery' Kayser there was Kasper Idland, a veritable man mountain. Like many physically imposing individuals, Idland was something of a gentle giant. At school he'd been bullied terribly. Worried lest he would hurt someone, he hadn't retaliated. But after one particularly bad day he'd asked his mother if it was all right to fight back. She'd told him it was. The next day he knocked down the two worst offenders. He was never bullied again.

Idland was a superb soldier, and he had what Ronneberg and Wilson prized above all else: an unshakeable loyalty. After 'gentle giant' Idland came the final member of the team – Hans

'Chicken' Storhaug, so named due to his thin, scraggy chicken's neck. Storhaug was an expert in the back country, and he was familiar with the terrain stretching all the way to the Swedish border. He would be a vital asset during their escape – that's if they made it in and out of Vemork alive.

Five good men and true; six with Ronneberg; ten – once they linked up with team Grouse; eleven, if Grouse One – Einar Skinnarland – should join their number. Eleven men on skis and equipped only with what arms and explosives they could carry across the ice-bound Norwegian wilderness: on these men rested the Allied efforts to stop Hitler from building the world's first atomic weapon.

As with the Grouse and Freshman teams before them, Ronneberg's force were rushed through specialist training, including a stint with a new and improved mock-up of the Vemork SH200 plant, at Brickendonbury Hall – Station XVII. They arrived at the grand country house to be shown to their dormitory. On each bed lay a kit bag, plus various equipment, including a brand new Colt .45.

Instinctively, each man went about checking the pistol's action. Ronneberg cocked his Colt, but when he pulled the trigger there was a deafening crash and plaster dust drifted down from a hole in the wall. Two of the Station XVII staff came running to investigate.

'What the hell is going on?' one demanded.

Poker-faced, Ronneberg pointed to the hole in the wall. 'I was just testing my weapon. It works perfectly.'

The Station XVII staffers glanced at each other, shaking their heads in exasperation. *Where did they find these crazy Norwegians?*

Ronneberg and his men would have one significant advantage over their predecessors. Just prior to the Freshman debacle, Jomar Brun – the bespectacled double agent at the Vemork plant – had been told to flee, lest he be swept up in the repercussions that would follow such an attack. Brun had recently arrived in Britain.

Working under an assumed name given him by the SOE – 'Dr Hagan' – he had been provided with a flat in London to house himself and his wife, who had fled to Britain with him. Dr Hagan was now the chief technical adviser for the coming mission. He'd brought with him a plethora of documents on the Vemork plant, from which the Gunnerside plan of attack could be polished and refined.

Wilson, meanwhile, was desperately seeking clear information on what von Falkenhorst might have learned from the Freshman captives. On 30 November he sent the following message: 'Information urgently required about details of bombers and gliders which came down in mountains ... Have some personnel escaped? Were aircraft destroyed by fire? Has part of equipment been caught by enemy?'

That message went to Swan, the code name for another resistance cell based to the north-west of the Vidda, in the region where the aircraft were believed to have crashed. With Grouse off the air, there was little point in trying to contact them, and in any case this was not their area. An answer came back from Swan a few days later.

'[Bomber] crashed on mountainside all occupants of aircraft being killed. Of glider's passengers 6 were killed in crash and 11 taken prisoner and shot. Other glider apparently made forced landing – 8 killed and 9 taken prisoner and shot at German camp ... Crews are described as "armed civilians".'

What Wilson needed to know was whether the Freshman captives had been forced to talk, and if so what had they revealed. It was then that an SOE agent – Norwegian Kirkeby Jacobsen, code name Crow II – managed to escape from Gestapo custody. By sheer coincidence Crow II had been used to question five captured British soldiers. It turned out that they were the injured Sappers from one of the Freshman gliders.

When Crow II reached London Wilson had him debriefed by MI5 to check his bona fides. They came back with confirmation: 'CROW reliable.'

Crow told Wilson that the Sappers had refused to divulge their objective, which was why he was forced to intercede on his captors' behalf. The Gestapo hoped that the presence of a fellow SOE operative and good English speaker might convince the British captives to talk. The Germans already knew where the Sappers had been heading: they'd retrieved maps from the glider wreckage with Vemork ringed in blue. Now they sought the detail.

Crow II outlined to the Sappers the less savoury methods used by the Gestapo. He explained that they wouldn't be able to hold out for ever. They were crammed into a dark, damp, unsanitary cell, and they'd received no treatment for their injuries. They were highly vulnerable. If they didn't agree to speak, they would be 'worked on'. With time, they would reveal all: their mission, their means and their numbers, their local associates, and their planned escape route.

In light of Crow's testimony, Wilson had to presume that General von Falkenhorst knew everything.

As if to confirm this, at dawn on 3 December 1942 air raid sirens echoed across the deep valley that houses Vemork. In truth, there was no bombing raid. Instead, the Germans used the blaring klaxon to keep the Rjukan residents indoors while they sealed off the town. Gestapo agents – supported by hundreds of regular troops – made house-to-house searches, rounding up dozens of 'suspects'. In particular, they were hunting for the local team that had been charged with helping to guide the Freshman force in.

The mastermind of the Rjukan raid was *Reichskommissar* Josef Terboven, Hitler's governor of Norway. A bespectacled, cold-blooded former bank clerk, Terboven was an early acolyte of the Führer. When Terboven had married the secretary of his good friend, Joseph Goebbels, Hitler was the guest of honour at their wedding. In Norway Terboven had a personal security force of around 6,000 at his command, and his brutality swiftly alienated the Norwegian people.

Terboven's apogee in terms of sheer cruelty was what became known as the 'Telavag tragedy'. Telavag was a small village on Norway's western coast. The inhabitants were found to have been hiding two men from the Linge Company. On 26 April 1942 German forces came to arrest those men, Gestapo officers rushing the loft where they were hiding out. There was a shootout, and two Gestapo officers were killed, including one infamous SS commander.

Terboven personally oversaw the reprisals. The villagers were forced to watch as their houses were torched, the boats in the local harbour sunk and their livestock killed. The men of the village were rounded up and either gunned down on the spot, or carted off to the Sachsenhausen concentration camp in north-west Germany. Few would ever return. Even the women and children of Telavag were imprisoned, some until the end of the war.

As Terboven's friend, Goebbels, had decreed, regarding the people of the occupied nations: 'If they cannot learn to love us, they should at least fear us.'

The day after the Gestapo's Rjukan raid, Terboven and von Falkenhorst paid a visit to the Vemork works. Speeches were given, and instructions issued about how security at the plant was to be beefed up. High-voltage wires would be mounted, running alongside the pipelines just above ground level. They would be perfect for electrocuting any would-be saboteurs. Further mine-fields would be strung across any possible approach routes, and the Skoland Marshes, the intended Freshman landing zone, were to be cordoned off under guard.

Maximum vigilance was required. 'Our security teams must be mobile and capable of fighting within the plant,' von Falken-horst stressed. 'They must be able to quickly pursue the enemy, overtake him in the course of his flight, and overpower him in hand-to-hand combat . . . The gangsters will choose precisely the most arduous approach route to infiltrate a facility, because that is where they expect to encounter the least protection and the flimsiest of barriers.'

The German general's words revealed how deeply he had come to understand commando and SOE doctrine, and how much must have been wrung out of the Freshman captives. 'The enemy spends weeks, even months, meticulously planning sabotage operations and spares no effort to assure their success. Conse-quently we too must resort to every conceivable means in order to thwart their plans . . .'

A third individual accompanied Terboven and von Falken-horst: *Obergruppenführer* (SS General) Wilhelm Rediess, chief of the SS in Norway. Like Terboven, Rediess was a diehard Nazi. He was an advocate of the *Lebensborn* ('Fount of Life') programme, which promoted the breeding of 'racially pure and healthy' Aryan children, most often sired by SS troops. During his time, around 8,000 *Lebensborn* children would be born in Norway, making it second only to Germany in the number of such births.

Acting on Rediess's orders, the Gestapo made a beeline for the Skinnarland residence on the shores of Lake Møs. The Skinnarland parents were in the midst of holding a party for one of their sons. The birthday celebrations were interrupted by the snarl of motorcycles arriving in their yard. Einar Skinnarland was absent, but Torstein was there. The Gestapo seized him, mistaking him for the 'radio operator and resistance leader' that they were after.

Reports on much of this reached Wilson's ears. Even for him it was hugely daunting. First Musketoon, and now this: the fallout from Freshman could hardly have been worse. Wilson had feared all along that Freshman was a suicide mission. He had been right. Those brave and courageous Sappers had been sent to their deaths in a tragic waste of human life. But the wider costs – they might determine the fortunes of the entire war.

In spite of this Wilson had no choice but to continue. The former Scoutmaster had given his word that Vemork's SH200 production would be stopped. He'd claimed this as an SOE operation, and Winston Churchill himself was keeping a watchful eye. The 17th of December was fast approaching: zero hour for Gunnerside.

There was one potential upside right now: much of what Wilson had learned from the field had come from Haugland, team Grouse's radio operator. In the midst of the German crackdown (*Razzia*) Poulsson and his men had risked breaking their silence to ensure that Wilson fully understood what they were up against.

In freezing conditions in a remote hut in the depths of the snowbound Vidda, Haugland crouched over his cipher key, finger tap-tapping away. 'On account of glider landing the Germans have carried out extensive raids in … Telemark … In Rjukan over 100 Gestapo and troops. State of emergency … Germans … appear to know that Vemork was to be attacked with Norwegian help.'

Detailing developments at the Vemork works itself, Haugland signalled: 'A.A. guns 20 mm. Searchlights … Gestapo continuing investigations … Rediess, Falkenhorst and Terboven have all inspected. Machine gun placed on roof of hydrogen factory.'

But for their dedication to the mission the Grouse team was suffering. As he hunched over his Morse key, working by candlelight alone, and in a hut in which condensation froze to icy tentacles on the inside of the walls, Haugland's hands were frozen right through. Yet he knew that he couldn't risk wearing gloves, for that would alter his radio 'signature', and that in turn could spell disaster.

Those who beavered away at the SOE's home station grew intimately familiar with a field agent's Morse signature. It was one of the ways in which they could triple-check that a message was genuine. One operator would cut his dots shorter than another, or prolong his dashes, and his or her 'fingerprint' was recorded in their file. If it changed, that might signify that the Gestapo had taken over a radio station and was using it to send disinformation to try to entrap others.

Such risks were very real, and Wilson was hyper alert to them. Earlier that month a fellow Norwegian radio operator – code name Lark – who was being hunted by the Gestapo, had suddenly gone off the air. Days later he apparently came up on his regular sked, but his signature had changed markedly. He'd sent the following message:

'Lost five figure code. Therefore use only the phrase from now on: "Not until the Norwegian flag waves". Number 3217. That's all.'

The message was riddled with errors. The 'phrase' – Lark's prearranged emergency communications sentence – should have read: 'Not until the Norwegian flag *flies over Berlin.*' It was both incorrect and incomplete. The number '3217' wasn't even Lark's correct operator code.

'The assumption is the operator, if he was our man, was doing everything he could to indicate that his message was being sent under duress,' Wilson concluded. Sure enough, he duly received a report confirming that Lark had been arrested and tortured, and his radio station taken over by the Gestapo. Heaven forbid that Haugland and the Grouse team should suffer a similar fate.

In mid December Haugland apparently sent a message in the middle of the night, but the signal didn't seem to match his signature, at least not to those who decoded it. Alarm bells began to ring. With the *Razzia* in full swing, had the Gestapo swooped on team Grouse and taken over their radio station?

The signaller decoding the message was seated in a comparatively cosy room in a quaint English village – a very different kind of environment from the Vidda in mid December. He ran through a series of checks, to all of which he received the correct answer. Then he fired off the final security question – the response to which had to be something that no Gestapo agent might ever guess at.

'What did you see walking down the Strand in the early hours of January 1st, 1941?'

Stiff fingers tapped out a reply. 'To Colonel. Three, repeat three pink elephants.'

In his Chiltern Court office – Wilson slept just a few paces along the corridor, and was permanently on call – the former Scoutmaster grunted with satisfaction. His radio operators were instructed to bypass all normal security channels if need be, and to come to him direct. Any message prefaced with 'To Colonel' was for his immediate attention, no matter what time of day or night it might be.

Wilson had been woken from his sleep and warned of the fear that Grouse had been captured and broken. Personally, he'd doubted it. Haugland's 'pink elephants' answer had proved him right. 'The German ... mentality could never have cracked so frivolous an exchange,' Wilson remarked. In truth, Haugland had sent the message while bundled up in his sleeping bag, and with bare hand tapping at his Morse key. His fingertips were so frozen that his 'signature' had changed.

But still Wilson was worried. He needed Grouse more than ever. He needed them to feed back vital intelligence to London and to guide team Gunnerside in. And this time he would need them to provide almost half of the force that was to hit the Vemork plant. Yet as Christmas 1942 approached Grouse was being hunted as never before, and it wasn't just the Gestapo, the SS and scores of German troops who sought to finish them.

As Wilson knew full well, his men had run out of supplies. Due to the terrible weather conditions over the Vidda, it had been impossible to fly any resupply airdrops, which was a widespread problem that winter.

'The requests from the field for . . . stores were continuous and not half of them could be met,' commented Wilson. 'Every effort was made to give . . . a reason when supplies could not be sent, but this was not always possible . . . Tobacco, coffee and chocolate were always in short supply. Many regard these as luxuries. To men living on mountain tops they were essentials.'

Cold and starvation stalked the men of team Grouse, pushing them to the most extreme measures in an effort to survive.

Chapter Twenty

Poulsson's pipe had long gone cold. Deployed to Norway for what had supposedly been a month-long mission, he'd run out of tobacco. But in truth, that was the least of his worries. As he surveyed the scene in their new redoubt – a bare hut known as the 'Cousin's Cabin' – he knew that his team's situation was utterly desperate.

They'd been reduced to scratching in the snow for 'reindeer moss' – the grey-green lichen that the reindeer herds graze on during the long winter months. Each of them was familiar with the moss, but not as a foodstuff: they'd used it as bedding during childhood camping trips.

The Norwegian wilderness harbours the largest reindeer herds in Europe. Poulsson reminded his men that in winter all those millions of animals survived pretty much on the moss alone. 'It's full of vitamins and minerals,' he told them, in an effort to bolster their flagging spirits.

Certainly, it was eaten by the native Sami people of the Arctic, well boiled and mixed with berries, fish eggs or lard. But unfortunately Poulsson and his men had precious little to add to the tough, bitter lichen. It made a thin, sour soup that did little to satiate their hunger, and it was debatable whether cutting the wood to boil the lichen used up more energy than the lichen gave back.

The Cousin's Cabin had actually been built by Poulsson, along with his cousin – hence the name. It lay amidst a 'finger lakes' region – an area crisscrossed by narrow spears of water, reaching across the land like the fingers of one hand. It was incredibly remote, wasn't marked on any maps, and no trails passed near it – making it ideal if you wanted to disappear.

In a drawer in the table Poulsson had found the guestbook. He'd flicked through it, wistfully: there were the names of all his dear friends and family. Many still lived in and around Rjukan, thirty kilometres south-east of the isolated hut. But, for all their loved ones knew of their existence here, Poulsson and his fellows might as well have been on another planet.

The last few days had seen one near-disaster after another. It was 'remarkable', Poulsson noted in his diary, that they'd somehow escaped death or capture. Haugland had been in the woods scavenging for food when German soldiers appeared. He'd dived for cover, and the search patrol had missed him by bare metres. Poulsson and Kjelstrup had likewise narrowly evaded capture when out tracking reindeer.

But it was Helberg who'd had the closest brush: he'd headed for the Skinnarlands' house just as the Gestapo had returned. Torstein Skinnarland was locked away in Grini concentration camp and his brother, Olav, had also been arrested, but the Gestapo were still on the hunt for Einar himself. Fortunately, a savage storm blew up, and Helberg was forced to turn back, so preventing him from stumbling into the clutches of the Gestapo.

Starving as these men were, they'd still had to carry all their weaponry, explosives, survival kit, heavy radio, the Eureka, plus batteries across the Vidda, to reach their new location. While laden down with the Eureka battery, Helberg had been caught in a blizzard. The man that Poulsson had hailed as being able to go on till he could do no more and then go twice as far, had finally buckled. As the weather worsened, he'd been forced to hide the battery in some woods and go to ground.

The winter of 1942–3 would be the worst in living memory. All four of the Grouse team were caught up in the storm that defeated Helberg. It blew into a monster – a snarling tempest that tore out of the dark heavens. There was no way any one of them could make it to the shelter of the Cousin's Cabin. Instead, they were forced to burrow into the snow and curl up inside their sleeping bags.

'We often had to crawl on all fours,' Poulsson remarked of that storm.

At one juncture they had to shelter beneath one of their old parachutes, to fend off the driving snow. At another, Haugland was almost driven into a patch of open, freezing water. The wind was so powerful that it blew him across the ice, his skis seemingly incapable of getting enough grip to fight back. Had he tumbled in during such a storm, it would have been the death of him.

Finally, the tempest blew itself out. All four made it back to the Cousin's Cabin more or less in one piece. They'd long exhausted the dog food – old, dried fish – that they'd scavenged from a farmhouse. Boiled, it had made a soup that had tasted delicious to men who were starving. In desperation they ate some salted reindeer meat that they'd discovered in a hut, but it turned out to be rotten. All went down with food poisoning.

Helberg had pushed himself too far. After eating the bad meat he developed oedema – a painful retention of fluid in the body, caused in this case by severe malnutrition. He put on twenty pounds. He was so bloated he couldn't button his shirt properly and was forever having to pee. Yet, incredibly, he still tried to sally forth each day, gathering their kit together and desperately seeking food.

A mid-December radio message to the SOE home station gave a sense of their dire situation. 'No contact. Charging of accumulator [battery] impossible. Current only about three hours. Send as little as possible. Draw home station's attention to this.'

In extremis, Grouse had pretty much shut down.

If it hadn't been for Einar Skinnarland, the four might not have made it this far. Hunted by the Gestapo, Grouse One had been forced to join their number in hiding. Better fed, resolute and of unflinching good humour, Skinnarland's very presence bolstered their spirits. He'd also brought with him what little food he had remaining, plus a freshly charged battery.

Helberg would write of his presence: 'It was a pleasure to be with him ... A matter of tremendous importance in circumstances so difficult as those we were in.'

After Skinnarland's arrival, Haugland blipped up for a rare moment on the air. His messages had to be brief now, for the longer he was transmitting the more chance there was of being captured. The Germans had mobile D/F units out, trying to pinpoint the radio signals emanating from the Vidda. They had search aircraft in the skies, and rumour had it that D/F units were also fitted to those.

The Gestapo would certainly be able to hear team Grouse. They knew that enemy agents were transmitting from somewhere in the snowbound wilderness of the Vidda. They just needed to find the source of the signals.

'Einar Skinnarland . . . was hunted by Gestapo . . ', Haugland's brief message read. 'He escaped to the mountains and joined us . . . Einar and his connections have been of great value.'

They certainly had been of great value, but not for very much longer. In arresting Torstein and sending Einar Skinnarland to ground, the Gestapo had cut off the one source of food that Grouse had been reliant upon. Starvation and the foul weather had become their chief enemies now, and they appeared to be winning.

On 10 December matters took a slight turn for the better. Haugland discovered a Krag rifle, plus some ammunition in a hut. Poulsson seized the rifle with undisguised joy: with a long-range weapon like this it should be possible to hunt reindeer. 'Just wait until there's game in the area,' he cried. The challenge would be finding the reindeer herds.

The very next day Poulsson set out with rifle in hand. But he seemed to be cursed by the weather. Fog had descended across the plateau like a thick soup. The higher Poulsson skied in search of the herds, the denser it became. He would never spot them in such godforsaken conditions. That evening he returned from scouring the Vidda empty handed, and to a dark hut reeking of hunger and of sickness.

Henceforth Poulsson set out daily, and daily he returned to four sets of expectant eyes, having failed to find anything. The Cousin's Cabin was warmed by a wood-burning stove, but the birchwood had to be dug from under the snow. For how much longer would his men have the energy to do that, Poulsson wondered? If the fire in the hut died, so would they. They would freeze to death and no one would be any the wiser.

The date of Gunnerside's insertion was fast approaching. Ronneberg and his team were scheduled to parachute into a flat patch of snow lying not far from the Cousin's Cabin. But what did Poulsson have to offer them? Five sets of hands that were listless and sickly, and barely able to hold a weapon.

Were he and his team even capable of manning the landing zone, and steering Gunnerside in? Poulsson just didn't know. And by no stretch of the imagination would they be able to ski thirty kilometres across the Vidda, to mount an assault on the Vemork plant. Indeed, he was worried if they could even hold out.

Either he tracked down some reindeer, and quickly, or they – and the mission – were finished.

In London, Wilson was facing his own problems. As further evidence emerged about Hitler's apparent order to execute all captured saboteurs, those in high office baulked at sending in yet more raiders. Mountbatten – already unsettled by the fate of the Freshman captives – was deeply troubled. Could he in all conscience continue to send out saboteurs, in the knowledge that any taken captive would be tortured and shot?

Mountbatten wrote to the chiefs of staff, seeking guidance. One way or the other, he felt he needed to brief Churchill. Wilson's riposte to all this was simple: Vemork was SOE business now. Having fully briefed Ronneberg on what he and his men were heading into, he felt absolved. In any case, the Vemork mission was far too important for any such considerations to come into play. Even if Gunnerside was a de facto suicide mission, the men concerned were more than willing.

A late December memo was circulated regarding the Freshman executions and Mountbatten's worries. Any action connected with 'the alleged executions of his troops in Norway, is dangerous until we have carried out operation GUNNERSIDE which . . . has the same objective.' Mountbatten was to be asked to 'delay any action until we have given the "all clear".'

In other words, they could afford to be squeamish once Hitler's nuclear programme had been stymied, and not before. And that meant Gunnerside had to go ahead come what may.

Spurred by such concerns, Wilson and Tronstad decided to bring the Gunnerside team further into their confidences. If they were to run such terrible risks, they should at least understand why. Tronstad showed a report to the Gunnerside men. It was marked with all the usual secrecy stamps, and addressed to the very highest in Allied command.

'It's the heavy water,' Tronstad remarked darkly, flicking through the pages. Haukelid got a good look at the contents: the report had to do with splitting the atom. 'It's manufactured at Vemork, and can be used for some of the dirtiest work that can possibly be imagined.' With it the Germans will 'win the war', Tronstad warned.

Incredibly, Jomar Brun had brought something else out of Norway, along with his blueprints and papers; he'd carried with him two flasks of the precious liquid itself. Those two kilos of SH200 had been delivered into the hands of the experts at Tube Alloys. Urgent tests were carried out. No doubt about it, this was the real thing. Take this, combine it with plutonium and the right scientific know-how, and you could build a nuclear weapon.

In America, Stephenson met with Roosevelt. 'What worries us more than anything is Niels Bohr,' he told the President, 'whose work is dangerously like atomic projects under way in the

United States.' He raised the risk of Bohr's research in his Danish laboratory being harnessed to the *Uranverein*'s needs.

'Could Bohr be whisked out from under the Nazi noses and brought to the Manhattan Project?' Roosevelt asked.

'It would have to be a British mission,' Stephenson replied. Another one, and Vemork was yet to be destroyed. 'Bohr is a stubborn pacifist. He does not believe his work . . . will benefit the German military . . . Nor is he likely to join an American enterprise which has as its sole objective the construction of a bomb.' Bohr had good friends in Britain – fellow physicists that he trusted. They could reach out to him.

A microdotted letter was sent to Bohr. He retrieved the pin-head message in the privacy of his Copenhagen lab. He sent back a reply: he would not leave Denmark, even for Britain, and he would certainly not join any project to build an atomic bomb. In any case, 'any immediate use of the marvellous discoveries of atomic physics is impracticable,' he concluded.

But Bohr's correspondence sounded an oddly contradictory note. He warned that the Germans – who treated him with kid gloves, for obvious reasons – were seeking more uranium and heavy water to build their atomic bombs. When word reached Churchill, Britain's leader took a very dim view. Here he was in London preparing Operation Peppermint, an Anglo-American programme to defend the nations' cities against a possible Nazi nuclear strike. In America, they were busy building radiation detection devices as part of that Anglo-American initiative.

Yet Bohr sat in his ivory tower preaching peace!

Bohr, Churchill fumed, came 'very near the edge of mortal crimes'. Lindemann, Churchill's chief scientific adviser, was equally worried. Germany 'increases its demands for heavy water and metallic uranium,' wrote Lindemann, 'and German scientists now submit proposals for the use of chain reactions with slow neutrons for producing bombs.'

Lindemann proposed getting the SOE to plant an explosive device beneath Niels Bohr's laboratory, where his cyclotrons whirred away, blowing all to smithereens.

But first things first: *Vemork*.

In Britain, the SH200 raiders had just received a massive fillip. Again, it had come from the amazing Jomar Brun. After Musketoon and now Freshman, it was clear that a force of just eleven men couldn't fight their way into the plant. Only by stealth and surprise might Ronneberg and his team succeed, and Brun just happened to know of a hidden way to access the target.

On the side of the plant that faced the plunging gorge there was a small, man-sized hatch. It opened into a cable duct, one that ran across the ceiling of the hydrolysis plant. Brun had come across it only recently, largely by accident, when, after heavy snowfall, he'd been searching for an alternative way into the building. If it had been missed in the post-Freshman security shake-up, it might just offer a secret means to gain entry.

There was another advantage of sneaking in that way. 'If you try and force the door to the basement,' Tronstad advised the men, 'you will likely trigger an alarm, which will result in a struggle with the German soldiers and many casualties. The killing of German soldiers will result in heavy reprisals . . . I therefore advise you to use the cable duct for entrance into the plant.'

There was one other juicy piece of intelligence, courtesy of Brun. Situated on the balconies that ran around the massive building were hydrogen burners. The plant workers called them 'cannons', because of the noises they made. When starting up, or if the flow of gas to the burners dropped, they would issue a small explosion, and sometimes even a large one.

Over time the German soldiers grew used to hearing such bangs. With luck, this might provide some cover for the Gunnerside force when their charges ripped apart the SH200 plant. At the very least it might buy them a little time.

Team Gunnerside's three weeks of frenetic preparations were done now. Their assessment was glowing: 'This was an excellent party in every way, and each member has a thorough knowledge of the target ... Their demolitions work was exceedingly good and thorough and their Weapons Training outstanding. If the conditions are at all possible, they have every chance of carrying out the operation.'

Wilson felt heartened. The trouble now would prove to be the wild and tempestuous Vidda. The harshest winter anyone could remember held the Barren Mountain plateau in its savage grip, and the Operation Gunnerside flights kept getting cancelled.

The December moon window came and went. Wilson's plan to strike on Christmas Eve had been sunk by the Vidda's inclement climate. For both a well-fed and eager Gunnerside team, and for the starving men of team Grouse, the weather was the chief enemy now. Ronneberg and his men grew sick of the sight of RAF Tempsford, the ghost airfield.

It was as if the place was mocking them, for theirs had seemingly become a ghost mission.

Chapter Twenty-One

Poulsson shaded his eyes. After so many days spent in the ice-grey twilight of the fog-bound Vidda, and countless nights in the Cousin's dark hut, he wasn't used to the glare. Sunlight. At last. It was 23 December 1942, and Poulsson had woken to a glorious dawn.

The fog had lifted. Rays had broken through. It was a perfect day.

For an hour or more he'd been following the reindeer tracks. It was a good-sized herd, and already he could feel his pulse quickening. If only. If only he could track them and make a kill – he would be the saviour of his men. He crested a ridge, the crust of snow breaking crisply under his ski poles, the air fresh and tight in his lungs. He scanned the whiteness below. Nothing. Where were they?

A phrase came back to him from his childhood. Reindeer: 'They are like ghosts. They come from nowhere, fill up the land, then disappear.' Maybe something had spooked them? A wolf? Humans? A German patrol? A herd in flight could travel twenty-five miles in an hour, easily. They might already be far away.

He pressed onwards, eyes glued to the distinctive tracks in the snow. He crested a second ridge. He stopped and pulled out his binoculars, wiping the glasses with a cloth he kept tucked under his watchstrap. He scanned the terrain below. The flat midday light played tricks, compressing everything and cutting out form and distance.

He swept the lenses back and forth across the sun-dazzled whiteness. He almost missed it. A group of rocks in a far valley. But wait, the rocks were moving. Slowly, almost as one, they drifted northwards across the snow.

He'd found it: the herd.

Pulse quickening, he set out once more. Being careful to keep downwind, lest they catch his scent, he skied across the intervening terrain. He climbed a second ridge. Halted. Removed his skis and crept into view. They were close now. Seventy or so of them, grazing on the moss that Poulsson and his men had grown sick to death of eating.

Well today, if only he could do this, they would feast like kings.

He wasn't yet within range. Between him and the herd lay open terrain. He couldn't risk crossing it. They were bound to see or hear him. He would have to lie in wait, hoping that they would come to him. An hour passed. The cold bit into his skin. He hated risking any movement, but he had to keep exposed flesh ice-free. He screwed up his face, shaking shards of ice from his thick beard and rubbing any areas that started to numb – the first signs of frostbite.

But no matter how long he waited, the herd just didn't seem to come any closer. Grazing on the moss fringing a small lake, most were like statues. With their thick whitish-grey pelts they melted into the surroundings, breath pooling in frozen gasps. He would have to risk making a move. The light would fade, and the last thing Poulsson could face was a long ski back in darkness, empty-handed . . . again.

He flitted into the valley, sticking to whatever cover he could find. Two bulls were nearest. He crept towards a small mound that would bring him within range. In theory the Krag was accurate up to around 900 metres. In practice, he needed to get to within a third of that distance to be sure of a kill. If he fired and missed, in that instant the herd would be gone.

Poulsson was almost at the mound behind the cover of which he would take aim and fire when his feet shot out from under him. Moments later he was sliding down the hillside in a mini avalanche. Up ahead the bulls stamped repeatedly, their alarm call pulsing across the hard snow like drumbeats. Within moments the valley was filled with the deafening sound of panicked hooves, and the herd was gone.

Poulsson sank back into the cold whiteness. He cursed this barren land. He felt utterly spent. Tears of frustration pricked his eyes. What he wouldn't give for a pinch of pipe tobacco, to bolster his frozen spirits. There was one spark of hope. When he'd first spotted the herd, he'd noticed a smaller group of reindeer grazing in a valley high above. It was just possible that they hadn't been spooked. It was his only chance.

He skied fast now. The light was dying. No point in finding that second herd if it was too dark to take a shot. He hit the slope leading up to the higher ground, removed his skis and began to climb. He tried to combine speed with utmost care. The last thing he needed was to take a second tumble and to scare off this herd – that's if it was still there.

He reached the lip of the rise and sank to his belly, inching his way upwards, praying that the wind would be in his face when he topped out. He raised his head, heart beating fit to burst. There. Ahead of him, maybe 300 metres. Reindeer. He counted thirty, skittish and unsettled as the wind kept shifting across the flat, exposed terrain. If it changed direction to behind him, they would catch his scent and be gone.

Poulsson belly-crawled ahead, rifle held before him. He would hit the first animal in the diaphragm. If his aim was true, the animal would fold gently into the snow, as if taken by the sudden need to rest. He might even get a second shot in. Who knew when the herds might return, and presently the hunger of his men knew no bounds.

He came within range and eased the rifle into his shoulder. He breathed deeply, calming his nerves and finding his centre, just as his grandfather had taught him. He took aim, the exhalations of the animals forming a cloud of warm mist enveloping them. He took up pressure on the Krag's trigger, and squeezed. The rifle barked.

The target animal didn't fall. Instead, it took to its heels. Poulsson fired again. And again. Still no animal fell. In a swirl of frightened snow they were gone.

Poulsson couldn't understand it. Had he missed three times? Was his physical condition so dire that he'd lost the ability to hold a rifle and aim true?

He skied after the herd. Almost immediately he discovered blood amongst the hoof prints. He hadn't missed. He figured it had to be the ammunition that was at fault. It was military issue steel-jacketed rounds, as opposed to the soft lead bullets that he more normally used for hunting. The shots must have cut clean through the animal, doing far less damage.

There were three blood trails. He picked one to follow. He came upon the wounded cow, legs scrabbling in the snow as she tried to stand. He raised the Krag and put her out of her misery. He tried to track the other blood trails, but it was almost dark now. He hated leaving two animals to die a slow death, but this was a matter of survival.

Poulsson returned to the cow. He grabbed a tin cup and filled it with her blood. He drank, rich warmth and energy coursing through his system. He drained the rest of the blood into a bucket, carefully setting it aside. He skinned the animal and quartered it, placing the head and tongue into his rucksack, plus the stomach, with its semi-digested load of lichen. From long experience he knew that these were the parts of the animal – rich in nutrients and flavour – that starving men craved.

He added the heart, liver, kidney and ribs and, crucially, slices of fat, for energy. He piled the leaner cuts in a heap, and roofed it over with snow. He'd return for that the following day. Finally, he cracked the small bones near the hooves, and sucked down the milky white marrow – a final burst of energy to prepare him for the long ski home under a crushing load.

He'd once commented that no man should ever carry more than thirty kilos across the Vidda, in such cold and at such altitude. He was close to that limit now, alone, and night was upon him. But he was buoyed up by the euphoria of the moment.

In the darkness of his return, he skied into the same herd that had first eluded him. The reindeer broke cover, thundering into the empty night. He arrived at the cabin, placed the blood-soaked rucksack by the door, and dusted his hands off in the snow. He walked in, head bowed and silent, as if – once again – he had failed. Poulsson figured he'd earned a little theatre.

Four sets of eyes turned to him dully. Any hopes they'd cherished had died several days ago. They felt sorry for him; more sorry for themselves. It was Kjelstrup who first noticed: there was blood on Poulsson's trousers. He glanced at the Grouse leader's emaciated features. He could tell that Poulsson was hiding something.

With a yell of excitement he darted outside and fell upon the bulging, bloodied rucksack. The others joined him, their wild cheers echoing across the dark Vidda.

Salvation.

With this, they would live. They were saved. This signified that the long-awaited reindeer herds had come. There would be more hunting. For now at least, life was assured.

Arguably, there were few others who could hope to survive here, in this harshest of lands. As Wilson had concluded, when sending out Skinnarland and then Poulsson and his men:

Even the most expert British skiers . . . could not have lived in the mountains across the North Sea . . . It would have been suicide to parachute our own people over on sabotage work. The enemy would have known about the landings in a matter of days, if not hours. Don't forget there were . . . Quislings over there, as well as many loyalists.

Norway, geographically, and in every other way, was just about the worst country in the world for undercover operations. The weather could change from favourable to decidedly dangerous in a few minutes. Areas suitable for landings . . . were few and far between . . . It was a country for mountain-trained men, who could merge into the local background, minutes after they hit the deck.

The following day, Christmas Eve, Poulsson and his men gathered at the hut's rough-hewn table, a juniper twig and some paper stars making a stand-in Christmas tree. To a background of carols played over the radio, and with the headphones set on a tin plate to amplify the sound, they feasted. Poulsson – the self-appointed Grouse chef – had prepared a soup made of reindeer blood and half-digested lichen, from the animal's stomach.

There would be no tripping over a reindeer pelt this time, spilling the precious meal. The soup was followed by fried reindeer tongue and liver. For the first time in weeks the men felt satiated. The animal had given its life so they might live. Arguably, it had given its life so the world might live in freedom and in peace, for such were the stakes in what was coming.

But for now, the survivors would celebrate the sheer fact of their survival. No one ever beat the Vidda. You had to learn to bend to its ways. If you did that, it would provide. Eventually. As it had done now.

As they sat back contented, one amongst them began to hum a tune that they had learned to love during the long months of Scottish training. All raised a voice – quiet, hopeful, re-energized. It was Christmas Eve and they had something very simple to celebrate: they were alive. Softly sung vocals echoed around the hut.

She'll be coming round the mountain when she comes,
She'll be coming round the mountain when she comes . . .

Humans cannot survive on meat and fat alone. They needed vitamins and carbohydrates, gleaned from fruit and vegetation. Poulsson and his men knew this, hence their eating the reindeer's stomach contents. Over the coming days they would consume every last morsel of the carcass, stewing the bones for forty-eight hours and pounding the residue into a thick, gluey 'porridge'.

'We ate everything except . . . the hooves,' remarked Poulsson of the reindeer that he had killed. And when that first animal was used up, they went out hunting again, for the herds had arrived in earnest now. Nothing went to waste. 'The skins we put on the floor, ceiling and walls to make the hut warmer.'

The failure of the December Gunnerside drop meant a wait for the January 1943 moon period. But with the reindeers' sacrifice, they would endure. A 14 January radio message reflects how Poulsson's team was reinvigorated. Typically, it downplayed the previous weeks of privation.

'Reason for our silence difficulties in battery charging ... Rations running short ... German force in district still 200. No change in forces at Møsdamm and Vemork. New ... D/F station at Møsdamm. Consider diversionary flying operations immensely important for the safety of the dropping. All lakes frozen and covered in snow.'

The last part of the message referred to the pending drop of Ronneberg and team. With the Germans scouring the Vidda and listening in, Haugland was suggesting that the aircraft should execute a diversionary ploy, to disguise the dropping of the Gunnerside team.

In London Wilson heeded Haugland's advice. He and Tronstad racked their brains for a suitable ruse. None came to mind. They would need to get their thinking caps on. In the meantime, Wilson radioed realism and encouragement, in equal measure, to team Grouse: 'Weather still very bad but boys eager to join you.'

The 'eager' Ronneberg paid a visit to his local ironmonger's. He and his men had already procured bespoke sleeping bags, boots, rucksacks, boot covers, ski caps and skis, all made to measure by various local craftsmen. They'd even got hold of some soft rabbit-skin jockstraps, to better protect their manhood from the trials and tribulations of the Vidda. But the right kind of bolt croppers – heavy, with insulated handles in case of electrification – had eluded them.

Now Ronneberg had them in his grasp. No lesson, however small, went unremarked. A note regarding the 'special pair of bolt shears' was sent to Wilson in London, along with the receipt, reference future operations. 'I am forwarding it to you in case you wish to take a note of the address of the suppliers . . .'

Over the preceding weeks the Gunnerside team had taken lessons from the SOE's training manual, learning the exacting dance of combat and turning it into an art form. The pivotal point of that dance was the Thompson sub-machine gun. Popularized by 1930s gangsters, the SOE believed the iconic weapon suited their purposes admirably.

The 'Tommy Gun' has a short barrel and fires blunt-nosed pistol ammunition . . . by reason of the heavy calibre of the bullets and the high rate of fire it is a valuable weapon for any type of close combat . . . such as Street and House Fighting . . .

In turning on to targets, the gun does not move independently of the body. It is brought onto the target by the body and feet moving . . . naturally to balance the body . . . you must get around on your target with tremendous speed . . . Note: Jumping round is a poor substitute for neat, precise footwork . . .

Ronneberg had reached similar conclusions about the weapon's merits. 'First we decided on Sten guns, because of the weight . . .' The Sten weighed seven pounds compared to the tommy gun's near ten. 'During training in Scotland we abandoned this idea, owing to the unreliability of the weapon ... We decided to take Tommy Guns instead, as these could be used as rifles up to 200 yards with good accuracy.'

At one stage Ronneberg and his men had been put through a firing exercise by a regular army weapons instructor. They were given 200 rounds each and told to advance down a mock-up street, taking out targets as they went. They started out, firing from the hip and pivoting gracefully as they'd been taught.

The instructor halted the exercise: they should stop, bring the weapon to the shoulder, and aim and fire 'properly', he explained. Ronneberg and his men demurred. They carried on as before. By the end of the course the instructor had lapsed into silence. He'd never seen such swift, accurate shooting.

Prior to the January moon window, Tronstad drew up a final briefing on their target. Entitled: 'GUNNERSIDE ... Approach to factory area', it laid out in incredible detail the means to fight their way into the Vemork plant, to seize it, and how to stop German reinforcements from driving them out again.

All ... lines of approach can be covered by a single or double post at the ... shelter just inside the main gate. This is a concrete affair with a ½ inch iron plate door fitted with a peephole ... Part way up the hydrogen gasometer runs a platform, which is reached by a staircase and affords an excellent view of the main gate. The ¼ inch iron plating gives some cover ... One may further assume the Germans will hesitate to shoot at the hydrogen gasometer for fear of an explosion ... The best place is on the level part between the gasometers, which gives ... lines of retreat either between them or through the compressor house. The field of fire ahead is excellent over all lines of approach.

The briefing covered point after point in similar detail. It was excellent: a step-by-step guide to how to seize and hold the Vemork works. Their equipment was ready. Their intelligence was as good as it could possibly get. The raiders were more than prepared. They just needed the weather to hold good over the Vidda to hit the next moon window.

On 23 January Ronneberg and team flew out of RAF Tempsford, heading north towards Norway, hoping that they would not be returning any time soon. They were to be disappointed. The Vidda proved to be as elusive as ever. Having failed to find the landing zone, the pilot refused to let the six men jump.

In one of the greatest of ironies, it was partly as a result of a new nickname acquired by Haukelid that the pilot had been adamant that the drop be aborted. Tiring perhaps of Bonzo, someone had given Gunnerside's chief rebel the teasing name of 'The General'. Apparently, the aircrew had overheard someone referring to Haukelid in those terms, and concluded that they were flying in some high-ranking Norwegian Army officer.

Upon landing back at RAF Tempsford, Ronneberg and his men had confronted the aircrew. The pilot glanced at Haukelid: 'I thought it looked too bad to drop a general.'

Either way, the January moon window had closed, and Ronneberg felt frustrated and let down. 'We wanted to drop,' he remarked. 'But the pilot would have none of it.'

Team Grouse would now have to hold out for another terrible month on the Vidda, and how were Ronneberg and his men to kill the long days waiting, trapped in Britain? Any further time at

Tempsford or similar, and they were going to go stir crazy. What they needed was to return to conditions as close as possible to those on the Vidda, or at least as Britain in January might offer.

Wilson concurred: he needed team Gunnerside to keep in tip-top condition, both physically and mentally. Repeated let-downs had to be eating away at their morale and their convictions, and that he could ill afford.

In America the turn of the year had brought news of dark promise and fear, in equal measure. The Manhattan Project's atomic pile – their experimental nuclear reactor - had gone critical, the point at which it became self-sustaining. This marked a huge milestone in the development of the bomb. A self-sustaining pile would 'breed' plutonium – at least if it was 'moderated' by heavy water. And with American scientists convinced that their German counterparts were well ahead of them, they had to presume that the Nazi pile had gone critical years before. Which begged the question: just how much plutonium had the Germans managed to acquire?

As Samuel Goudsmit – a key Manhattan Project figure – put it:

Since the Germans had started their uranium research about two years before us, we figured they must be at least two years ahead of us. They might not have the bomb yet, but they must have had the chain-reacting piles going for several years. It followed they must have fearful quantities of artificial radioactive material available. How simple it would be for them to . . . sow death wholesale amongst us . . .

Of the Manhattan Project people Goudsmit wrote: 'Some of the men . . . were so worried they sent their families to the countryside. The military authorities were informed and fear spread . . . scientific instruments were set up . . . to detect the radioactivity, if and when the Germans attacked.'

Such worrying reports were heard in Britain. Reluctant to acknowledge these grimmest of fears, still Churchill felt obliged to push forward with Operation Peppermint. Geiger counters and teams equipped to use them were to be stationed around Britain, in case of such an attack. Peppermint was cloaked in layers of secrecy. If word leaked out there would be panic on the streets, and in January 1943 that was something that the Allies could not allow.

All this served to increase the pressure on Wilson.

Right now he needed a place of respite for the Gunnerside team. He sought a remote and private hideaway where six men might wind down and recharge batteries. He found it at Crispie, a remote and rambling house facing west across Loch Fyne – Britain's longest sea loch – the only intruders being the red squirrels that abounded there. A Mr Mackenzie lived at Crispie, a veteran of the First World War who'd been involved in intelligence work.

'The atmosphere and surroundings are, of course, particularly suitable to Norwegians, being wild, rough and rugged,' a 'Most Secret' report recounted. Of Mr Mackenzie, it concluded: 'Being unable to take a very active part in this war on account of a "gammy leg" . . . he would be well disposed to rendering any assistance he could.'

Crispie was secretive. It was private and remote. It was set within scenery that evoked the Vidda. 'This sounds like the place we want,' Wilson declared. In late January Ronneberg and party were whisked north to Crispie. There they could tramp the moors to their hearts' content, and fish and hunt game.

Having got the Gunnerside party out of the way, Wilson now had to keep Grouse onside. He radioed Haugland, begging the team to hold on for another month, and another moon window.

'Deeply regret weather conditions have made it impossible to land party. Do hope you can manage to keep going until next standby period . . . Take care. We all send you our thanks and our admiration.'

Haugland radioed back an unflinching and pragmatic response. 'On account of turning of crank handle the correspondence goes a bit more slowly . . . If possible we require for killing game Krag ammunition . . .'

Team Grouse were running short of ammo for hunting reindeer, but they were most certainly hanging on. Marooned in the Cousin's Cabin, Einar Skinnarland had even cobbled together a charging mechanism for their battery, one that was operated entirely by hand – the so-called 'crank handle'.

Yet Wilson was feeling the pressure. General Groves – the American in charge of the Manhattan Project – had been in touch with General Eisenhower, Commander-in-Chief of American forces in Europe. The Vemork SH200 facility had to be put out of action at all costs. If sabotage wouldn't do it – if the British couldn't pull something out of the bag – would a massive US Air Force bombing raid not suffice?

Wilson had to get this done, for others were itching to take over.

As January blew into a rain-lashed February, Crispie it seemed had done a fabulous job. 'My dear Mackenzie,' Wilson wrote, 'I wish to thank you for the arrangements you made in order to ensure that this party were kept fit and in good condition . . . I feel that this opportunity of getting amongst the hills will prove of greatest value to them in the work which they have to do on the other side.'

With the February moon window fast approaching, Wilson, Tronstad and Ronneberg agreed that enough was enough. They could brook no further delay, and neither by any stretch of the imagination could team Gunnerside. They would insist on the aircrew doing the forthcoming drop, no matter whether they could find the landing zone or not.

Once they were down amongst the snow and rock of the Vidda, Ronneberg felt certain they could find their way.

Chapter Twenty-Two

Torrential rain sheeted across RAF Tempsford – Gibraltar Farm. The tin-roofed hangars, disguised as ramshackle farm buildings and barns, reverberated to its incessant drumbeat. Ronneberg and his men stomped about soggily. One thing lifted their spirits: this time, there would be no turning back. They'd hijack the aircraft if they had to, but they were going to make the jump.

The six figures appeared somewhat incongruous: white snowsuits and ski caps, plus white rucksack covers. Even their tommy guns had been painstakingly painted white. Snowmen in a rain-lashed British February.

Tronstad gathered the Gunnerside team. He was speaking on behalf of Wilson, and in a sense on behalf of all freedom-loving peoples of the world. 'For the sake of those who have gone before you and fallen, I urge you to do your best and make the operation a success . . . trust that your actions will live in history for a hundred years to come . . . What you do, you do for the Allies and for Norway.'

There was a weighty silence. Ronneberg levelled his gaze at the Professor, his eyes gleaming. 'You won't get rid of us that easily.'

It was 16 February, and the moon window had just reopened. It was hard to believe, conditions at Tempsford being as they were, but the weather over the Vidda was supposedly perfect: calm, crisp and clear. Tronstad and Ronneberg fell into step: there was one matter they needed to deal with, prior to departure.

They headed for Squadron Leader Gibson's office, the pilot who would be flying team Gunnerside in. Gibson indicated a map on the wall, and talked them through the flight plan. Ronneberg heard him out, then asked for one significant modification: if the drop zone marked by Grouse could not be found, Gibson was to release their party anyway.

'We'll find our way ourselves on the ground,' Ronneberg assured him.

Gibson checked with Tronstad. The Professor concurred.

Those who executed the moon flights had immense respect for their charges. While they might risk the lonely and dangerous skies, they were at least likely to return to a warm mess and breakfast. The SOE agents were leaping into the unknown, to spend months on end in hostile territory. It was hard enough to let them jump on a verified drop zone, but near impossible to kick them out when there was no reception party to be seen.

But Squadron Leader Gibson understood. Tonight was different. Tonight, these men would drop, no matter what.

At the apron, Tronstad bade his farewells and wished them luck. Six men mounted up the waiting Halifax, squeezing between steel tubes stuffed with kit, explosives and weaponry. One of those containers was packed with rucksacks, which in turn were crammed with all the kit they would immediately need. *Good to go.* Others held skis for the six men, plus four replacement sets for the Grouse team.

Another container held fireman's axes, for hacking apart the telephone switchboard at the Vemork plant. That would be far quicker, easier and quieter than using explosives. And several were jammed with food rations: enough to last the six men '130 man days', and with extra for the Grouse party. These were listed as: 'Army biscuits; Dehydrated food blocks; Slab Chocolate; Dried fruit (raisins, apricots, figs); Lump sugar; Butter; Salt; Tea, Coffee.'

And of course, there was tobacco. There would be hell to pay if they forgot something for Poulsson to stuff into his beloved pipe.

The aircraft taxied to the end of the runway and turned, nose into the wind. The men waited in silence, the atmosphere febrile, pumped with tension and excitement. So much preparation. So much training, frustration and disappointment. But not tonight. Tonight they were on. They could feel it in the air.

The fuselage began to shake and vibrate, the noise of the four engines rising to a thunderous roar. Finally, the pilot released the brakes, and the bomber accelerated, gathering speed. At the moment of take-off the Gunnerside party felt the mass of the warplane shift from wheels to wings.

They were airborne, and clawing into the grey skies.

The Halifax climbed to 3,000 metres, weaving its way through holes in the cloud cover. It levelled out at that altitude and thundered over the North Sea. As they pushed onwards the clouds disappeared, moonlight glinting off the waves far below – the stretch of ocean that these men had crossed long months ago. Now they were returning to strike a blow for freedom such as none had ever imagined possible.

The warplane crossed Norway's western coast, distant breakers flashing silvery-white in the moonlight, staying high to avoid the first of the snow-clad peaks. Then, those in the aircraft's hold felt her descending, as Squadron Leader Gibson steered a course towards a deep valley, one that should hide them from German radar.

The thunder of the Halifax's Bristol Hercules radial engines echoed across the valley walls. The six men took turns at the aircraft's small window. Below were the snow-dusted forests, frozen lakes and rivers, and the ice-spangled slopes that they had talked about with such longing back in Britain. Beside inlets and streams upturned boats glistened. A dog chased the aircraft's moon shadow through a field. At villages and farms faces stared skywards, curious at their passing.

Just prior to midnight the Halifax thundered across the border of the plateau of the Barren Mountains. Squadron Leader Gibson gave the warning: 'Ten minutes.' Ronneberg and his men had no idea if their pilot had found the Grouse landing zone or picked up on their reception party's Eureka signal.

Regardless, they were still going to jump.

As they readied themselves, each man was acutely aware of the risks. Recently, one Linge Company team had dropped onto the Vidda only to land on a partially frozen lake. The ice had broken and all had drowned. As they gathered at the dark slash of the Halifax's open bomb bay, they tried to blank such fears from their minds.

The six crowded closer. All knew the order of the jump: first Ronneberg; then Hans 'Chicken' Storhaug; then the 'grandfather', Birger Stromsheim; next cheery Fredrik Kayser; then gentle giant Kasper Idland, and keeping the boldest to last, Knut 'Bonzo' Haukelid.

The jump light flashed green. Ronneberg, Storhaug and Stromsheim leapt, their bodies silhouetted for a brief instant against the moonlit snow. Packages containing tommy guns, ammo, skis, a sniper rifle, rations, a sledge and sleeping bags followed. The Halifax executed a graceful turn and came back for a second run.

The last of the containers were kicked out of the dark hole, and Kayser and Idland jumped.

Haukelid was just about to follow when he stopped on the very brink: his static line was snagged around the dispatcher's leg. If he jumped the man would be dragged with him, and both would plummet to an untimely death on the Vidda. Without breathing a word he shoved the dispatcher aside, sending him tumbling into the Halifax's innards, freed the line, and leapt.

Below him, Haukelid counted sixteen parachutes – seventeen with the one that blossomed in the darkness above his head. Six men. Eleven containers. All floating earthwards suspended beneath a wide skein of silk. And between them enough raw explosive power and warrior spirit to tear the Nazi nuclear programme to shreds.

Some thirty kilometres away four figures had gathered. After their epic sojourn on the Vidda, team Grouse had assumed the countenances of true mountain men: long, unkempt hair; heavy, matted beards; skin weathered and rough-scoured; eyes distant, searching far horizons for reindeer herds. They had endured here for one day short of three months, and tonight they were expecting company.

Earlier that day Haugland had received the 'crack signal' from London, the coded message – a three-digit number, 211 – that signified the drop was on. But tonight, apart from the faint drone of an aircraft engine, they had detected nothing. The Eureka was powered up, the L-lights were illuminated, but no parachutists emerged from the moonlit skies.

In the early hours they retired to their hut and their sleeping bags. Poulsson gazed wistfully at his pipe. Others rubbed their bellies. Having survived for two months pretty much on reindeer alone, they were desperate for some proper sustenance. Until they could raise London they would have no idea what had befallen the Gunnerside team, not to mention the promised tobacco and food supplies.

At dawn Ronneberg and team reached the deserted hut that they'd spotted. By luck, it lay a mile distant from their drop zone. No one could agree exactly where they had landed. Ronneberg had checked with Haukelid, for Bonzo knew the Vidda better than anyone.

'Any idea where we are?'

Haukelid had glanced at their flat, snowbound surroundings, and shrugged. 'We may as well be in China for all I know.'

A strong wind was blowing. One container had been dragged by its parachute a mile across the snow, coming to rest wedged in an ice crevasse. It contained three of their precious rucksacks and sleeping bags. They dug a trench, cached their excess kit, and marked the position with rods driven vertically into the snow.

The only way into the hut was to use axes to prise open the doorframe. By hunting shack standards it was sumptuous: there was a sleeping loft, a kitchen area and a stack of dry birchwood. They got the stove roaring and crawled into their sleeping bags. They needed rest ahead of the trek to the Cousin's Cabin, to make the rendezvous with team Grouse.

That evening, prior to setting out, Ronneberg had the men check their British Army-issue watches. For whatever reason, perhaps the intense cold, two had stopped working. There was no fixing them and so they were dumped. It was irksome. Ronneberg knew how crucial timekeeping would be when they went to hit the plant. Exact timing would be essential. He had to hope that upon linking up with Grouse, Skinnarland might procure some replacement timepieces locally.

With Ronneberg leading, the six set out eastwards, the direction in which they figured the Cousin's Cabin had to lie. They were laden down with heavy packs and dragging two sledges each piled with 110 pounds of gear. Barely had they begun the journey when the wind stiffened to their rear. Soon it was blowing fiercely, driving hard needles of snow into their exposed backs.

Visibility was worsening, but they pressed on. After all, this was what they had trained for: to take on and conquer the Vidda. At one point Ronneberg noticed twigs sticking out of the snow. He pulled at one. It didn't budge. Tree tops. How could there be trees here? They'd figured they must have landed on a frozen lake called the Bjornesfjord. But if they had, how could they be skiing over trees?

He stopped. The others gathered. 'We have to turn back—' The last of Ronneberg's words were torn away by the wind.

He signalled an about turn. Now they were cutting into the teeth of the storm. With one frozen hand Ronneberg gripped his compass, their only guide. The driving snow had obliterated their tracks. With the other, he tried to shield his face, as ice particles tore into his exposed skin. Those long days spent on the hills above Crispie paid dividends now: by a miracle of navigation Ronneberg led his team back to the mystery hut.

They stamped inside. It was still blissfully warm. Frozen limbs began to thaw. Frost had even formed on the inside of their nostrils. Ronneberg had few illusions as to how dire their situation would have become had they missed finding this place of sanctuary.

Having set a sentry rota, Ronneberg reached up and removed a map from the wall. Before it had been framed, the sheet had been well used. By torchlight he pored over its surface. Eventually he found it: one part of the map had been so well fingered it was discoloured and almost worn through. He stared at that point, trying to figure out the name: Lake Skrykken.

The hut had a locked side room. Ronneberg broke it open. Inside was the guestbook. The hut was named Jansbu, and it belonged to a Norwegian ship owner. It was indeed positioned on the shores of Lake Skrykken. That put them a good thirty kilometres from their intended drop zone, and the rendezvous point with team Grouse.

There was nothing any of them could do about it now. Outside, the wind howled and screamed its rage. None of the six had experienced a storm like it. It was as if some maddened beast was tearing at the roof in an effort to get at those sheltering inside. They didn't doubt anymore what would have happened had they pressed on. Without shelter, they would have perished, claimed by the savagery of the tempest.

They remembered the vital lesson of the Barren Mountain plateau. You didn't fight the Vidda – at least not if you wanted to survive. There was no option but to lie low and shelter from whatever it might throw at you.

In London, Wilson had received the news with relief: the Halifax crew had filed an upbeat report on Gunnerside's insertion. 'Party dropped in accordance with leader's arrangements with pilot . . . on frozen lake surface . . . Exit according to plan and in perfect order. Highly successful, with men in good spirits . . . All seven-teen 'chutes counted . . . Dummy run made 15 miles to the N.W. after dropping.'

But since then, nothing. Or at least, nothing from Gunner-side. Haugland had sent a message, but that had only confirmed that there was no sign of Ronneberg's force anywhere. Which left Wilson stumped. Laden with explosives, weaponry, food and survival kit, Ronneberg's team hadn't carried a radio. Their intention was to link up with Grouse, at which point Haugland would become the Operation Gunnerside signaller, ably assisted by Skinnarland.

Another day passed and still not a squeak from Gunnerside. Just as had happened with Grouse, Wilson began to fear that they had plunged into the Vidda, only to be swallowed without trace.

For if not, where in the name of God were they?

Ronneberg's notes on his mission revealed exactly where they were – holed up in the wind-lashed hut beside the shores of Lake Skrykken. 'The snowstorm still raging with undiminished force . . . impossible to go outdoors.' Such was the reality of life on the Vidda: the weather could switch in an instant and no forecast held good for long.

It was day two of Operation Gunnerside, and they were trapped. The storm was all-consuming. Tearing in from the west, the air was laden with moisture from a long passage across the Atlantic. It hit the cold of Norway's coastal mountains, dumping angry blasts of snow.

Inside the hut it felt as if they were marooned beneath a part-frozen waterfall. Fifty-mile-an-hour gusts thick with snow pounded into the hut's wooden frame, threatening to pluck it from its foundations and hurl it across the iced-up lake. Outside, visibility was zero. A whiteout.

'The cabin seemed about to be lifted,' Ronneberg remarked, 'even with all six of us, over half a tonne of weight, inside.'

The temperature plummeted to ten below zero. Snow piled against the hut into drifts many feet deep. On the afternoon of the nineteenth, day two of the storm, they cracked open the door to icy blasts. Their surroundings had been transformed. Bizarre snow sculptures rose before them, as if some primordial monsters had risen from the lake and become frozen in time. In between, wind-blasted pans of ice were scoured clear.

'The same weather,' Ronneberg noted. 'Storm and driving snow. We made an attempt to reach the depot to fetch more food . . . This had to be given up for danger of losing our way.'

The following day, a second attempt was made to reach the cache, but the storm had so altered the terrain that the men were lost in an alien land. On the third attempt a container was found, and a little precious food retrieved.

It was only the shelter of the hut and the warmth of the fire that was keeping them alive. Then the stove began to billow smoke. Something was wrong with the chimney. Ronneberg ventured forth to investigate. He climbed through a churning mass of blasted whiteness, levering himself onto the roof. Every which way he turned the air was dark with snowflakes, some the size of giant moths. Visibility was nil, and from such a height the impression was doubly disorientating.

In every direction everything looked exactly the same. Ronneberg felt as if he were marooned on a flying carpet in a world formed of snow. He gripped the roof with frozen hands, his anchor amidst a frightening sea of freezing, blinding white. He crawled towards the chimney. A brace had been torn away by the wind. By feel alone he tried to reattach it. As he struggled to do so, the wind buffeted him one way and then the other, in some bizarre and fearful tussle with nature.

Finally, the storm won. A blast of unbelievable power lifted Ronneberg up and blew him off the roof. He landed deep in the snow, like some rock thrown from a giant's hand. He struggled to his knees, but the storm knocked him down again. And again. His greatest fear now was being driven further from the hut. Where was it? He couldn't see his hand in front of his face, let alone make out that precious wooden sanctuary.

He turned into the cruel, taunting face of the wind and began to crawl. Feeling with his hands like a blind man, his fingers made contact with a frozen wooden upright. His heart skipped with joy: the wall. He was drawn towards the warmth and safety inside, but knew he couldn't go there. He forced himself to climb back onto the roof, where he finished fixing the chimney, only to be blown off for a second time. Eventually he groped his way back to the hut door.

On the morning of 21 February team Gunnerside awoke to an extraordinary blissful stillness. They cracked the door, to discover a landscape with a dreamlike, *Alice in Wonderland* quality. They'd never seen anything like it. Everything was snow. The windows of the hut were blinded by snow; its walls were built of snow; the entire structure was roofed over with snow; and giant, wind-sculpted slabs of white lay like stranded icebergs scattered across the frozen lake.

The calm belied Ronneberg's feelings. He was worried. They'd flown out from Britain five days earlier, and in the interim they'd managed to move barely a mile from their drop zone. Team

Grouse would have been in contact with London. They would have no way of knowing that Ronneberg and his men had found shelter, and anyone caught out in such a storm would surely have died.

It was imperative that they make contact with Grouse. Ronneberg ordered his men to gather up their supplies. Speed was of the essence, and they would need to travel relatively light. They would take only enough to ensure that they could survive the coming journey, and wreak havoc on the heavy water plant. By mid afternoon they were ready. Their packs weighed twenty-five kilos, and there was seventy kilos of kit split between the two sledges.

It was as light as they could risk.

Ronneberg was about to give the order to move out, when the most unbelievable thing happened. There on the snow-sculpted lake before the snow-sculpted hut, a figure appeared. He was alone, moving on skis and dragging a sledge behind him. Ronneberg could not have been more surprised had one of the primeval ice forms come to life before his eyes.

It was as if that lone figure had been vomited out of the storm.

Chapter Twenty-Three

It hadn't at first seemed very likely, but the lone stranger turned out to be an excellent guide. He'd approached the Lake Skrykken hut, apparently convinced that he was the only human being moving on the Vidda. Instead, he'd come face to face with six unshaven men in uniform, brandishing weapons. Unsurprisingly, he'd all but had a heart attack on the spot.

Ronneberg had proceeded to question him relentlessly. His ID card had revealed him to be one Kristian Kristiansen, forty-eight, from Uvdal, a town to the east of the plateau. He was a reindeer hunter, he explained. He carried a rifle, plus a list of customers for the animals he intended to cull. He had one reindeer carcass on his sledge already. Then Ronneberg had hit him with the million-dollar question: was he a member of the Nasjonal Samling, the Norwegian Nazi Party?

While he wasn't exactly a paid-up member, that was the party he supported, Kristiansen averred. Ronneberg suspected the man – frightened and in shock – was lying, perhaps because he had mistaken them for German soldiers or members of the Hird, the quisling Nazi guard. Who else would be out on the storm-blasted Vidda heavily armed and in uniform?

But no matter what Ronneberg said, the man didn't seem to want to admit to any loyalty to the king, or any desire to overthrow the German invaders. Ronneberg, it seemed, was left with two stark choices: either kill him, or take him with them as a captive. Finally, he hit upon a ruse. If they spoke to his neighbours, in Uvdal, would they confirm that Kristiansen was a good and loyal Nazi?

Kristiansen prevaricated. It seemed that there was no one in Uvdal who would definitely vouch for him. It was clear that he was lying about his Nazi sympathies in an effort to save his own skin. Finally, they managed to convince the man that they were fellow Norwegians, and about as anti-Nazi as it was possible to get.

At that Kristiansen broke into a broad grin: 'God, but it's great to see you fellows! Here on the Vidda, of all places!'

That evening they set out, with Kristiansen leading. More than anyone he knew the region like the back of his hand, no matter how the storm had warped its horizons. He quickly proved to be a skier without equal. 'He could criss-cross his way up a hill, using every contour to his advantage,' Ronneberg remarked, describing the 'smooth, seemingly unthinking ability of that simple man in the mountains.'

There wasn't much in that snowbound wilderness that Kristiansen's eye missed. By daybreak, they were approaching the long valley leading to the Cousin's Cabin. They topped a rise, their guide leading, and a graceful sweep of snow-swept terrain opened before them. Almost immediately Kristiansen raised one hand in warning. Coming up the valley were two men on skis.

As one, the seven dropped behind the cover of the ridge. Ronneberg pulled out his binoculars. Together with Haukelid, he studied the approaching figures. Bonzo had trained with the Grouse team, for he was originally supposed to deploy with them, but he'd accidentally shot himself in the foot during training. He should recognize the two mystery figures, it they were indeed Grouse men.

Neither seemed familiar. But with their massive beards and ski caps pulled so low, that didn't mean a great deal. With the rest covering him – and Kristiansen hiding behind some rocks, in case there was any gunfire – Haukelid set out to investigate. He skirted around the lip of the valley, keeping out of their line of sight, and was able to edge up behind the two mystery figures.

When they reached the high ground they paused. Leaning on their ski poles one pulled out a telescope, and surveyed the land beyond. Clearly, the two men were looking for something or someone. They were the right height for Claus Helberg and Arne Kjelstrup, Haukelid told himself, but neither had been anything like this woefully thin.

His hand on his hidden pistol he coughed deliberately, loud in the stillness. The two figures swung around, hands on their own weapons. It was Helberg and Kjelstrup all right, but each was barely recognizable: skeletally thin, their clothes hanging in rags, red eyes staring out of wild, unkempt beards.

From their place of hiding, Ronneberg and his men heard the wild whoops of joy. They gathered – nine, including Kristiansen – and broke out some of the goodies they'd brought from England to celebrate: raisins and figs, washed down with melted snow, mixed in a tin mug with powdered milk and chocolate. Delicious. And, afterwards, some cigarettes.

The Cousin's Cabin was but a few miles away. Their dilemma now was what to do with Kristiansen, their unexpected companion. Ronneberg sent him away with some British rations, including a slab of chocolate – an unheard-of luxury in those straitened times – and a dire warnings ringing in his ears. 'He could resume his hunting if he wished, and stay as long as he wanted in the mountains, but when he did return he was to say nothing about what had happened – absolutely nothing to anyone.'

They had his black market customer list, and it was strictly forbidden by the Germans to carry a weapon. If he breathed a word of what he had seen on the Vidda, that would be the end of him.

As Kristiansen skied away, they wondered if they had done the right thing. Wilson had warned them repeatedly not to jeopardize the mission in any way. If Kristiansen reached Uvdal and hit a bar and got drunk, he might talk. Word would rapidly reach the ears of the Gestapo. Should they have killed him, to ensure his silence? Or had their instincts been the right ones?

Only time would tell.

They reached the Cousin's Cabin at four in the afternoon on 22 February. Ronneberg and his men had covered forty-five kilometres in eighteen hours and under crushing loads. Their mission was a week old, and it was time to celebrate. The reunion in the hut proved high-spirited and raucous, though it did take a while for the newcomers to get accustomed to the surroundings.

The Cousin's Cabin was like charnel house. It was surrounded by bloodstained snow, discarded reindeer antlers and hoofs. Inside, the cabin was dressed floor to ceiling in reindeer skins. On the stove stood a soot-blackened cooking pot, purring wisps of steam. Seemingly all of the reindeer's organs – eyes, brains, fat, stomach contents – had been stirred into a witch's brew, one that the men of team Grouse eyed with gusto.

It revealed more about the last few months than words ever could.

Much of the food the Gunnerside team carried consisted of 'K-rations', named after their inventor, Norwegian professor Leiv Kreyberg. Working out of Cambridge University, Kreyberg had developed a means to compress dehydrated food into solid blocks to make compact, high-energy combat food.

Ronneberg had paid a visit to Kreyberg, explaining the kind of distance they would have to travel to reach the Swedish border and safety, and that every ounce of weight would count. K-rations would help reduce their loads. They were made ready by adding water, and all that was required to eat them was a tin mug and a large spoon, which cut the weight still further.

But right now was not the time for K-rations. Now, it was time to dig out their tin mugs and spoons and tuck into some serious reindeer gruel. In Norwegian culture, providing hospitality to guests is paramount. Poulsson and his men needed to feel as if they had welcomed the newcomers properly, and that meant serving up a meal. But all they had to offer was reindeer – every last bit of the animal.

Once the newcomers had made a show of feasting, they shared the precious goodies from Britain, and laughed like old friends. Finally Haukelid – as forthright as ever – posed the question uppermost in the newcomers' minds: had the Grouse boys experienced any particular trouble over the long months marooned on the Vidda?

'Nothing,' Kjelstrup replied, simply. 'Nothing.'

All understood then to drop the subject.

That first evening, no one so much as mentioned the forthcoming mission. It was what had brought them all to this unique time and place, but for now they wanted to celebrate the simple fact of having found each other – which meant that the past weeks of struggle and endurance beyond measure had been worthwhile.

There was one – tangential – reference to Gunnerside, but it was made more by accident than design. Haukelid had brought a special message of encouragement for team Grouse, penned by a very senior Allied commander. He read it aloud to the men, then balled up the note, ready to throw it into the stove.

Haugland – Grouse's radio operator – reached out a hand to stop him. 'Is that edible?'

It was a fair question. Sensitive SOE documents were generally printed on rice paper, so the bearer could eat them if at risk of capture.

Haukelid eyed the ball of paper. 'Quite digestible, I would imagine.'

'Well, we don't throw away food here.'

Haugland took the paper and began to chew. It may have been a little tough and unpalatable, but it was nothing compared to reindeer lichen.

Having munched down the missive from on high, Haugland composed a message of his own, to be sent to London in the early hours, the time of his next sked: 'The party arrived yesterday evening. Everything in order. The spirits are excellent. On the air again after the operation. Heartiest greeting from all.'

That night the men bedded down like sardines, curled up nose-to-toe on the pungent reindeer skins that lined the hut floor. No one seemed to mind the cramped conditions. They were together. Operation Gunnerside was fully manned. *Not long now.*

At dawn they brewed coffee and got down to business. It was time to decide their plan of attack, and to do that they first had to contemplate the challenge that lay before them: Vemork. From memory, Ronneberg sketched out the location of the plant and the fearsome natural defences that made it so impregnable. He had never visited the place, but during rehearsals in Britain he had got to know it more intimately than many who had.

The plant stood like some ancient fortress, perched on a shelf of rock blasted out of the precipitous surroundings. The dark, sunless chasm in which it lay – the Vestfjord Valley – had been formed millennia ago, when an earthquake had torn the Vidda apart. The Måna River had swirled into the knife-cut ravine, the high walls of which remained untouched by the surging waters, and little worn by their passing.

So sheer was the valley that a stone dropped from the rock-hewn platform of the Vemork plant would fall uninterrupted two hundred metres to the icy waters of the Måna River below. Above, the mountains rose to over 1,000 metres, the Vemork works perched halfway up their dizzying flanks.

Only three routes led into the plant: the first, across the suspension bridge from the road on the valley's far side; the second, descending the water pipelines, which ran to the rear of the plant; the third, via a single-track railway that threaded along a narrow ledge hewn out of the mountainside, linking the plant to Rjukan town.

Those obvious routes of ingress were heavily defended: mines, guards, barbed wire, electrified fences and booby traps abounded. If an ancient Viking king had sought a place to build an impregnable fortress, he could not have chosen better than the shelf of rock that housed the Vemork SH200 plant.

Ronneberg began to populate his sketch with details of the defences, shading wide stretches of terrain that were to be avoided at all costs – the minefields. His pencil flashed across the paper, tracing the concentric rings of fencing that surrounded the plant – its second line of defence – plus the single heavy line of the railway, cross-hatched to indicate its purpose.

As he scribbled, he gave a running commentary. 'The railway track is used only occasionally, for bringing equipment and machinery to and from the plant. It extends right into the plant's yard, after passing through an iron-barred gate in the fence . . .'

He drew a small square adjacent to the giant one that marked the position of the SH200 plant, their key target. 'There is a barracks here, housing fifteen German soldiers. And over here, twenty yards from the barracks, are the storage tanks that will give us cover if we are detected.'

As he sketched and talked, Ronneberg was relying in part on Tronstad's detailed briefing, 'GUNNERSIDE . . . Approach to factory area', in which every possible firing position and patch of cover had been delineated. Jomar Brun's sage advice was also prominent in his thoughts. He drew a tiny square in the southern wall of the SH200 plant, marking it 'hatch'. That, he explained, was the entrance to the cable duct leading into the bowels of the building.

He eyed his men. 'I'm told that few people even at Vemork know about the cable duct. There is just enough space for one man at a time to crawl through, but we'll use it if we have to.'

Ronneberg paused. There was no easy way to put this. They had all the weaponry and explosives necessary to do the job; no team could be better trained or prepared. The challenge would be getting into the plant to place their charges, and then getting out again. The previous mission, Operation Freshman, had been predicated on sheer force of firepower. In a full-frontal assault they would rush the bridge, fight their way in and blow the place to kingdom come.

As a result of the tragic failure of that mission, the defences at Vemork had been massively strengthened. Gunnerside would need to find a different way: it would require subterfuge, concealment and guile to get them within striking distance. Ronneberg made it clear that nothing was off limits: if any man could think of anything, he was to speak his mind.

Claus Helberg – Poulsson's childhood classmate – had a suggestion. He was the born trouble-seeker and adventurer of the party – the one whose curiosity got him into scrapes, and whose innocent-faced charm got him out again. When Helberg spoke, others tended to listen, if only because he was likely to come up with a different slant on things.

It was obvious that the bridge was a non-starter, he explained. 'The other option is to cross the gorge . . . climb the cliff to the railway tracks on the far side, and follow the tracks into the plant unseen.' The railway was unlikely to be mined or heavily guarded, 'since the Germans don't expect anyone to attempt a crossing of the gorge.'

In numerous reports and briefings, every man in that hut had read about how 'impossible' it was to scale the sheer walls of the gorge. Indeed, such a route of attack had been considered for Operation Freshman, and discounted just as quickly. Defenders and attackers alike had concluded that that route of approach was unfeasible, which was pretty much why Helberg was proposing it now.

How many times had Ronneberg and his men been told that the gorge was unscalable? But if it was even remotely possible, it made sense to do the utterly unexpected.

Ronneberg fired a series of questions at Helberg. Was the railway line guarded? How regularly was it used? Was the point where the tracks met the fence breachable?

To each question Helberg gave pretty much the same answer. Their latest information was that none of those factors should cause them any great trouble. But the Germans were changing their routines and defences daily. Security was being forever tightened.

Ronneberg decided that they would need the most up-to-date information possible, if they were to even contemplate Helberg's suggestion. Helberg himself offered to get it. He had a contact in Rjukan who worked at the plant: he should be able to tell him everything. Helberg didn't volunteer the name of that person, and no one thought to ask: you never divulged the identity of a source unless you had to.

A plan of sorts was made. Not for the first time since parachuting into the Vidda, Helberg would shave, dress in the smartest civilian clothes anyone still possessed and ski into the valley of shadows. When heading into civilization it was crucial to shed the battered look of the Barren Mountain fugitive. 'A bearded face on a man in uniform or civilian clothes will give rise to suspicion at once,' the Grouse team had noted. 'A neat and tidy appearance was essential.'

The shaven and spruced-up Helberg would head for Rjukan and seek out the definitive intelligence they sought. Once he was done, he'd link up with the others at a lonely hut, set to the western end of the gorge, where the valley met the high ground of the Vidda. That hut, called Fjosbudalen and known to them all, was bound to be deserted at this time of year.

All being well, they would RV there in three days' time.

In London, Wilson felt a burning jolt of excitement upon receipt of Haugland's message. He penned a note to his boss, McVean Gubbins, noting that the Gunnerside team had surfaced very much alive and well. Gunnerside had made their 'rendezvous with the reception committee,' he wrote, '. . . and were said to be in excellent spirits.'

It had been a torturous week's wait, but now the mastermind of Operation Gunnerside had been rewarded with the news that he'd been desperate to hear. Wilson sensed that they were close now. He sent a detailed set of instructions to the home station about any further messages from the field: 'All information to be reported . . . with the least possible delay.'

The next message would declare either the much longed-for success of Operation Gunnerside, or another dismal failure. Pray God that it would be the former, for rarely had a mission run this close to the wire.

In recent days Nazi propaganda minister Goebbels had delivered his *Totaler Krieg* – total-war – speech in Berlin, to an audience of thousands. 'I ask you: do you want total war?' he demanded. 'Do you want a war more total and radical than anything we can even imagine today?' His audience roared out their support for such measures.

Goebbels shook his fists and ended with this: 'Now, people, rise up and let the storm break loose!' The thrust of his speech was reported widely. To those Allied leaders in the know the message couldn't be clearer; if, as many suspected, the Reich had nuclear weapons, or even crude radiological bombs, they were ready to use them.

There had to be a counter-strike, and all hopes rested on the eleven men now gathered on the Vidda.

Chapter Twenty-Four

Helberg inched his way down the treacherous slope, taking the very greatest care possible. In the back of his mind was one of the key lessons learned from Operation Musketoon. The team that had so successfully sabotaged the Glomfjord power station was criticized for not determining exactly how they would make their getaway.

'The party apparently did not have time to recce the immediate . . . escape route . . . if time is short at least one of the party's job must be to recce this route while the remainder are carrying out the attack.'

Taking the lesson to heart, Helberg was doing just that right now. His mission in Rjukan was already done and dusted. He'd met with his contact, Rolf Sørlie, a construction engineer at the Vemork plant, and secretly a very active member of the resistance. He'd secured answers to the questions that Ronneberg had raised, not that some of Sørlie's responses hadn't proved worrisome.

Now to check out their means of escape, and that meant finding his way into the depths of the shadowed gorge. To Helberg, their best route to attack the plant was also going to be their best route of escape. Admittedly, they would have to scale the 'impossible' cliffs twice – but better that than a full-on battle to cross the bridge.

By the time he was done with his recce, Helberg had quartered the banks of the Måna River, which over the winter months had been transformed into a broad ribbon of ice. He'd tested its frozen surface. It was treacherous, but with care it should hold a man's weight. He'd studied the sheer rock on the far side – by far the most daunting of the two precipitous slopes they had to cross.

Looking carefully, he'd mapped out the route that they would have to climb. He'd made a mental note of the key points, and then retraced his steps. Once he was done he'd thrown on his skis and headed for the RV with his brothers-in-arms.

Helberg got there first. He broke into the deserted cabin, and did what he always did on such occasions: he searched the place for food. After forty-eight hours on the go, and constantly dodging Gestapo patrols, Helberg felt utterly spent. He had a massive sugar craving.

As he rummaged through the cupboards, he reflected upon his clandestine visit to his hometown. The most disquieting thing had been seeing the house where he grew up, the schoolroom that he had shared with Poulsson and others, the homes of family and friends, yet not being able to so much as slip a note through anyone's door. He'd had to skulk about like a fugitive in his own home. What a vile thing this war was; what an evil cradling.

In one cupboard Helberg found a bottle of Upper Ten, a Norwegian brand of whisky. He decided he'd leave it untouched, so they could enjoy a celebratory tipple at mission's end. *That's if it all ended well.* Then his eyes alighted upon a tin of syrup. Perfect. Great for energy. Comfort food to truly lift the spirits.

He grabbed a spoon and levered off the lid. What a disappointment: the gooey surface was crusted with dead ants. He stared at it for a long minute. He was sorely tempted to throw caution to the wind and dig in, but he'd had enough of rotten, sickly food on the Vidda. He replaced the lid and set the tin back on its shelf.

He'd wait for the others and their thick slabs of chocolate.

At six o'clock that evening a single file of skiers pulled into the dark clearing outside the Fjosbudalen hut. There were eight in total, a reluctant Haugland having been left with Einar Skinnarland to form the signals party secreted on the Vidda. Whether the mission was successful or not, it was vital that someone got news through to London.

For a change, a gale was blowing on the high Vidda. Regardless, Poulsson had led the party some sixty kilometres through driving snow and poor visibility, unerringly finding his way. Having greeted Helberg, and ensured that the hut was absolutely blacked out – windows shuttered and any light-emitting cracks stuffed with rags – Ronneberg set a watch rota. Extra care would need to be taken to ensure that their presence wasn't detected at the eleventh hour. Vigilance was everything.

The cabin huddled at the base of a giant peak. It felt as if they were still in the midst of the barren wilderness, but in truth they were just seven kilometres from their target. To the north lay the shadowed valley, which of course was both inhabited and patrolled by the enemy.

The hut offered a view right into Rjukan itself, but not of Vemork, which was hidden deep in the chasm. From the doorway the lights of the town could be seen twinkling away. So many of the party had friends and family living there. It was another reason to strike by stealth and surprise: the fewer Germans killed, the less likelihood of any local reprisals.

They were all acutely aware of the Telavag massacre, and *Reichs-*

kommissar Terboven's visits here made it clear how much he had invested personally in Vemork. Ten months ago he had wiped Telavag off the face of the earth because two SOE agents had killed a senior Gestapo officer. What might Terboven be capable of when the SH200 plant was blasted into ruin?

Such concerns made their mission a delicate – some might claim impossible – balancing act: they were to hit hard at what was very likely the most sensitive target in the entire Reich, while at the same time minimizing enemy casualties. Ronneberg hoped that Helberg's intelligence-gathering mission might help them determine how exactly they could do that.

After a snatched meal, Helberg cleared the table. He produced, as if by magic, a large-scale map. This, he declared proudly, had been purchased from a Rjukan stationer's, and pretty much under the nose of a German officer. In the nearby house of his 'friend', Helberg had even got it marked up with all the key points. This was vintage Helberg: cheeky beyond measure, risky in the extreme, and cocking a snook at the enemy.

The map was a mass of light blue swirls and whorls, delineating the contours of the hills and troughs of the Vidda. But it was dominated by one feature: a dark slash cut the map in two, marking the course of the Måna River as it thundered onwards to the sea. Using the width of his thumb as a measuring stick, Helberg indicated the key features.

'The suspension bridge: seventy-five feet long and it spans the ravine gouged out by the river. Vertical sides to the riverbed, as you all know. That's where they expect the attack to come.' Helberg glanced up, his eyed crinkled with laughter lines. 'And that would be like committing suicide.'

Eight sets of eyes returned a questioning look. 'Why?'

'There are always two sentries patrolling end to end of the bridge. They could trigger off the searchlights and alert the machine-gunners on the factory roof before we were halfway across. That would bring out patrols and trigger more flood-lights to light the Rjukan road, that's if there were any of us left to retreat.'

Helberg paused. No one said a word. Something of a showman, Helberg had them gripped.

'Even if a battalion attempted to storm that bridge, a massacre would be the result.' For a moment he searched the map in silence. Then: 'I think I can put my finger on the weak spot – here!'

He stabbed at a certain point lying downstream of the bridge, maybe halfway to Rjukan town. 'As a boy I crossed the Måna many times at this season, just below that bend in the river.' He eyed Poulsson quizzically. 'Remember, Jens?'

Poulsson frowned. 'Only too well. I had to fish you out a couple of times.'

'We dump our rucksacks there,' Helberg explained. 'We go over the precipice, cross the river, and up the other side. Nobody in their right mind would think it possible. But I've checked and it just is. It will be difficult. Much more difficult. But it can be done.'

Poulsson and Helberg – former Rjukan classmates – shared a close bond, but still the Grouse leader wasn't convinced. Scaling the gorge would be daunting enough in summer, in daylight and moving under light loads. But in the depths of an ice-bound winter, laden down with packs stuffed full of explosives and weaponry, and in darkness: was it even possible?

'It allows them so much longer to spot us,' someone objected, giving voice to everyone's concerns. 'Miles and miles more.'

'We have to get in there *undetected*,' Ronneberg growled. 'It doesn't matter a damn how far around the houses we have to go.'

Ronneberg, Poulsson, Haukelid and the others watched as Helberg's finger traced their route 'around the houses'. It dropped from the cabin through a gap in the fir woodland, turned away from their target, kinked around the small hamlet of Vaer – a cluster of wooden-walled houses set at the near end of the suspension bridge – and stopped at Helberg's chosen spot, the point where he'd recced the route across the chasm.

From the valley floor Helberg had spotted a faint line of stunted trees, hanging doggedly to the far wall of rock. If trees could climb that dark and ice-bound slab, so could their party of nine, Helberg reasoned. Once they reached the top they'd follow the railway line in, 'and hit the plant via the back door'.

Eight sets of eyes stared at the map, trying to grasp what Helberg was proposing.

'What about the escape?' someone asked. 'Do we leave via the suspension bridge still?'

Helberg shook his head. 'Easiest way to have the guard force on our heels.'

They would depart by the same route as they had come, Helberg explained, the climb across the gorge. It would be exhausting and fraught with natural hazards, but it would be utterly unexpected.

Poulsson shook his head, worriedly. 'Will we really be able to climb the gorge twice in the one night?'

Ronneberg looked equally unconvinced. 'We'll be trapped in the valley if we try to escape the same way. The explosion will almost certainly alert the guards, and they in turn will alert the troops in Rjukan. We'll be trapped in the valley if German troops get to the top before we do.'

'What about when we're back where we started?' someone else queried. 'At the rucksacks? Where do we go from there?'

During his helter-skelter recce mission, Helberg had checked out one other wildcard option. Because Rjukan was sunk in dark shadow for much of the year, Norsk Hydro had built the Krossobanen cable car as a present to the townsfolk, to carry them from the darkness to the light. It ran up one side of the valley, topping out at 800 metre and offering a splendid view of the sunlit mountains.

These days the Germans controlled the cable car, of course, but Helberg wasn't about to propose that they use it themselves. Running beneath the cables was a zigzagging maintenance track, known as the Ryes Road. It was little used other than by a few locals. The Ryes Road would carry them right to the lip of the Vidda, leaving few traces for anyone to follow.

'Means a hell of a hard climb,' someone objected. 'About 500 metres from the Rjukan road to the peak.'

Helberg agreed that it did. It wasn't the easy option. But the easy option would be obvious to the enemy, and draw pursuers. By contrast, no one would even think to search the Ryes Road. In any case, what was the alternative?

'To go straight up the side of the mountain through a metre of wet snow will be almost impossible,' Helberg pointed out, 'even if we did use the suspension bridge as an escape route. We'd become separated long before we reached the top.'

A momentary silence settled over the scene, each man lost in his thoughts. Whichever route they decided upon, they knew how slim their chances were. With searchlights sweeping the valley and troops fanning out from the Vemork plant and from Rjukan, they would be caught in a giant pincer.

Ronneberg declared himself for fighting their way across the suspension bridge. It offered the quickest and most immediate means of escape. But as the mission commander he didn't want to force it. Every man deserved to have his say; to own the plan and believe in it wholeheartedly.

Ronneberg asked each man in turn for his opinion. Kasper Idland offered the most surprising response of all.

'I don't much care which escape route we take,' Idland remarked, quietly. 'I don't put much faith in the idea of escape. I don't expect to reach Sweden anyway.'

Idland – the gentle giant who'd once been bullied at school – was the least proficient skier in the group. For a while now he'd been worried about his ability to stick with the others. But mostly he was convinced that theirs was a suicide mission. They might get in and wreck the target, but they stood little chance of escape. Secretly, others shared his fears, but it did little good to voice them now.

'Where there's life there's hope,' Helberg told him, in an effort to cheer his spirits.

The votes were cast. Idland and one other abstained. Ronneberg voted for the bridge. The remainder were for retreating via the gorge, and for scaling the Ryes Road thereafter.

'It's decided: we cross the gorge,' Ronneberg confirmed. 'Now, let's get on with it.'

They would split the force into two groups, Ronneberg explained. One, a demolitions party of four, led by himself, would concentrate on blowing the SH200 apparatus. The other, a five-man cover party, including Poulsson, Helberg and Haukelid, would provide covering fire – if and when the enemy attacked.

'If all doors into the building are locked, and the cable duct blocked, we'll use explosives to blow one of the steel doors,' Ronneberg declared, 'in which case the cover party must be ready for anything. Once inside, the demolitions party should complete the operation in about seven minutes.' That was how long it had taken during their rehearsals at Station XVII.

'The only sure signal the cover party will have that the job's been done will be the explosion itself. If the demolition party is killed before the plant is reached, the cover party has to take over placing the explosives. Everyone must act on his own initiative. Someone must reach the objective and do the job.'

Ronneberg paused for an instant, eyeing his men. 'To repeat what was said in Britain: Hitler has ordered every saboteur or commando, whether in uniform or not, to be shot. So, if any of you is wounded or about to be taken captive, you must end your own life.'

During the months spent fighting for survival on the Vidda, none in the Grouse team had given much consideration to the suicide pills they carried; the same was true of the Gunnerside force during their long weeks of training. Now, all minds turned to the cyanide capsules stuffed in their breast pockets. It was all very well agreeing to death by one's own hand, but what if you were too badly injured to get to the capsule in time?

The final briefing done, Ronneberg took Idland to one side. He explained what was self-evident. Over the past weeks Idland had stuck with the others through some of the toughest skiing conditions imaginable. He needed to put all thoughts of inadequacy to one side. No one was going to be left behind. They would stand or fall as brothers.

Zero hour was set for eight o'clock the following evening. Between now and then they could look forward to a sleep in cramped conditions, interspersed with sentry watches, plus final mission preparations. Ronneberg was determined that each man should get as much rest as possible and eat well. They would need every advantage if they were to endure the epic that was coming.

The following morning Helberg took a seat outside the hut, squatting on a conveniently placed log. Grenades and weaponry had been flown out packed in their original factory grease; all needed to be thoroughly cleaned. Sheltered in a heavily wooded valley, there was little chance of their being detected, and with sentries set he should have ample warning if anyone did approach.

As he cleaned and oiled his tommy gun, the sun beat down. It felt unseasonably balmy, and for a few moments Helberg basked in the unexpected warmth. His mind drifted to thoughts of the Ryes Road – the escape route to which all were now committed, thanks to him. The risks of using it were legion. All it would take was for the Germans to realize what they were doing and put a force of infantry into one of the cable cars: it would beat them to the top and they would be trapped.

Helberg moved on to cleaning his Colt .45. It was flecked with rust, the result of three months on the Vidda. He sensed that the wind was stiffening. To a large extent everything now depended on the weather. When Helberg had last checked, the Måna River had been treacherous but fordable. Yet all it would take was a sharp rise in temperature and the ice bridge would disintegrate.

He sensed that the breeze on his face was a warming wind. Heaven forbid that it presaged a *foehn*. The *foehn*, or 'snow-eater', was a dry, downslope wind, caused by air dropping its moisture over high ground and warming rapidly thereafter. It could raise air temperatures by as much as 14 degrees Celsius in a matter of minutes. The name 'snow-eater' referred not so much to the heat of the wind as to its dryness: it sucked up moisture like a giant hairdryer.

If a *foehn* hit the shadowed valley they could be trapped, and the Germans would hunt them down at will.

Chapter Twenty-Five

Helberg grasped the stunted, springy fir tree and used it as an anchor from which to carefully lower himself downslope. Little moonlight filtered through the dense vegetation and it was as dark as the grave here. He was leading, and so far all was well. The round-the-houses approach route that he'd mapped out the previous evening seemed to be working just as he'd intended.

There had been only the one major scare. As they'd descended from the hut, a pair of buses packed with night-shift workers had loomed out of the darkness, taking the road from Rjukan to the bridge leading into Vemork. The saboteurs had narrowly escaped plunging onto the roofs of the vehicles, only saving themselves by grasping onto the trees.

But now would come the real test: the drop into the gorge – something that Ronneberg described as being 'like a gigantic trap'.

A few dozen metres higher up the slope, Helberg and the rest of the assault party had slipped out of their skis and dumped all extraneous gear in a cache. Each man was stripped down to the bare minimum now: his main weapon, pistol, grenades, explosives, plus their chloroform knock-out pads (for subduing any Norwegian guards), and a little water and food.

As his boots bit into the snow, Helberg felt the breeze cutting through the woodland. Ever since that morning when he had cleaned his weapons, it had been stiffening. He figured it had strengthened a good dozen knots or more. The snow felt damp and claggy underfoot, the air unseasonably muggy. It made for hard going.

Helberg could feel the sweat trickling down his back and soaking into his thick woollen British Army fatigues. It wasn't just the physical exertion that was causing him to perspire: the wind carried with it a real sense of heat. It picked snow off the ground where he'd disturbed it, and whisked it away, greedily. Above him, it dislodged heavier clumps, which fell with a hollow, ghostly whoomp.

The lower he descended, the stronger the wind gusted: hotly, moodily, unpredictably. There was no denying it: it had all the characteristics of a *foehn*. If it blew hard enough and hot enough, snowmelt from above would surge into the gorge, first inundating and then breaking apart the river ice, with catastrophic consequences.

But they were committed now. No turning back. Votes had been taken. It was this way, or no way.

A fresh gust pummelled into Helberg with the power to blast him off his feet. It carried with it something else: something eerie yet strangely intoxicating, all at the same time. Helberg detected a deep, hollow throbbing. It seemed to reverberate through the dark air all around him and the cold rock at his feet, as if coming from all directions.

He knew instinctively what it was. He recognized it from his childhood. It was the heartbeat of the hydroelectric plant; the pulse beat of the turbines. Unmistakably Vemork.

Then, as clouds blew clear of the moon, far below them their target suddenly appeared, lying on the far side of the chasm and bathed in a silvery, gunmetal-blue light.

'There it was, less than 1,000 yards away,' Ronneberg recalled, 'this great concrete factory, looking like a fortress . . .'

As if by an unspoken command, all came to a halt. The nine saboteurs stared, transfixed.

Seven storeys high and constructed of 800 tonnes of steel and 17,000 barrels of cement, the electrolysis building was built from massive blocks of rock hewn out of the mountainside. Above rose the pipelines, each five and half feet across, and together channelling 1,750 cubic feet of water per second to the plant below. The friction of the water's passage was so great it heated up the steel pipes, melting the snow to either side; their bare forms glistened in the moonlight, like giant serpents.

It was the rushing of the water, and the resulting churning of the plant's machinery, that they could hear. To the local boys, who had watched in childish wonderment as the plant had risen from the mountainside, block by block, it seemed almost unreal that they were back, and this time intent on wreaking havoc in the bowels of that massive structure. To the outsiders, it just seemed impossible that they were so close, and poised to strike such a blow in freedom's name.

It was Ronneberg who brought the men's minds back to the moment at hand. 'Birger, you have your set of charges?' he whispered.

Stromsheim – thirty-one years old, the grandfather of the group – nodded. He and Ronneberg were each carrying a full set of Nobel 808 explosives, put together by the SOE's demolitions experts back in Britain, and shaped to fit the giant electrolysis cells. If one of them was killed going in, the other would still be able to plant his charges and destroy the target.

Ronneberg turned to Helberg, his eyes glinting with excitement. 'All right, let's go. Lead the way.'

Helberg turned to the narrow groove in the rock-face – the one by which he had descended not so many hours before – and dropped out of view. One by one the others plunged after. The darkness swallowed them, the raiders vanishing into the abyss.

At times Helberg sank up to his waist in a deep drift, where snow had piled thick on a perilous ledge, and he had to fight his way out again. Moments later he found himself struggling to remain upright, where the precipitous rock had been transformed into a sheet of treacherous ice. He was forced to make a wild grab at the juniper bushes, or the low-lying branches of spruce and birch, to save himself from a fatal plunge.

Without the tree cover, this descent would be impossible.

Finally, his boots touched solid, level ground. Or rather, sticky, squelchy ground. He was down in the bowels of the gorge; above him the starred heavens consisted of a narrow slash of sky squeezed between sheer walls. Here, where the hot breath of the *foehn* was at its fiercest, the effects of the thaw were far more noticeable.

Water trickled down the rock face in runnels. The air was full of the sound of the thaw and of dripping. The few remaining patches of snow were sodden and spongy underfoot. The meltwater drained into the river, turning its partially frozen surface into a wet and treacherous ice rink. As Helberg turned towards it, searching for the solid ice bridge he'd discovered earlier, he knew how nightmarish this crossing could prove.

Signalling the others to follow – but to move one by one, to limit their weight on the ice – Helberg stepped out onto the frozen surface. Strangely, he almost relished the risk. As he placed one foot in front of the other, feeling for the strongest, thickest ice, it felt like a game of Russian roulette. One false move and he would he sucked into the freezing water below.

At the river's edge the ice had been sculpted into bizarre forms – ripples frozen in time. The clear, translucent ice had entrapped vegetation – grasses, ferns – freezing them fresh in its glassy embrace. Further out the ice turned a greyish-blue as it thickened and toughened, but here and there cracks were visible.

The question was, which force of nature, the freeze or the thaw, would triumph?

The ice bridge creaked and pinged, voicing its discontent at Helberg's crossing. But finally he was over. As those behind began their odd, fearful dance across the river's frozen surface, Helberg surveyed the way ahead. This side of the chasm was far steeper. The slope they had descended was only vertical in places. Between were rock shelves, and steep slopes garlanded with trees.

Here, it was all sheer. As others joined him to stare in awe at the rock face, Helberg noted whichever dark fissures and chiselled corners might offer a little purchase. Here and there an odd spruce or pine grew, stubborn as the rock to which it clung. They would have to feel for and test every hand- and foothold, each a step into the unknown.

Helberg glanced at the riverbank. It was littered with sharp boulders, caused by the repeated freezing and thawing of the cliffs above. If a man lost his footing and fell, he would come to grief in one of two ways: either he would smash into the river ice, or impale himself on one of those knife-cut rocks.

To left and right shadowy figures reached up and tested handholds. The saboteurs placed their feet into grooves in the sheer rock, rehearsing the first moves they would make. In a strange way, making the descent in darkness had served to sharpen their sense of feel and touch, plus it had yielded an instinctive sense of what rock might give good purchase, and what vegetation might hold fast under a man's weight.

When all nine were gathered, Ronneberg gave the order to move. As one, the figures began the climb towards the railway tracks 200 metres above them. There was no following the leader now. While Helberg had rehearsed the descent, he hadn't tested the climb. It was every man for himself.

Throwing his tommy gun onto his back on its sling, Helberg reached up and grasped the slippery rock face. The *foehn* sang a siren song as it whipped along the slab-sided gorge, its warmth turning icicles into mini waterfalls. To all sides Helberg could hear water spurting and cascading downwards. *Damn this foehn.* But there was nothing they could do about it now.

Helberg found a couple of toeholds and thrust himself upwards, his hands grasping for the next outcrop of rock or stubborn veg-etation that might conceivably hold his weight. One thing their mountain warfare instructors had stressed when training in the Cairngorms: *never look down*. Every man amongst them repeated that mantra as they grabbed sharp edges of rock, slid boots into cracks running with meltwater, and levered bodies and heavy packs upwards.

Of course, in Britain they'd trained on routes that had been scaled countless times before. Every hand and foothold had been tested ad infinitum by the previous trainees. This was virgin territory.

They'd been taught to ensure they had four good holds on the rock, before relaxing one and reaching higher. There was no doing that now. Instead, desperate lunges towards a promising clump of roots or a lip of rock were the order of the day. One precious handhold was swapped left to right, freeing the other hand finger by finger so it could grope higher in the search for grip. At times a foot was swung free, only to toe its way across the rock face in a desperate effort to make contact with something – anything – that might offer firm support.

In training, they'd been told repeatedly that use of knees and elbows was a strict no-no. It might help in the short term, but it would manoeuvre the body into a contorted position from which it was difficult to move on. How did you get off your knees, when suspended two hundred feet up a sheer cliff? All such lessons went out of the window here in the grip of the shadowed valley. Elbows, knees, even faces sometimes – all were scraped across dirty rock slick with moisture, in the search for a handhold or a scrap of vegetation to latch on to.

Figures seemed to freeze in mid move. Cramp seized muscles unused to such constant and punishing exertion. Faces gazed up into the moonlight, searchingly, only to receive a shower of rock and detritus dislodged by the man above. Climbers fought their way upwards through cascading water as thick as any waterfall.

Several minutes into the impossible ascent, Kasper Idland froze. He'd reached a point where his feet suddenly went out from under him. He was reduced to hanging on to the cliff by one precarious handhold. Idland – the gentle giant – was immensely strong. But not even he could hold out one-handed for ever.

With his free hand he felt along the contours of the slab, fingers spidering for the slightest crack or outcrop. Nothing to the left: only a shallow fissure packed full of flaky rock, repeatedly shattered by the freeze, and now rendered into a slippery sludge by the thaw. He swapped hands, inching the fingers of his left to replace the hold of his right, while trying to brace with his feet against the smooth, sheer surface.

To the furthest reach of his right, his fingertips felt the tantalizing promise of vegetation: tree roots, burrowed deep into a fissure in the rock. It was just too far to grasp, but the longer he hesitated the more the strength in the fingers of his left hand seemed to drain away. Jolts of pain shot through his shoulder as he began to do the only thing possible – to swing by his one arm in an arc across the cliff.

He made a final swing and forced himself to let go with his left hand. For an instant his body arced through the air, unsupported in any way. Then the fingers of his right hand made contact with the base of that small tree, and, fighting through the mulch of rotten pine needles and dirt, he held fast with all he was worth. Both hands gripped the precious hold, as a sudden blast of warm wind howled down the gorge, tearing at him, moodily. If he hadn't made the jump he'd have been caught one-handed by that gust, and it would very likely have thrown him into the abyss.

The desperate move had taken precious seconds, and Idland was falling behind the others. He shook the sweat from his eyes and moistened cracked lips. The fear of the fall drove each man onwards, propelling him upwards at a precipitous rate. Dread drove them on. Idland moved, chasing the underside of the boots clambering higher above him.

Relentless, driven, feverish; nine men swarmed ever higher. Three hundred feet; four hundred; the impossible end point drew ever closer. But even as it did, fatigue began to drag at their resolve. *Never look down. Don't look down. Do not ever look down.* The mantra played through their minds, even as pain-racked limbs cried out for a brief rest on a narrow ledge, and a squint at what lay below. After all, a glance downwards would show how far each man had come and how little there was to go.

Three did look down. Ashen-faced, their features smeared with muck and flecked with bloody scratches, they took a glimpse into the shadowed abyss. The Måna River was a twisted sliver of silver far below, the dizzying drop to either side framing it in empty, beckoning darkness. Intoxicating, irresistible; how much easier it would be to jump, rather than force the body to go on.

Never look down. To left and right their brother saboteurs hissed the climber's prayer; the mountaineer's mantra. *Never look down.* It served to break the spell. The very sight and sound of their fellow warriors struggling ever higher drove the down-lookers back into action, and back to the climb.

Five hundred feet. Five hundred and fifty. With bruised hands and knees the leading ascenders hauled themselves over the lip of the railroad cutting, driving those below to ever greater efforts. Amongst the first, Helberg and Ronneberg sank to their knees on the level, hard surface. Even though they had made it, the reality of their achievement – proving the impossible possible – seemed difficult to grasp.

Here and there a figure reached out to touch the cold, hard steel of the tracks – proof that they were indeed at the shelf of rock on which the railway ran all the way to the gates of the Vemork plant. So far at least, they seemed to have made it here undetected. Apart from the wind and the growl of the plant, all was night-dark silence and stillness.

To the west stretched the tracks, straight and level some 900 metres to their target. The building rose stark, angular and greyish white in the moonlight. It was utterly alien in these wild and rugged surroundings. As the nine caught their breath and fought to bring the feverish pounding of their hearts under control, so the roar of the Vemork plant seemed to grow in intensity.

Carried on the *foehn* wind, the sound served to focus minds. The night shift would be at work now, each at their stations within the plant, and at their guard posts would be the German soldiers. All were blissfully unaware that a force of nine saboteurs had infiltrated their defences.

'All right, let's get closer,' Ronneberg announced, once the nine were gathered on the rock shelf. 'The cover party will lead the way.'

Haukelid and Helberg shouldered their packs. Together they set out, heading west into the teeth of the gathering wind. In doing so they were consciously taking their lives in their hands: if the railway was laced with landmines, they would be the first to know.

Haukelid discovered some footprints in the snow: someone had walked this way recently. He placed his feet in the prints of those who had passed before, for surely they must know where any minefields might lie. Behind him, Poulsson did the same, and so they advanced in single file, aping each other's movements. Ronneberg waited until they were a good fifty metres ahead before signalling the demolitions team to follow.

In that manner they came to a small iron shed, housing some kind of electrical installation. Here the heartbeat of the Vemork plant was that much louder. To those who had spent so long in the wilds of the Vidda, the churning of so much giant machinery sounded unnatural and foreboding. It served to further focus minds on what was coming.

Ronneberg ordered a halt in the cover of the shed. 'We've got a good view from here. We'll wait until the guards on the bridge are relieved. That will be at midnight, so thirty minutes from now.'

The entire Vemork complex was laid out before them. Directly across the valley the light of a vehicle snaked along the Rjukan–Vemork road. Below and to their right, the suspension bridge threw a narrow thread across the gorge. At one end, they could just make out the distinctive silhouette of two German guards. Directly ahead lay the railway gate and beyond that the two massive buildings: to the rear, the generator hall; in front, the SH200 plant. And, sandwiched between them, the squat black form of the guard barracks.

'The wind carried the deep humming of machinery to us,' Ronneberg remarked of the moment. 'Now and then we could hear a door being opened or shut.'

The seconds ticked by. Some munched on chocolate to replace energy lost in the gorge. Others eyed the zigzag course of the Ryes Road as it climbed the valley in a series of convoluted hairpins. Helberg sought to calm their worries about that untested escape march by regaling all with the story of the ant-encrusted syrup tin. Ronneberg gazed at his men, amazed and not a little humbled by how calm they appeared to be; how primed and ready.

He felt so close to them, yet somehow also a man set slightly apart. One half of his mind was in London, where he knew that the highest in the land were longing for tonight's mission to succeed, where before had come only failure. The raiders were so close now. So much hinged upon this moment. And here Ronneberg's men were, listening to a tale about an ant-infested syrup tin, as if they had not a care in the world.

He felt a massive surge of confidence. If anyone could do this, surely they could. Having scaled the gorge with such calm determination, what were his men not capable of?

At 11.57 the door to the barracks swung open, bleeding light into the darkness. Two figures, their helmets and their weapons utterly distinctive, moved across to the bridge. Nine sets of eyes tracked their movements. They reached the bridge, exchanged greetings with the sentries, who then moved back towards the barracks. One was taller than the other, and talkative. As they walked, he thrust out his chest to emphasize a point he was making.

There was something thrilling about spying on their heedlessness to danger. None had an inkling of what was coming. Ronneberg ordered a few more minutes' wait, just to let the new guards settle into the routine and the boredom of their shift. Then, the nine would make their move.

The Gunnerside leader was a man who thrived on the tension of coming action. He became calmer as the moment of danger drew closer. He walked from man to man, softly reminding them of their role in the coming attack, and the key points to remember. With each he reiterated the need to try to minimize German casualties, in the interests of their fellow Norwegians.

At 12.30 Ronneberg gave the word: the cover party was to advance up the track and cut their way through the gate. 'Once the gate is open, signal. We'll stand by to follow up immediately.'

Five figures turned and headed into the windswept darkness, Helberg, Haukelid and Poulsson leading. One gripped a pair of powerful bolt croppers that their leader, Joachim Ronneberg, had discovered in a British ironmonger's store.

Soon now.

Chapter Twenty-Six

Everything was still and quiet. Maybe too quiet. Kjelstrup bent to the bolt croppers, his shoulders tensing. The powerful teeth closed around the ¾-inch steel of the padlocked chain that secured the Vemork railway gate, as the raiders tensed for the gunshot snap of steel cutting steel.

Ronneberg's bolt croppers sliced through the chain as if it were a human finger, the innards showing silvery in the moonlight. As the steel thread broke Haukelid caught it, lest the loose metal clank against the gate itself. But still, the noise of the cutting had sounded deafening to the saboteurs.

No sooner was the steel severed than Kjelstrup eased the gate open and the first of the saboteurs crept through, flitting onwards into the darkness. In truth, the throbbing of the Vemork plant was deafening now, and it had doubtless masked the noise of their entry.

They were in.

Haukelid and Poulsson led the party forward to take cover amidst the thickest of the shadows. They came to a halt less than fifty metres short of the SH200 plant. While it had seemed large from a distance, at close range it was truly monolithic. It towered above them, its sheer size and scale emphasizing the dangers of where they were and what they were about to attempt.

Behind them, Ronneberg and his three-man demolitions team

cut their way through a second chained gate, opening up an alternative route of escape.

'I stopped and listened,' Ronneberg recalled. 'So far we had not been detected. The hum of the machinery was steady and normal. There was good light from the moon, with no one in sight except our own men.'

Ronneberg signalled for his teams to head for their pre-assigned positions. Helberg melted into the darkness by the fence, sandwiched between the two gates; he was to guard their escape route. Kjelstrup turned left, towards the mountainside that towered to the rear of the plant. He was to keep his eyes peeled for German sentries patrolling the pipelines who might be drawn to the plant by the coming explosions.

Storhaug – the Chicken – pushed ahead right, to where a track wound downhill, linking the plant to the suspension bridge. It was from that direction that the Germans would send in reinforcements. In a crouched run, Haukelid and Poulsson advanced towards the main threat – the squat black form of the German barracks. They edged their way along the rear of an office block, broke cover and dashed for the wall of the generator hall, then flitted from there to the first of a series of giant storage tanks.

Poulsson gripped his tommy gun, finger tight on the trigger. In his trouser pocket Helberg had one of their chloroform knockout pads at the ready. If they stumbled across any Norwegian workers, he'd use that to disable them. With rubber-soled boots flitting over the gritty yard of the plant, the two men advanced from tank to tank, seeking the best position from which to menace the barracks.

Poulsson gave a signal and they came to a halt. The door to the barracks block was but a few metres away. Should the German guards come piling out of there, he and Haukelid would be nicely placed to put some long bursts of tommy gun fire their way, and at very close range.

'Good spot,' Poulsson whispered, eyeing the doorway. 'Only a few feet away.'

For a moment he glanced at the SH200 plant, which lay just a few dozen metres to their right. From this angle – they were several feet lower than the heavy water works – the blacked-out windows bled slivers of light. Here and there the dark terrain was sliced apart by slits of beamed illumination, as if the earth had grown eyes.

To their left, Ronneberg paused for a second and listened hard. He could barely believe it, but still there wasn't the slightest indication that their presence had been discovered. His eyes scanned the darkness, lingering on the odd speck of illumination, but still there was no movement to be seen anywhere.

The machinery of the plant drummed out its steady heartbeat. The very earth seemed to vibrate. So far, so good.

As Kayser covered him, Ronneberg stole ahead towards the SH200 plant, the rucksack of explosives heavy on his shoulders. Stromsheim followed, back likewise bowed by the weight of his charges. The two men with the demolitions gear were to be protected at all costs by the others.

They reached the corner of the electrolysis building. Flecks of light escaped from where the blackout paint didn't quite reach the edge of the window frames. Ronneberg bent to one of those, placing his eye to the glowing chink. Suddenly, he was gazing into a real-life version of what he had practised on so often at Station XVII: a rank of steel vats filled one, massive wall, each stuffed full of the most valuable – and dangerous – liquid in the world.

He snatched his eye away, but not before he'd noted the lone figure keeping watch.

The four men pressed ahead until they reached the solid metal door that gave access to the SH200 plant. With one hand gripping his pistol, Ronneberg reached out and grabbed cold steel. He flicked his wrist to the right, but the handle didn't budge. The door was barred.

'Locked,' he hissed.

He glanced at Stromsheim and Idland, and signalled to the concrete stairwell that ran up to the floor above. 'Try the door on the ground floor.'

They hurried up the steps but returned just as quickly. Idland shook his head; that door too was locked.

What options remained, Ronneberg wondered. They had grenades to blast open the steel doors, or to blow in one of the windows – but that was bound to alert the German guards. And the longer they stayed here, right at the entryway to the SH200 works, the more chance they would be discovered. As yet, they hadn't been spotted. But their luck couldn't last for ever.

The answer had to lie in the cable duct, if only they could locate it. Ronneberg ordered the parties to split up, to see if they could find that tiny entry point. He and Fredrik Kayser headed right around the plant, Stromsheim and Idland going in the opposite direction. The plant was so massive, it felt as if they were searching for the proverbial needle in a haystack.

A snowplough had been at work recently, clearing paths around the building. The snow was pushed into high banks. If one of those had inadvertently covered the cable duct entry hatch, they were in serious trouble.

Near the far corner of the building, Ronneberg spotted a steel ladder several feet deep in a drift. He glanced upwards. The top-most rungs terminated at a small, dark, empty square. Cut into the side of the massive stone wall, it looked like the entrance to a troll's cave.

He gestured excitedly. 'There it is!'

He raced across to the ladder, kicked the snow aside and began to climb. The beanpole figure of Kayser followed. Ronneberg reached the top and knocked away the snow that blocked the entrance. There was no time to risk a call to the others. Strom-sheim and Idland would have to find their own way.

Ronneberg leant forward, threaded his head and shoulders into the darkness and began to wriggle his way further inside. It was darker than hell and there was a fetid, dank airlessness to the narrow space. Beneath his knees whatever ran along the floor of the duct dug in uncomfortably. There was no way he could risk proceeding without a light.

He pulled out a torch and flicked it on, using one hand to shield the beam. The duct stretched ahead of him: too narrow to turn around; too long to countenance backing out again; too constraining to linger indecisively. Heaven forbid if either he or Kayser discovered they were prone to claustrophobia halfway.

This had to be the route that Jomar Brun had alerted them to, back in Britain, but it was several months since he had ventured this way, and who knew what might have changed in the interim as a result of von Falkenhorst's security upgrades.

Above the maze of pipes and tubes there was just enough space to crawl ahead. Ronneberg set off. Behind he could hear Kayser panting as he tried to catch his breath and keep up. Ronneberg tried to focus his mind. He scanned the route ahead with his torch beam, identifying any cables, piping or loose debris that could be shoved out of the way. It gave him something to focus on.

At the back of Ronneberg's mind was the nagging worry that even now he and Kayser were crawling across the ceiling of their target, with no direct route of entry unless the duct actually led somewhere – to a point where they could exit. Surely it had to, for that was what Brun had told them. But maybe all that had changed in the interim.

If they were heard or otherwise detected while trapped in this narrow tunnel, Ronneberg didn't want to think about the consequences. One burst from a Schmeisser sub-machine gun from the far end of the duct, and he and Kayser would be in trouble. And there was zero chance of reaching for their suicide pills, constrained as they were.

He blanked all such thoughts from his mind and crawled onwards. Halfway down he came to some water pipes. They passed through the duct, draining into the room below. Presumably they carried a lesser concentration of SH200 from the floor above to the final stage – the high-concentration cells. As Ronneberg went to crawl over the obstruction, he froze. The pipes didn't make a tight seal with the roof, and through the gap he could see directly into the SH200 plant; right below him, and seated at a desk making some notes, was the lone guard.

Barely daring to breathe, Ronneberg inched his way across. Having made it, he paused to regain his equilibrium. Behind him, Kayser moved to cross the pipes, but when he was halfway he must have leaned too far over. His heavy Colt slipped out of its shoulder holster and clattered onto the water pipes, the noise of steel striking steel ringing out like a clanging alarm bell.

Both men froze, terrified that they might be discovered this close to the target. To be thwarted at this point – it was too bitter to contemplate.

Finally Ronneberg risked a peep through to the floor below. He was just in time to see the guard turn back to his paperwork. He must have concluded that this was just another of those odd noises that the massive plant tended to make. He gestured to Kayser to fasten the pistol properly, so it couldn't fall out again.

Ronneberg turned and pressed onwards, his mouth dry, his heartbeat firing like a machine gun. He squeezed past several thick webs of cabling, before finally he reached an open hole in the floor. Just as Brun had described, the cable duct ended in a hatch, which was kept unbolted and opened into the high-concentration floor of the plant. Below Ronneberg was a ten-foot drop – an easy leap for someone recently out of training at Crispie.

Every second was precious now. Discovery was surely only a matter of time – if not for them, then for the cover party. With no sign of Stromsheim and Idland – the others tasked with the demolitions – Ronneberg decided to press on and attempt the job with just himself and Kayser.

With hands placed to either side of the manhole-like gap, Ronneberg lowered first his legs and then his torso through the floor, and dropped. He landed like a coiled snake, his gun out of its holster almost before he'd come to rest. He swept the room to either side. It was deserted. They'd reached a side chamber to the main high-concentration plant, which now was but a bare few steps away.

'NO ADMITTANCE' read the sign on the doorway.

Kayser having vaulted down beside him, Ronneberg reached for the handle. As Kayser covered him, Ronneberg pulled the door open wide and the hallowed confines of the SH200 high-concentration room swung into view. It felt strangely familiar and alien peering into that room; the rehearsals at Station XVII had prepared them for this moment, but not for the sense of penetrating the heart of the Nazi nuclear dream.

'There were the cells,' Ronneberg remarked of the moment, 'looking just like the models we had attacked during our training, but they were the real thing at last.'

The night watchman, an overweight, grey-haired Norwegian, was sitting with his back to them, and still he hadn't noticed that anything was wrong. All around them the plant hummed and purred reassuringly. Kayser strode forward, his gun at the ready.

'On your feet,' he barked in Norwegian. 'And hands up.'

The guard turned, abruptly. His consternation was accentuated by his need to remove his glasses. He was obviously long-sighted and couldn't make out who his unexpected visitors were. He fumbled, removed his specs, then stared, open-mouthed.

'On your feet,' Kayser repeated. 'Keep your hands above your head. And where's the key to the door leading to the yard?'

He meant the steel door via which Ronneberg and party had tried to gain entry. They would need to exit through it after they had triggered the charges. They certainly wouldn't be able to crawl back out through the cable duct, not with the explosives detonating right beneath them.

'The key!' he repeated. 'Nothing will happen to you if you do as you're told.' He tapped the British insignia on his shoulder flashes. 'See. We're British soldiers.'

'Keep talking to him about Britain,' Ronneberg barked at Kayser, deliberately speaking English.

The more they could impress upon this man that they were

British, the less the likelihood of any reprisals – or so the two hoped. As Kayser dealt with the guard, Ronneberg bolted the door they'd just come through, pulled the desk over, opened his rucksack and laid out his twenty charges of Nobel 808 – one for each electrolysis cell, and two spare.

His hands worked feverishly, but with a practised authority: he was only doing now what he had rehearsed so many times before at Station XVII. Each charge was sausage-shaped, about twelve inches long, with a fuse and detonator inserted into it. Pulling on some rubber gloves, to protect against electric shocks from the SH200 cells, he turned to the first and got to work.

It towered above him, a mass of pipes, tubes, seals, rubber connectors, anodes, cathodes, water jackets and flanges, all wrapped around a large metal cylinder – the stainless steel SH200 container. He reached up and moulded the first charge around the base of the container, where it stuck fast like sticky plasticine.

When it detonated, it would rip the guts out of the equipment and send the precious SH200 gushing down the drain. The explosives 'seemed to be made to measure and fitted like a glove', Ronneberg remarked. He turned for another set of Nobel 808 charges, moving onto the second steel cylinder.

'What's your name?' Kayser asked the night guard. Anything, to keep the man calm.

'Gustav Johansen', he replied, but his eyes were glued to Ronneberg, a mixture of fear and shock writ large upon his features.

Kayser kept chatting to the night watchman, regaling him with stories from England. They'd had reports that Johansen was a good, loyal Norwegian, and they wanted to give him as many reasons as possible to believe that the raiding party was British.

'Have a good look', Kayser told him, fingering the sergeant's stripes on his shoulders. 'Notice those marks? Now you can tell the Germans what an English uniform looks like. I don't suppose there are so many of the *Übermensch* who've had the chance of getting close to an Allied soldier!'

Ronneberg had reached the ninth cell in line, halfway through his task, when a sudden crash of breaking glass cut through the steady hum of the SH200 plant. A boot had crashed through one of the windows to the rear of the room. Kayser whirled away from the night watchman, his weapon at the ready, finger bone-white on the trigger.

In a flash Ronneberg drew his pistol, as he too prepared for battle.

Chapter Twenty-Seven

Bonzo Haukelid and Jens Poulsson eyed the barracks block warily. What the Grouse leader wouldn't give now for a long pull on his pipe. Haukelid tapped his watch: twenty minutes in, and still no sign of the sabotage party.

'What can be keeping them?' Poulsson hissed.

Haukelid shrugged. 'I wish I knew.'

It had taken seven minutes to plant the charges when they'd rehearsed this back in England. Ronneberg and his men must have hit trouble getting access to the plant.

Poulsson had his tommy gun levelled at the barracks doorway. If there was any sign of movement he would start 'pumping lead into the hut'. Haukelid had half a dozen hand grenades within easy reach; if the Germans raised a hue and cry, he would dash forward and hurl them through door and windows. But he would have to be careful: the wooden walls of the barracks would offer precious little protection from the blast.

'Remember to shout Heil Hitler when you throw your grenades,' Poulsson muttered, his eyes not leaving the doorway.

The suggestion was only half in jest. That cry of allegiance to the Führer might buy them a few extra seconds in which to wreak their carnage.

For an instant Haukelid's mind flipped back to an incident etched deep in his memory. At one stage during the fighting against the German invaders Haukelid and party had surrounded a section of enemy troops. The Germans had taken cover in a wooden house, not realizing what little shelter it offered. By the time Haukelid and his fellows had ceased fire, there were dead Germans hanging out of the windows. This wooden barracks blocks would give equally limited protection.

The steady throbbing from the generator hall seemed to taunt Haukelid. What was keeping the sabotage party? It felt as if he and Poulsson had been waiting here for ever. It had to be worse for the others. Helberg, Kjelstrup and Storhaug were utterly isolated at their solitary posts. As the minutes ticked by they each must be thinking: had Ronneberg and his party got trapped inside the plant?

A short distance downhill Storhaug stared with unblinking eyes at the two sentries on the bridge. He was so close that he could hear their night-time chatter. They clearly had no idea that a force of 'British' soldiers had infiltrated the SH200 plant. The trouble was, Storhaug had no idea where the sabotage party had got to, or even if they were still at liberty.

It was all just so nerve-racking.

Inside the high-concentration room, Ronneberg and Kayser eased off the pressure on their triggers. One of their number – Stromsheim; the grandfather of the group – had thrust his head through the freshly broken windowpane, and he'd almost got it blown right off. They'd only just recognized him in time.

Stromsheim, who was carrying the second set of demolition charges, had despaired of finding the cable duct entryway. Instead, he'd decided to smash his way in: the noise of the breaking glass, plus the shaft of light that would have suddenly pierced the darkness, lent Ronneberg's task an even greater sense of urgency now.

With his rubber gloves to protect him, Ronneberg removed the remains of the shattered window pane, to help Stromsheim in. He ordered the man's companion, Idland, to head around to the main steel door and take up a position there, to guard their exit. But as he pulled a final fragment of glass free and went to guide Stromsheim through, Ronneberg felt a sharp stab of pain in his hand.

He glanced down to see a spurt of oozing red. A shard of glass had pierced the rubber glove, and it looked as if he'd cut himself badly. For the briefest of instants his mind flashed to the gorge, and the sheer climb he would have to execute to get out of here. Now he would have to attempt it with an injured and bloodied hand.

He forced such thoughts from his mind. Enough time had been lost already. Ordering Stromsheim to help, Ronneberg turned back to his task. Two sets of hands should make light work, and with luck they'd have the final explosives set within the next couple of minutes. Feverishly Ronneberg and Stromsheim worked away, moulding their Nobel 808 charges to the remaining SH200 chambers.

As he worked, Ronneberg's mind was racing: each package of Nobel 808 came equipped with a 120-second fuse, but he didn't want to risk such a lengthy delay. If they fled the room leaving two-minute delays, it was just possible that a guard might make it in here and disable the fuses. He decided to cut the time short – very short. They'd use thirty-second fuses instead.

That would leave them only half a minute to get the hell out of the room. They'd also be left with zero chance of making it out of the Vemork grounds before the explosions ripped the SH200 plant asunder. But Ronneberg figured that was a risk worth taking to ensure the sabotage was successful.

Fuses and charges set, Ronneberg and Stromsheim ran through one last set of checks, ensuring that all was as it should be. Then Ronneberg turned to Kayser.

'Right, let's get the door onto the yard unlocked.'

At gunpoint, Kayser ushered the night watchman towards the exit. The heavy steel door was encased in thick reinforced concrete. He got it unfastened, then swung it open a fraction, just to ensure there was nothing that would obstruct their escape. Thirty seconds didn't leave a lot of time for something to go wrong.

Ronneberg put the final touches to his handiwork. He pulled out a handful of British parachute wing badges and scattered them over the floor – the commandos' calling card. That done, and with blood oozing from his cut hand, he grabbed a box of matches.

The first flared, and still there wasn't the slightest sign of alarm from anywhere around the plant. But as Ronneberg bent to the fuse, the night watchman cried out in alarm.

'One moment! My glasses. I left them on the desk. I must have my glasses.'

Ronneberg froze. From Jomar Brun's intelligence reports he knew there were German guards stationed within this building. At any moment one might arrive, on patrol. Every second was precious. But he also knew that the Germans had seized all of Norway's optical manufacturing facilities, so there was no way this man would get replacement glasses any time soon.

He killed the match, hurried to the desk and grabbed the man's spectacles case. 'Here.'

'*Tusan takk*' – a thousand thanks – the watchman replied.

Ronneberg turned back to the charges and struck a second match. The voice rang out again.

'Wait! I beg you! My glasses! They're not in the case!'

Silently, Ronneberg cursed. Was he really to endanger their mission for a pair of eyeglasses? Roosevelt, Churchill, the Norwegian king and so many others in high office were waiting on his actions. If they failed now – if a German guard intervened and raised the alarm – there surely would be no second chance. Not for them, nor for any other raiding force, and possibly not for the free world.

He blew out the second match. 'So, where are you damn glasses?' he hissed.

He rushed to where the man indicated, and found them jammed between the leaves of a logbook. He thrust them at the watchman. 'Take them!'

The man repeated his thanks.

Ronneberg struck a third match. *Third time lucky*. But as he crouched to light the fuse he heard the noise that he had most dreaded: heavy footsteps thundered down the iron stairway from the floor above. He felt the hair on the back of his neck prickle. A German soldier was coming. Should he throw caution to the wind and light the fuse? Or wait and disable the guard?

For a moment the flame hovered indecisively, before Ronneberg snuffed it out. He turned to Kayser and Stromsheim; all had their weapons ready. The three men tensed for battle. A figure strode through the doorway. The three raiders breathed a collective sigh of relief. It wasn't a German in uniform. It was a Norwegian – the plant foreman doing his rounds.

The foreman stared at the scene before him in utter disbelief.

His eyes took in the watchman, Johansen, with his hands above his head; three rough-looking soldiers in what appeared to be British uniform, guns levelled; and the Nobel 808 charges, threaded around the eighteen SH200 cylinders like a long string of sausages.

It was impossible. The plant was ringed with barbed wire, electrified wire, minefields, alarms, searchlights, machine-gun posts and German guards. So how could all this be happening here, at the heart of this facility that was of utmost importance to the Reich?

There was no time to ponder this. Instead, the foreman was forced to put his hands up, under the menace of three gaping muzzles.

'Get the both of them over to the stairs,' Ronneberg ordered. 'After I light the fuse tell them to run. They should reach the second floor before the charges blow, so they should be safe enough ... Tell them to lie down and keep their mouths open, or they'll lose their ear drums.'

Almost as an afterthought Ronneberg scattered about some of the tools that he'd been using, each of which had 'Made in Britain' stamped into its metal parts – yet more evidence of who exactly had wreaked the carnage here.

That done, Ronneberg set his match to the fuse and yelled: 'Go!'

At the stairway, Kayser delayed for a few seconds, just to ensure his two captives couldn't do anything to interfere with their handiwork. Then he shoved them up the steps, his words chasing after their heels. 'Run! Run! As fast as you can!'

With that he, Ronneberg and Stromsheim yanked open the steel door, darted out of the plant, slamming it shut and locking it after them. They turned and ran, legs pumping and pulses racing, heading east into the beckoning darkness. They'd made no more than twenty metres when there was the flash of an explosion. The noise of the blast was muffled by the massive walls of the building and the thick steel door, yet inside the SH200 room was all a mass of flame.

The force of the explosion burned hot upon their backs as they sprinted for safety. The shortened fuses had made sure that 'no desperate or misguided German' had had a chance to spoil their work. But having struck at the heart of the Nazi's greatest – and darkest – of secrets, now they had to make their getaway.

To Poulsson and Haukelid, standing guard over the barracks block, the explosions had sounded somewhat subdued. The noise was 'like two or three cars crashing in Piccadilly Circus', noted Poulsson. Yet the white-orange flash of the blast had cut through the darkness like lightning, and they had to presume that the sabotage team had done their work.

The two men tensed, waiting for the reaction from the German guards. A few moments passed before the door was flung open. A single figure stood there, silhouetted in the light. Bareheaded and without a visible weapon, he glanced at the balconies running around the SH200 plant – those that housed the hydrogen burners, the 'cannons', which were well known for issuing their sporadic explosions.

The guard shook his head, as if the burners' erratic behaviour must account for the noise that he had heard. With shoulders hunched against the chill he wandered over to the SH200 plant's steel door. He tried it, found it locked as usual, and returned to the warmth of the barracks. Haukelid and Poulsson relaxed their grip on their weapons and readied themselves to take flight.

But then the barracks door was thrown open for a second time. The same figure stepped out, only now he looked decidedly more businesslike. He was armed with a rifle and had a torch gripped in one hand.

'The bastard's back,' Poulsson hissed. 'He must smell trouble.'

'Could prove fatal,' Haukelid growled.

With the torch held before him, the German began to play the beam back and forth across the ground. Steadily he approached where Poulsson and Haukelid lay prone, weapons at the ready. Poulsson thought of his parents and his brother and sisters in nearby Rjukan. If he blasted this fellow with his tommy gun, others would follow, and there would be a bloodbath. The reprisals would be correspondingly brutal.

'Shall I fire?' he whispered, as he stared down the barrel of his tommy gun.

Haukelid, gripping his grenades, shook his head. 'Not yet. He might not see us. Leave it for as long as possible.'

For an instant the guard flashed the light up towards the balconies that housed the cannons, before bringing it down again to quarter the ground to the rear of Poulsson and Haukelid. All he needed to do now was sweep the beam forward onto the prone figures, and he was a dead man. The German hesitated, as if trying to puzzle something out, glanced at the balcony again, then turned and stomped back into the barracks.

The moment the door closed, two silent figures rose from the ground and melted into the darkness. Haukelid and Poulsson raced for the railway gate, feet flashing across the ground. They were met there by Helberg and Kjelstrup, who confirmed that they were the last; everyone else was ahead of them and making their way down the railway tracks.

Haukelid swung the gate shut and wrapped the severed chain around it several times, so at a casual inspection it might appear to be intact. For an instant Haukelid and Helberg paused. Had they really left enough evidence that this was a British sabotage operation? Surely a little something scattered along the escape route wouldn't hurt?

Haukelid decided to dump his chloroform pads and tube. But before doing so, he gave the equipment a wipe over with a handkerchief. No sense in leaving any finger prints for the Gestapo. They'd taken Haukelid's prints when he was arrested in 1941, and he didn't want to risk any reprisals against his family.

Helberg, meanwhile, laid his beloved tommy gun gently in the snow beside the tracks. He'd nursed that weapon through three terrible months on the Vidda, but now was the time for their parting. There was nothing more symbolic of the commandos than a tommy gun, hence his leaving it behind.

'All right, let's go!'

The last two saboteurs took to their heels, heading east along the glistening line of the tracks.

Up ahead Ronneberg waited, making certain that everyone had made it out of the plant. 'For a moment I looked back down the line and listened,' he remarked. 'Except for the hum of machinery that we had heard when we arrived, everything in the factory was quiet.'

It was hard to believe, but they appeared to have got in and out and to have blown the SH200 plant to pieces without the defenders even realizing it. Even now, the impossible promise of escape beckoned. But in the euphoria of the moment, the nine saboteurs had overlooked one thing. There was a sense of real heat to the air; a fetid hotness to the wind.

The *foehn* – the snow-eater – was hungry and intent on feeding.

'Helberg – lead the way,' Ronneberg ordered, as they turned towards the chasm.

Helberg found a place where the cliff looked noticeably less treacherous, compared to the place where they had climbed. He led the nine over the edge, scrambling from one snowdrift to another, and leaping from ledge to ledge in a semi-controlled scramble towards the floor of the gorge. Above and behind him figures stumbled after, in a helter-skelter dash for the low ground.

Helberg reached the banks of the Måna first. His gaze was drawn to the groaning river. It looked as if an earthquake had torn apart the ice. Slabs had been thrown free and piled against each other, as the sheer volume of water released by the snow-eater threatened to carry it all away. The noise was deafening: fresh meltwater rushing over slabs of ice that were tearing themselves apart under the strain.

Helberg searched for a point where they could chance a crossing. At all junctures angry waters eddied and swirled. Wave crests foamed white in the moonlight. The river roared and the ice wailed. And then, over it all rang out an even louder screaming.

Rhythmic, piercing, unearthly – the new sound echoed deafeningly down the length of the gorge. The German guard force had sounded the siren, raising the alarm.

The hunt was on.

Chapter Twenty-Eight

Chief engineer Alf Larsen swept his torchlight around the heaps of steaming, ghostly wreckage. Ten minutes previously, this had been the world's most prized and heavily protected industrial plant. Now . . . The eighteen stainless steel tubes lay in twisted ruins, their stands torn apart by the raw power of the blast, their forms ripped from the wall.

The white-painted room was scorched black, its windows shattered, its doors left hanging drunkenly. Water gushed from above, ruptured pipes emptying their contents into the debris-strewn room. Telephone cables and electrical wires had been torn from the ceiling, to be left hanging in twisted and deformed clumps – hence the pitch darkness. Outside, pumps and other machinery had stopped working, electrical surges from the explosion having fried the plant's circuitry.

Engineer Larsen had replaced Jomar Brun at the Vemork works, after the latter's mystery disappearance of a few months ago. He glanced at his watch: an hour after midnight. He'd been drawn here by the explosion. Inside the giant building, its effect had been far from muted. The power of the blast had been felt practically everywhere, reverberating throughout the entire seven-storey structure.

But still Larsen had never expected to discover anything quite as cataclysmic as this. He poked through the debris, getting soaked by the water that streamed from above. Shrapnel from the explosion had peppered the room, cutting through the SH200 plant's intricate cooling system. Standing here was like being under a cold shower.

He made his way gingerly towards what had once been the high-concentration cells. The beam of his torch glinted upon the shattered remains of the first of the cylinders. It looked as if a giant had attacked it with a massive tin opener, desperate to get at its contents. He checked the cells in turn. Sure enough, each had had its guts ripped out.

Beneath his feet floor grates gurgled, as the last of the priceless liquid drained away.

Outside, stairwells and balconies rang with the clanging tread of scores of hobnailed boots. The Germans were convinced that the British saboteurs must still be on the premises. No one had crossed the suspension bridge or ascended via the heavily mined route of the pipelines. As the gorge was 'unscalable', the attackers had to be here still, hiding out somewhere.

But as engineer Larsen surveyed their handiwork, somehow he doubted this was the case. It was, as he would later report, 'a perfect sabotage'. The work of true professionals. The saboteurs had known exactly what they were doing. Men like that didn't tend to leave their escape to the whims of chance.

Larsen was right: the saboteurs had planned their escape in exacting detail. But still chance, or fate – the *foehn* – might foil their getaway.

Right now, those nine men struggled across a fast-disintegrating ice bridge. The 'ground' beneath their feet was as treacherous as the devil himself. Angry water foamed around their legs, as white as any snow. Figures stumbled and slipped, grabbing at rocks and boulders and slabs of shifting ice.

At their head were Helberg and Poulsson, driven onwards by the wail of the siren as if they were men possessed. They knew from the intelligence briefings that the alarm would trigger searchlights, which could sweep the entire length of the gorge in a blaze of blinding illumination. If they were caught under that they would be helpless – sitting ducks to be picked off by the German machine-gunners at will.

'It was as if we were being pursued across the river by the shrieking sound itself,' Poulsson remarked of the wailing sirens. 'We slipped and fell, grabbing onto rocks and blocks of ice, it didn't matter which.'

Somehow, with their weapons held high to avoid the churning meltwater, all nine reached the far side . . . and still the gorge was cloaked in darkness. What had happened to the much-vaunted searchlights? No one knew. But there was no time to tarry now and question their good fortune. They climbed – straight up, grasping onto trees, shrubs, rocks and boulders, hauling tired bodies onwards.

'It was already more than an hour since the attack,' Ronneberg remarked, 'and we were still at the bottom of the trap. Very much depended on good luck now . . .' When he glanced towards the plant, 'car after car roared along at maximum speed heading for Vemork. We made ready to defend ourselves at any moment . . . should we meet any patrols.'

To their front the growl of powerful engines cut the night, as truckloads of reinforcements sped along the road leading from Rjukan to the Vemork works. To their back the fleeing saboteurs spotted a line of torchlights bobbing along the route of the way.

One or two sporadic shots rang out through the distant trees. The Germans were shooting at wraiths and at ghosts.

As the nine saboteurs gained height headlights flashed through the forest, blinding them. They were being hunted on all sides.

'Nice of the bastards to keep their lights on,' someone growled. 'At least we can see where we're going.'

Fighting against a crushing burden of mental and physical fatigue, with their uniforms soaked and feeling frozen to the marrow, the nine made it to the main road that cut through the woods. Once over this obstacle they could swing east and head for the Ryes Road – the cable car switchback track leading to the high plateau.

Helberg waved them across, one at a time, checking that the coast was clear. Even so, the last two had to dive into the ditch that lined the road, to avoid a car that rounded the bend unexpectedly with dimmed headlights. They reached their cache of equipment and donned skis, whereupon the nine set out through the cover of the pre-dawn forest, heading for the road beneath the cable lines.

Behind them at the plant, a mortified sergeant of the guards was still searching for the switch that would operate the floodlights. He couldn't seem to find it. Finally, he was forced to collar a Norwegian worker and ask where it was situated. By the time they'd found it and the searchlights had sparked into life, Ronneberg's force was deep in the forest and too distant for any such illumination to reach them.

It was a stroke of good fortune. It wouldn't be their last.

160 kilometres south-east, in Oslo, General von Falkenhorst was woken from his bed, as were *Reichskommissar* Josef Terboven and

SS chief General Wilhelm Rediess. They were not best pleased. News of the sabotage landed like a bombshell. All three responded similarly: they would make an immediate journey to Vemork to investigate. If things were as dire as they sounded, Hitler would be apoplectic. Heads would roll, and none of them wanted to be the one to lose theirs.

In his Baker Street headquarters a scar-faced former Scoutmaster longed to hear news, good or bad, of Operation Gunnerside. Others in far greater positions of power waited on his word. And in a remote hut on the Hardangervidda, Knut Haugland and Einar Skinnarland were poised to send a message winging across the airwaves.

But they would only do so if one of the nine saboteurs made it out of the shadowed valley alive.

It felt as if they had been skiing for hours: upwards, ever upwards, around switchback bends that never seemed to end. After the superhuman efforts of that long night's action, this was sheer torture. Skis had little purchase on the wet, sticky, *foehn*-plagued snow. Dragged down by their rucksacks, harried by exhaustion, the nine fell often. But they rose again and again and they kept going.

Helberg and Ronneberg set the pace, leading from the front. Speed, they knew, was of the absolute essence – the difference between death and survival. They had to make the summit by daybreak. To be caught on the Ryes Road in broad daylight would prove fatal. They pushed onwards, criss-crossing beneath the wires of the cable car station, gaining height; always gaining.

'Up we climbed,' remarked Ronneberg, 'and every time we came to a bend we looked down . . . to see if anything was going on. With every bend we got nearer the top, until at last, five hours after the attack, we were able to . . . make for the high plateau. Now we had the mountains of Norway as our great ally.'

As they topped the last ridge opening onto the Vidda, the pine forests thinned to nothing. A savage wind cut into their faces – the all-too-familiar embrace of the Barren Mountain plateau. It carried with it the promise of heavy snow. Within minutes the nine were forced to shield their faces as wind-whipped ice particles laden with grit cut into exposed skin. The storm became a howling blizzard. It was agonizing, but still the nine skied willingly into its icy blast.

Helberg turned to Ronneberg. They had made it to the Vidda, and with this welcoming storm his thoughts had turned to that bottle of Upper Ten whisky and a celebratory drink. It lay eleven kilometres due west, at the Fjosbudalen hut, in the heart of the strengthening blizzard. What better place to hide up as the storm raged, and the German generals raged impotently?

'They will never send search parties out in this!' Helberg cried. 'They'll never dare the mountains in such a storm.'

Helberg's words were whipped away on the thickening wind, but the Gunnerside leader recognized the sense in them. The storm was now their greatest friend. The dense, driven snow should obliterate the saboteurs' ski tracks. The nine pressed onwards into the teeth of the gale, which howled out of the western skies. As they disappeared into the raging whiteout, they gave thanks for their second stroke of good fortune.

They were swallowed by the storm with barely a trace of their passage left for anyone to follow.

SS General Rediess was the first of the Nazi big guns to arrive at Vemork. Consumed by a cold fury, he was here to demand answers. How had such a sabotage operation even been possible? No one seemed able to say.

The saboteurs hadn't crossed the suspension bridge and they hadn't used the pipelines to gain access. Halfway along the route of the railway all signs of their passing – including a trail of blood indicating that one at least had been injured – seemed to disappear. So what on earth had happened to them?

Rediess knew from security reports that scaling the gorge was impossible, so how had they attacked and made their getaway? And where were they now, so he, General Rediess, could better direct the hunt? In the absence of any answers he ordered mass arrests. Fifty of the plant's workers and technicians were taken in for questioning. Worse still, ten of the luminaries of Rjukan town were seized. They would be shot the following morning, Rediess declared, if he didn't get answers.

General von Falkenhorst came hot on Rediess's heels. He immediately saw the raid for what it was: a slick and professional military operation carried out by soldiers in British uniform. He surveyed the devastation, shaking his head with grudging admiration. 'British gangsters,' he muttered, declaring the attack to be 'the finest coup I have seen in this war'. He countermanded Rediess's orders; as this was clearly the work of *Britischers*, and a British military operation, no reprisals were to be taken against any locals.

Von Falkenhorst reserved his fury for the German guard force. In front of the twisted and still-dripping wreckage of the SH200 works he berated them: 'When you have a chest of jewels like this, you plant yourself on the lid with a weapon in your hand!' He ordered his men to stand permanent guard over the plant from now on.

His anger spiked when he heard how the plant's guard dogs had not been out on patrol due to the foul weather. But he reached the absolute apex of his rage when the sergeant of the guards admitted that the searchlights hadn't been turned on because no one could find the switch. He ordered that man to be sent to the Eastern Front, with immediate effect. That done, he stalked the length and breadth of the Vemork works, decreeing a series of measures be taken to bolster security.

Rediess meanwhile shifted his focus to Rjukan town, where he was joined by *Reichskommissar* Terboven. They declared a state of emergency and a night-time curfew. The telephone exchange was shut down and house-to-house searches begun. There were dozens of arrests. Posters were pasted on every corner. They warned the town's residents that if there was a repeat of the Vemork sabotage, 'the sharpest measures will be taken against the civilian population'.

The following morning, 1 March 1943, some thirty-six hours after the Gunnerside saboteurs had struck, Wilson got the first hint of their success. In a telegram to the key military and political leaders of the land, he outlined a Swedish radio report that had been – partially – intercepted by the BBC:

The following was received over the telephone from the B.B.C. Monitoring Service . . .

(First sentence has been missed by the B.B.C. and they are doubtful whether they will be able to get it.)

'. . . perpetrated against Norwegian hydro installation. The damages are said to have been extensive, but at the point where the attack was made the destruction is said to be complete. The attack was made by three Norwegian-speaking soldiers in British uniform who are now being searched for . . .'

At the point where the attack was made the destruction is said to be complete. The intercept was tantalizing. It suggested that team Gunnerside had succeeded where all others had failed. It suggested that Wilson's great gamble had paid off. If that was true, an incredible blow had been struck in freedom's cause.

But Wilson needed more. He needed absolute verification. He was soon to have it, and from the most unlikely of sources. The following morning a copy of the *Daily Mail* newspaper landed on Wilson's desk. The headline and dateline screamed out at him:

Daily Mail, 2 March 1943

CAME-AND-LEFT BY AIR:
Nazi Works Wrecked

The Norsk Hydro works, which were the target of airborne wreckers on Saturday night, is a subsidiary of the famous I.G. Farben chemical factory. The plant produces sulphur and nitrogen for high explosives for Germany.

PLANE LANDED ON LAKE

Three Norwegian patriots in British uniform were landed from a plane on a frozen lake, 80 miles northwest of Oslo, during the half-moonlight of Saturday night.

The men, skilled saboteurs, succeeded in blowing up part of the great German-controlled Norsk Hydro Electric plant at Rjukan.

Then the patriots returned to the ice-covered lake, clambered aboard. The engines revved and the journey back to Britain was begun . . .

Spite at being outwitted led the German SS and Rediess, Norway's chief of police, to seize 17 hostages.

The attack on the factory, producing quantities of nitrates and fertilizers, is the most sensational case of wrecking since the commando raids on Lofoten and St Nazare.

At least one section of the giant factory has been totally destroyed . . .

The explosions were timed so that only German and Quisling night-watchmen were killed . . .

The report, filed by Ralph Hewins, the *Daily Mail*'s Stockholm correspondent, was remarkably accurate, considering its publication less than seventy-two hours after a top-secret mission. Somehow, Hewins seemed to know more than Wilson, the architect of Operation Gunnerside, which rankled. How had a reporter beaten the SOE to such earth-shattering news, and only to place it slam in the public eye?

Admittedly, there were errors. No aircraft had picked up Wilson's saboteurs from any frozen lake, of that he was certain. There were likely to be other mistakes too. But right now Wilson could verify few of the details, because he had no contact with his raiding party. Where was Haugland? Skinnarland? His superlative communications team? Why the silence?

Had they been captured? Injured? Killed? He just didn't know.

He would have to wait for them to come on air. In the meantime, he would try to do something about this breach of security. Someone had briefed the *Mail* reporter, and in significant detail – that much was clear. The saboteurs were reported as 'knowing the country intimately', and needing 'no help from local agents'.

Who had done so and why?

It turned out that the *Mail* article was based in part upon reports that had appeared in the Swedish newspapers. The *Dagens Nyheter* (Today's News) gave extensive detail of the Vemork raid. There was an obvious benefit to the coverage. The Swedish reports told of how the 'three' raiders 'have now been picked up and returned to England. The German search for them has been fruitless.'

What if the Germans were to believe this? If so, it was fantastic disinformation. It might well result in the Germans calling off their search, which would be a magnificent outcome. On balance, Wilson decided that the press coverage was a good thing.

On a 2 March security briefing about the *Mail* article, Wilson was able to scribble a handwritten note: 'No breach of security involved.' Later that day a formal memo was circulated, which concluded that those on high were: 'Delighted at the newspaper reports of the Gunnerside operation.'

Wilson may have taken a pragmatic line about the breaking news, but he remained desperate for absolute and irrefutable confirmation of the raid and its outcome. A Mosquito squadron was ordered to undertake a recce flight over Vemork. Wilson briefed its commander about how anxious he was for 'factual evidence of the damage done'.

But securing photographic proof would be no easy undertaking. 'It is possible that no outward sign of the explosion will show,' Wilson explained. 'On the other hand, there is a possibility that owing to the ignition of certain gases, considerably greater damage may have been done. As you are probably aware, this was the highest priority target in Norway.'

While he awaited the outcome of that air recce, Wilson longed for some kind of direct confirmation from team Gunnerside.

Those nine men had skied across the storm-lashed Vidda, making their way by stages to the Cousin's Cabin. There they'd prepared a message for Haugland to send to Wilson, before they split up. Five, led by Ronneberg, were to ski for the Swedish border, in a bid to return to Britain. Four – Bonzo Haukelid, Kjelstrup, Poulsson and Helberg – would remain on the Vidda, with the intention of making life very difficult for the German occupiers.

On 4 March Ronneberg's group set out, heavily laden, heading east across the Vidda. Haukelid and Kjelstrup, meanwhile, also took off on skis, to link up with Haugland and Skinnarland and get the good news to Wilson. Poulsson set off south towards Oslo, to rendezvous with Helberg – the man who had played such a key role in leading the Gunnerside team on the ground – who would make his way by a separate route to that city.

But little did they know that they were skiing into a whole world of trouble.

Chapter Twenty-Nine

It was the chocolate that had given him away.

Kristiansen – a simple, warm-hearted man of the mountains, certainly no political animal – had decided to give it to some local children. When was the last time any in his native town of Uvdal had had any chocolate? And if the force of gunmen that he had blundered into – whether British or Norwegian, he still wasn't entirely certain – had been good enough to share some with him, he would do likewise.

But with a dark inevitability the news of a local man bearing gifts of chocolate for the children of Uvdal reached the ears of the Gestapo. Kristiansen was arrested and 'persuaded' to talk. And so, bit by bit, he revealed the story of his reindeer-hunting expedition, and of the mystery force of gunmen that he had run into on the Vidda.

His Gestapo interrogators sent a report to their boss, General Rediess. It read: 'Days before the Vemork incident eight men were seen on skis on Hardangervidda, going towards Rjukan . . . carrying, amongst other things, sub-machine guns. All had white camouflage clothing on. A hut at Lake Skrykken was broken into . . . After, the tracks of five pairs of skis and a sledge were seen running from Rjukan and avoiding inhabited areas.'

Rediess flew into Uvdal, followed by Terboven and von Falken-horst. All of a sudden this small town set to the east of the Vidda had become the nerve centre of their operations. Obviously, the reports in the Swedish media were wrong: no British agents had landed on a frozen lake and taken off again, all in one night. The attack on Vemork had been long in the making, far more enemy agents were involved, and on some level at least it had been masterminded from the Hardangervidda.

The German commanders named the coming initiative *Aktion Adler*: Operation Eagle. Over 10,000 German troops were drafted in, including Alpine mountaineering specialists, ski patrols, tracker dog units and spotter aircraft crews. By now, rumours abounded of 'hundreds of British commandos' hiding out on the Barren Mountain plateau. Von Falkenhorst, Rediess and Terboven were determined to leave no stone unturned. They would hunt down every last one of them.

Fortunately, word was sent to the saboteurs – or at least, those that could be reached. Local farmers skied into the wilderness to issue warnings to Haukelid, Kjelstrup, Haugland and Skinnarland, four men who had just succeeded in radioing their hurried but triumphant message to Wilson.

'Operation carried out with 100% success. High-concentration plant completely destroyed . . . The Germans do not appear to know whence the party came or whither they disappeared.'

Wilson telegraphed back to them: 'Heartiest congratulations on excellent work done. Decision to continue your work approved. Greetings from and to all.'

'The measure of relief brought . . . by that brief signal is difficult to imagine', Wilson would remark of Haugland's short radio message. 'The news was flashed to the War Cabinet, the Chiefs of Staff and other interested circles . . .'

In a 10 March memo marked 'Most Secret and Urgent', Wilson

reported that 'Information has been received today . . . that the high-concentration plant was completely destroyed . . . I have spoken to Professor Tronstad, who confirms complete destruction would effectively prevent further production of the liquid for a considerable period.'

Churchill read the message to his War Cabinet. Cigar smoke danced in the shadows as those figures gathered around the giant table received his words in absolute silence. For a rare and glorious moment they dared to contemplate some of the most momentous news of the war so far – and not all had gone well for the Allies. Hopefully, Hitler's nuclear ambitions had just been thwarted.

Tronstad, the brain who had designed and built the heavy water works, believed that they had. He estimated that the SH200 plant would be out of action for eighteen months. Wilson ended his note by pointing out that a number of the saboteurs were heading for Sweden, 'after a snowstorm had effectively wiped out all tracks connecting them to Vemork'.

It was an entirely positive report, pointing to success on all levels. But still Wilson fretted about those of his saboteurs who had chosen to remain on the Vidda. 'I worried about them. The audacity of the raid on Vemork must have infuriated the enemy.'

Wilson was right to be worried. Haugland contacted him again, and the tenor of his radio message was much changed. News of Kristiansen's Uvdal chocolate bungle and its consequences had reached their ears.

'Dropping place . . . occupied by Germans. Gunnerside met a reindeer hunter after dropping who was kept under guard . . . He promised to keep his mouth shut and was given money and food. Everything points to his having notified . . . the Germans.'

Both the Gunnerside drop zone and the Lake Skrykken Cabin had been overrun by the enemy, and the hunt was very much on. In light of this, the four saboteurs collapsed their base at the Cousin's Cabin, hid their communications gear in snow caves, and packed up their tents, sleeping bags, food and weaponry. Then they melted into the wasteland of the high Vidda, terrain where no right-minded individual would ever dare to venture.

Camped on the highest peaks amidst the freezing snow and ice fields, they watched as the German patrols flooded in below – obliterating ski tracks they should have followed, shooting at each other by mistake, torching cabins and bombing them from the air, blundering into treacherous terrain, and generally trying to conquer the Vidda.

In attempting to beat the Barren Mountain plateau, the German forces attracted only its very worst predations: their patrols were plagued by frostbite, blood poisoning, starvation, drownings and exhaustion.

But one of the Gunnerside party knew nothing of the massive *Razzia* sweeping the Hardangervidda. That man was trouble-seeker-cum-escape artist Claus Helberg. Post-Gunnerside, and after linking up with Poulsson, Helberg had gone to ground in Oslo, losing himself in the welcoming anonymity of the city. Now, he was drawn back to the Hardangervidda, for there was work to be done.

Alone, Helberg skied for the Lake Skrykken hut: there were arms and food still buried in the cache there. In doing so, he was unwittingly heading into the epicentre of *Aktion Adler* – Operation Eagle.

Helberg had spent months living on the Vidda, and he felt glad to have left the crowded confines of Oslo and to be moving into its wild embrace again. He'd been skiing for some fifty kilometres when the Lake Skrykken cabin hove into view. He decided to rest and recuperate there, before paying a visit to the cache. The first signs of trouble were the unlocked door and the wreckage that lay inside. Tables and chair had been upturned, mattresses slashed open, and the contents of cupboards and drawers emptied onto the floor.

For a moment Helberg felt stunned. The Hardangervidda was *their* territory. This was the raiders' sanctuary. Never once during his time here had the hated occupiers even been close. But clearly the enemy had been to the cabin, and recently. A worrying thought struck Helberg: maybe they were still here, lurking somewhere nearby? Maybe they were waiting to pounce?

He hurried to the door, running his gaze across the snowy wastes outside. Sure enough, several hundred metres away a group of figures could be seen. There were five of them, grey-uniformed and armed, and they were skiing fast in Helberg's direction. Armed with only his Colt .45 pistol, Helberg could hardly put up a fight.

As he threw on his skis, not for the first time he regretted leaving his tommy gun behind at Vemork. He'd done so in an effort to prevent local reprisals; to leave a quintessentially British commando signature behind. But as he set off, Helberg wondered if it was about to cost him his life.

It was late afternoon and he set a course due west, into the low sun, which should dazzle his pursuers' eyes, making him a less easy target. From behind he heard the staccato bark of rifle fire. Bullets snarled past, kicking up angry plumes in the snow.

For a moment Helberg figured he was dead, and he gave thanks at least that he had played his part in destroying the SH200 plant. But as he zigzagged across the snow, the Germans couldn't seem to get their shots on target. Finally, the gunfire petered out. In the silence that followed, Helberg felt certain they were coming after him.

One glance behind proved him right. He turned back to the way ahead – his only route to safety. It was a mass of unmarked, virgin snow. Presumably the Germans had fresh legs, whereas he had been on the go since early morning. Picking a route through the contours to maximize his speed and advantage, he set to his task.

As he weaved his way through wind-sculpted drifts and past ice-encrusted cliffs, in the back of Helberg's mind were thoughts of the suicide capsule still secreted in his pocket. The very worst would be for his pursuers to score a lucky hit, disabling him with a shot from one of their rifles in such a way that he would be prevented from killing himself. The fear of being taken alive drove him onwards.

An hour into this life-or-death race three of his pursuers began to falter. One by one they gave up the chase. But two remained and they seemed to keep pace with him, matching ski stroke for ski stroke. Across hills, ridges and sweeping valleys they followed in his tracks. Helberg realized his greatest disadvantage now: he was beating a path of flattened, firmer snow for them to follow.

For sixteen kilometres they pushed onwards, Helberg and his two hunters neck and neck. Then one of them must have suffered a debilitating cramp. One moment he was there, skiing power-fully after him; the next he was gone. It was one-on-one now. A manhunt.

'He was fresher than me,' Helberg would remark, 'and a good skier, too. So the race went on for another hour, maybe two . . .'

For all that time the distance between the two barely wavered. One moment Helberg would increase his lead on the German; the next that lead would be cut. Eventually Helberg realized that his pursuer could briefly close the gap whenever they descended a slope, but Helberg seemed to regain much of his lead as they climbed hills or ridges. The German was far fresher, of course; indeed, Helberg felt on the verge of exhaustion. But it was clearly a question of technique.

Helberg sought out the highest ground possible, so as to establish a more commanding lead. He scaled ridge after ridge, and sure enough he started inching away from his pursuer. But then he crested a final rise, to discover that only descent beckoned. It was all downhill for a good way now.

'I started down, pushing off with all my strength,' Helberg recalled, 'trying to use every twist or turn to my advantage, but after about a quarter of an hour I could hear his skis and poles behind me. He got closer and yelled "Hands up!" in German.'

Helberg came to a halt, drew his Colt .45 and spun around. The German stopped and stiffened in surprise. He clearly hadn't expected the man he was hunting to be armed. In his own hand he gripped a Luger, the iconic German pistol. Forty metres separated the two men; the German's intent had clearly been to take Helberg alive. Now he knew he faced a duel, with himself set on higher ground.

In fact the terrain favoured Helberg. He had the setting sun to his back, so right in the German's eyes. It would be glinting off the snow and ice, doubly blinding the enemy. For an instant the two adversaries hesitated, each wondering what the other might do. And then Helberg fired. It was a single shot, well aimed, but at such range he knew he had little chance of hitting the man.

The shot was a provocation, designed to infuriate and instil fear.

It did both. Summoned to fight, the German opened up with his Luger. As Helberg's stomach knotted with tension, the first bullet tore past him. A second whipped by his head. The German fired again and again, two more bullets missing their mark by bare inches. Helberg tried to comfort himself with the thought that the German would be as breathless as he was, weak with fatigue, and with sweat running into his eyes. But even so, being under fire at close range like this felt terrifying.

Should he try to move? Dodge the man's aim? Before he could decide the German fired again. The fifth bullet tore a path through the air to the side of Helberg's arm. Had he moved, it might well have got him. Helberg's finger itched to pull the Colt's trigger, but he forced himself to hold his fire. He knew that whoever had bullets left after this duel would win. But it took a superhuman effort of will to stand and take the fire, even as his adversary unleashed two more rounds.

The German fired his last shot. It buzzed past Helberg's head, close enough for him to feel the hot breath of its passing, then struck a rock to the rear, ricocheting with a loud ping. Did the German try to pull his trigger again, only to realize he was out of ammo? Helberg wasn't sure. But the look on the man's face spoke volumes. All of a sudden the roles were reversed. The hunter had become the hunted, and he had only one way to flee – uphill.

The German turned and fled. If he could reach the crest of the hill without Helberg catching him he would be free. He knew it and the knowledge seemed to lend him wings. But Helberg was faster. He was following in the German's tracks now, where he had beaten down the snow. Helberg kept telling himself that he was the better man uphill; he had to get near enough to make his shots count.

The gap kept closing. The sun was setting red on the distant horizon, illuminating the enemy soldier perfectly. The German knew he was losing the race, which made him ever more frantic, and thus less effective over the steep ground. Finally Helberg caught the man just before he reached the summit.

Aiming at the middle of his back – the target that gave most room for error – he fired, repeatedly. 'He began to stagger and finally stopped,' Helberg recalled, 'hanging over his ski sticks like a man on crutches. I turned around and pushed on, to get away before the others came. The sun was setting. It would soon be dark. I was safe, at least for the time being.'

Helberg knew the hunt wasn't over. The four surviving German soldiers would have kept following their comrade's ski tracks. Those would lead them to Helberg's, and they could track him even through the darkness. He must have skied a good eighty kilometres or more, and he was on the verge of collapse. He needed terrain in which to lose his pursuers.

He headed for a nearby lake, Vrajoen. There he could ski across the ice, leaving no trace. The night was clear and still but there was no moon. Perfect for hiding; not so good for navigation. In the thick darkness, Helberg skied over an unseen cliff. One moment he was gliding across firm ground; the next, airborne. He fell for several metres, landing in an agonized heap and rolling further downhill.

When he finally came to a halt he lay in the snow, waiting for the pain. It hit first in his right shoulder, stabbing down the entire length of his arm. A bone had to be broken. When he tried to move that arm, nothing seemed to work properly. He tried to assess his situation dispassionately. He was alone, injured and armed with only a pistol. He could not defend himself against the four who remained of the hunter patrol, or any others that he might encounter. He needed help, and fast. Most of all, he needed a doctor.

He clambered to his feet, relieved that his legs still seemed to work, as did his skis. If he went carefully, he could manage – just – with one ski pole.

Injured and alone, he set out into the darkness.

Chapter Thirty

Helberg marvelled at the utter impossibility of it all. Here he was enjoying a fine dinner of fried trout in the dining room of the Bandak Tourist Hotel, in the town of Dalen, with *Reichskommissar* Josef Terboven and General Rediess occupying adjacent tables, set against the roaring fire. They were so close that he could listen in on their conversation.

The *Reichskommissar* and the SS general had demanded that two pretty Norwegian girls join them for dinner. One, Åse Hassel, had cold, defiant eyes – at least when she addressed the Germans. She told them to their face that her father was in England, serving as a colonel in the Royal Norwegian Army. And when they suggested she might like to come to their rooms for a nightcap, she laughed in their faces with scorn.

Rediess and Terboven reddened with rage. As for Helberg, he could barely hide the admiration he felt for her barefaced defiance. His journey to this place and moment had been vintage Helberg. Cradling his injured arm he'd managed to ski his way off the Vidda, eventually running into a German patrol. Acting on instinct, he'd told the commander that he had been helping in the *razzia*, serving as a guide to a German search unit. He'd got injured in the hunt.

Helberg was a consummate bluffer; he could be incredibly persuasive and the German sergeant had believed every word.

He'd sent Helberg into the local town to be treated by a military doctor. Helberg had got his shoulder bandaged, whereupon he was scheduled for evacuation to Oslo for further treatment. A boat was leaving Dalen for Oslo in the morning, and Helberg was booked on it. He'd been billeted overnight at this hotel, only to discover that the two German commanders had decided to base themselves here too.

So it was that he came to be dining alongside the SS general and the *Reichskommissar*, who were even now involved in the hunt for the Vemork saboteurs, of whom Helberg was arguably the leading light. So much had been achieved by bluff, cheek and chutzpah, and once he reached Oslo Helberg intended to lose himself in the city, as he had done many times before. But Ase Hassel's spirited defiance was about to bring all of his plans to a sudden and unexpected end.

Later that night the hotel's Norwegian residents were rounded up and told they were being sent to Grini concentration camp, for questioning. They had insulted the *Reichskommissar* and this was their punishment. At gunpoint they were herded aboard a bus. Helberg knew that once they got to Grini, the game would be up. When fighting against the German invaders he had been taken as a prisoner of war, and they would have records. The Gestapo would use all possible means to establish exactly what an escaped prisoner of war like him had been doing during the three intervening years.

Helberg took a seat at the rear of the bus, which was flanked at either end by motorcycle outriders. By chance he was close to Ase Hassel, the young Norwegian woman who had so defied Ter-boven. He fell into conversation with her, explaining in whispers that he had specific and urgent reasons to get away. With a wink and a nudge she signalled her willingness to help.

They began talking in a loud and gregarious manner, laughing and joking all the way. Everyone else was silent and grim-faced, wondering what fate might hold in store. Naturally, Helberg and Hassel became the centre of attention. The German guard sitting at the front of the bus was clearly irritated. He marched to the rear, looming over them, his face dark with anger.

'What are you two up to?' he barked.

Ase Hassel frowned. 'Up to? What on earth do you mean, up to? We're talking, that's all.'

She'd spoken in the fine, fluent German that the soldier had been taught to respect. It was far more educated than his own.

'Are we not allowed to talk?' she added.

The German guard was lost for words. He stomped back to his seat at the front. Ase Hassel cracked a joke in Norwegian about her confrontation with Terboven over dinner, and a ripple of laughter ran around the bus, which only served to stoke the guard's rage.

In a moment he was back again. 'Move! Up to the front,' he barked at Helberg. 'From now on I sit here.'

Helberg slung his rucksack over his shoulder and moved to the front. It was an ancient-looking bus, with a door operated by a hand lever. He was now seated next to the handle. Ahead, the motorcycles ploughed through the pre-dawn darkness, keeping a constant twenty metres' distance. Helberg knew the rear riders would be doing the same. He would need to choose his moment carefully.

The driver slowed to negotiate a steep hill. Dark forest crowded in from either side. Helberg tensed, said a quick prayer for Ase Hassel, yanked the lever backwards and jumped. There were yells in the darkness and the squeal of brakes as Helberg got to his feet and ran. He had a short patch of open ground to cross before he reached the cover of the beckoning forest.

Bullets tore after him. He dodged to right and left to distract the shooters' aim, his legs pumping as he darted from one patch of cover to another. He was just at the fringes of the woodland when a grenade thumped into his back. He dived for the trees, tensing for the blast that should rip him limb from limb. But nothing happened. The grenade was either a dud or the German soldier had forgotten to pull the pin.

As Helberg rose to his feet and sprinted onwards, further grenades were hurled into the forest, but they exploded harmlessly to his rear. Moments later he was deep into the woods, and the sounds of pursuit faded away. He stopped for a moment to check if he was hurt. He'd been running on fear and adrenalin, which blinded him to any injuries. Miraculously he seemed to be unscathed.

Helberg had no weapon, no food and no skis. He had to get away before the bus reached Grini and a search party was sent out to track him down. He trekked through the snow. By chance he knew of the house of a loyal farmer not so far away. He headed in that direction, the ache in his shoulder and arm growing more intense the whole time. He'd tried to land on his good side, but he'd rolled hard, compounding his recent injury.

He needed help, shelter, sanctuary and medical treatment, and all as soon as possible. There happened to be an asylum for the insane situated a short drive away. From the farmer's house Helberg was smuggled to the asylum, riding in an ambulance. By that day's end he had been 'committed' – locked in a padded cell, with a sign outside declaring Helberg to be a 'DANGEROUS LUNATIC.'

He recuperated in the asylum. Once his shoulder was healed, Helberg smuggled himself cross-country to the Swedish border. He would remark of his reception there: 'When I reached Stockholm with four of my proverbial nine lives squandered – the parachute drop, the ski chase, the crash over the cliff, the jump from the bus – I was still pretty shaken. Then I just relaxed. Everything was so pleasant.'

From Sweden, Helberg was flown back to Britain. Wilson had received reports that Helberg had been shot, so it was as if he had come back from the dead. He would write of the man the following tribute: 'Helberg was, from all points of view, one of the key members of the sabotage party.' His subsequent escape from the enemy was, 'an epic of cool-headedness, bravery and resource'.

By now, all of the Gunnerside saboteurs had been accounted for. Ronneberg and his party had completed a marathon, eighteen-day ski to the Swedish border and escaped the German *Razzia* unscathed. And the four stay-behinds – Bonzo Haukelid, Kjelstrup, Haugland and Einar Skinnarland – were still hiding out on the Vidda, dodging the *Razzia*, and keeping watch over Vemork.

Ronneberg and team had reached London in late March. Based upon their accounts of their actions, Wilson penned a detailed report entitled: 'Attack on Heavy Water Installation'. That report was sent to Churchill, amongst others. Britain's wartime leader read its contents, responding in a personal minute to the chief of the SOE with a simple, yet telling query: 'What rewards are to be given to these heroic men?'

Wilson drew up the recommendations. His citations, running to half a dozen pages, proposed awards of two Distinguished

Service Orders (DSO), three Military Crosses (MC), and four Military Medals (MM), amongst other honours for the Gunnerside team. But more than that, the citations reflected how intimately Wilson understood each of the men who were involved in the mission, and how well he appreciated their strengths and qualities.

Wilson lauded Ronneberg's 'courage, coolness, ability and leadership'; Poulsson's 'spirit of resistance which is beyond all praise'; Haugland's 'first class' radio work and 'coolness' while 'exposed to danger from the elements and the enemy'; Helberg's fantastic 'final reconnaissance of the Works'; plus Bonzo Haukelid's 'considerable self-control as well as military skill'.

Churchill's response to Wilson's recommendations was a one-word, hand-written imprimatur: 'Good.' The honours had been approved. As the great man's assistant explained in a written note to Wilson, the lengthy citations comprised 'A wonderful story [but] I do not think that the Prime Minister has time to read more about this operation, though he would greatly enjoy it.'

Operation Gunnerside had scored a double success: for now at least it had put an end to the German ability to manufacture SH200, as well as destroying the Nazis' existing stocks of heavy water – or at least those then stored at Vemork. But in the late spring of 1943 – and even as the fortunes of the war began to turn in the Allies' favour – Churchill remained troubled by Germany's nuclear capabilities.

Churchill and Roosevelt were chiefly worried about what the *Uranverein* – the German nuclear club – might have achieved *prior* to Gunnerside's success. Facing a series of defeats in North Africa and on the Eastern Front, Hitler and his cronies were increasingly desperate for a weapon to rebalance the conflict, and there were worrying reports that they were poised to get it.

One Allied intelligence bulletin cited widespread rumours in Germany of 'a new-fangled bomb. Twelve such bombs, designed on the principle of demolishing atoms, are supposedly enough to destroy a city of millions'. At the same time the German intelligence services had established beyond doubt that the Manhattan Project was pursuing its own route towards an Allied atom bomb. The nuclear race was raw and real, and whoever won it would vanquish the other.

Allied reconnaissance flights had picked up tantalizing evidence of the building of launch sites for an unknown weapon, pointing at Britain. These were, of course, the V1 ramps constructed in Germany and across occupied Europe, so that the *Vergeltung* flying bombs could start raining down onto British homes. How difficult would it be to fit such weapons with a crude nuclear or radiological warhead?

From a detailed report produced in the US, Roosevelt and Churchill knew of the threat that a working Nazi heavy water reactor posed: short-term it would produce 'colossal amounts' of radioactive material. Dropped over a city centre, radiological bombs could enable the Germans to 'completely incapacitate' entire urban centres. London would be evacuated; Washington reduced to a ghost town.

'Germany is contemplating using this weapon against Britain, in the near future,' the Americans warned. The threat was especially real, 'if Germany thought herself faced with the possibility of defeat . . .' Reports described how 'fission products would be spread over an area by discharge from an aircraft . . . against thickly populated areas, either indiscriminately as a terror weapon, or over selected targets such as dock areas or factory districts.'

In an urgent and 'Most Secret' telegram, Stephenson's New York SOE headquarters alerted London's Tube Alloys about defensive measures that should be taken. 'In view of possible use of radioactive products as weapon it is desirable that manufacture of adequate number of detectors should be taken in hand ... Instructions for use of detectors and for steps to be taken in various degrees of contamination should be formulated, in readiness for future action.'

In America General Groves met with Roosevelt to brief him on the status of the Manhattan Project, but Roosevelt also wanted to know where the Germans were in the race for the nuclear prize. Groves's answer, as always, was direct and to the point. The *Uranverein* were 'doing serious work on this before we were ... they might still therefore be ahead of us.'

Groves knew about the success of Operation Gunnerside. However, he wasn't sure that the British saboteurs had gone far enough: the Vemork plant hadn't been totally destroyed. Roosevelt made it clear that whatever measures could be taken to sabotage the Nazi nuclear effort would get his blessing. Groves was about to be gifted the perfect target, as Nazi scientists arrived at Vemork, tasked to get the SH200 plant up and running again, and on a massively more ambitious scale.

According to Allied intelligence reports, plans were in place to raise productivity at Vemork to 500 times what it had been prior to the Gunnerside attack, using I.G. Farben personnel and technology to rebuild the plant. Knowing of I.G. Farben's reach and expertise, Groves found such reports highly credible, not to mention alarming. He'd got Roosevelt's blessing, and decisive action would have to be taken.

In London in that summer of 1943, Churchill screened a cine reel captured from the Germans. It showed the atrocities inflicted on the Jews and other victims of the Reich in the occupied territories, revealing a catalogue of dark horrors. Churchill was visibly moved. He ordered the film to be screened to all US servicemen arriving in Britain; they were to be told that this was what they were fighting for – to free Europe from such unimaginable evil.

Churchill wrote to Roosevelt, urging that more be done to assist those fleeing Nazi persecution. 'Our immediate facilities for helping the victims of Hitler's anti-Jewish drive are so limited that surely the ability of removing some to safety is all the more incumbent upon us.' Roosevelt concurred.

Churchill would go on to call the Holocaust 'the greatest and most horrible crime ever committed in the whole history of the world'. But allowing the Reich to build a nuclear arsenal would doubtless facilitate an even greater one. Heaven knows what the architect of such evil would be capable of with an atomic or radiological weapon to hand. Every effort had to be made to stop Hitler.

Wilson, too, was feeling the heat. In one August 1943 memo to him marked 'Personal and Most Secret', concern was raised over 'several reports about the German secret weapon . . . which will do everything required of it to win the war . . . The date of availability of the secret weapon was stated . . . to be November.' This 'secret weapon' had the full backing of Goebbels, amongst other top Nazis, and SH200 production was vital to its completion.

Clearly, Vemork needed to be kept out of action. Any attempt to resuscitate heavy water production had to be prevented. But at the same time Wilson feared a general panic amongst the British public. A 24 June article in the *Daily Express* talked of the

Vemork laboratories in which 'the Germans are experimenting with the so-called "heavy water bomb" intended to surpass all explosives hitherto known.'

Wilson declared himself unconcerned 'with the security aspect' of such press reporting. What worried him was the British media revealing 'matters which could so easily cause considerable alarm and even despondency amongst a section of the community'. The prospect of a Nazi atomic attack was too frightening for most of the public to contemplate. Wilson remained convinced that the best – the quietest – way to deal with the threat was by using his team of stay-behinds.

Those men hiding out on the Hardangervidda were watching Vemork, and they awaited his call to arms.

Chapter Thirty-One

Life on the Vidda remained harsh. Of the Vemork saboteurs who had stayed behind, only two, Bonzo Haukelid and Einar Skinnarland, remained. The others had been driven away by the weather, starvation, the German *Razzia*, or had returned to Britain for further specialist training.

It was 14 February 1944 when Haukelid skied towards Rjukan, at Wilson's behest and on a top-priority mission. Much had happened over the intervening months since Operation Gunnerside had scored such signal success. Niels Bohr had finally seen the light, and not a moment too soon. In the summer of 1943 the Nazi regime had finally shown its true colours in Denmark: Jews and other enemies of the Reich were rounded up and carted off to the concentration camps.

No longer could Niels Bohr – the grandfather of atomic physics – bury his head in the proverbial sand. He had been wrong about the Nazis and Hitler; they were far from being a benign presence in Denmark. In September 1943, just before the Gestapo came for him, Bohr fled Copenhagen for neighbouring Sweden.

When he reached Stockholm he appealed to Princess Ingeborg, the sister to the Danish King Christian, to save Denmark's Jews by making a royal appeal to the German leader's 'better instincts'. Secretly, Princess Ingeborg was part of Stephenson's spy network, and she was a tough and plain-speaking woman.

'You are out of touch with reality,' she told Bohr, bluntly. 'You lived in the Third Reich, but you never understood it.'

Bohr tried to protest. 'But surely an appeal to Hitler—'

Princess Ingeborg rounded on him. 'Dear God! An appeal to Hitler is an appeal to the Devil himself. If we draw attention to those Jews, Hitler could kill every one of them . . . Your laboratory has been a fool's paradise.'

The Princess's words cut through the fog of Bohr's delusions. Seeing the Nazi regime for what it was, he agreed that the only course of action left open to him was to travel to Britain and join forces with the Allies. In spite of his naivety and his misguided loyalties, he was wanted on the Manhattan Project badly. If Bohr would cooperate, he could help win the nuclear race for the Allies.

The Allies' need for Bohr was too urgent to countenance a lengthy sea voyage. So it was that a Mosquito aircraft took off from RAF Tempsford – Gibraltar Farm – scheduled for a midnight rendezvous with the Danish scientist on a remote and deserted Swedish airstrip. The Mosquitoes executing the moon flights had been converted so that the bomb bay could carry one passenger, slotted in and breathing on oxygen.

'SOE had priority as far as the allotment of seats . . . was concerned,' Wilson remarked, of these flights. 'It was possible to send in a limited number of men to make their way into Eastern Norway, and more important, to bring out many . . . such as Professor Niels Bohr, the nuclear physicist, travelling in the bomb rack.'

Bohr almost didn't survive the nerve-racking journey.

On a deserted airstrip the wooden-framed aircraft awaited, its engines still turning. From the bowels of the Mosquito had climbed a mysterious young woman, an SOE agent on a secret assignment. She briefed the Danish scientist hurriedly, leaving little to the imagination: he would be isolated from the Mosquito's aircrew for the duration of the return journey to Britain, and if the unarmed aircraft were attacked he could expect little help.

If he were wounded, there were morphine and medicines packed into a small, hand-held kit. He would need to medicate himself and to hang on until arrival in Britain. The converted bomb bay would allow little room to move. If the plane went down in the icy waters of the North Sea he would be trapped, but at least, like the aircrew, his suffering would be short, before death from exposure.

Her briefing delivered, the young woman peeled off her snow-suit – designed to keep a human warm at high altitude – and handed it to the world's pre-eminent nuclear physicist. It was 7 October 1943, and Bohr had just turned fifty-eight. Taking her helmet and mask – still warm from her body heat – he clambered into the dark and constricting hold. Moments later the bomb doors hissed closed, the twin Rolls-Royce Merlin engines snarled and Bohr was whisked into the dark skies.

As they climbed to altitude the pilot checked the airflow to his mystery passenger, but the dial was stuck stubbornly on zero. Either it was faulty, or the man in the hold wasn't breathing any oxygen. The Mosquito's only protection against enemy fighters was speed and altitude, but if his passenger wasn't getting any oxygen and they remained at this height, he would die.

The pilot had no option but to push his nose downwards and dive towards the sea. He recalculated his route. If he turned further north he had just enough fuel to make Scotland at full speed. Probably. He would need to juggle throttle and speed with the remaning fuel supplies, to nurse them into an airfield like Wick.

When the Mosquito finally touched down it was sipping on fumes. An ambulance tore across the tarmac. The bomb bay whispered open to reveal an unconscious Niels Bohr. Waiting on the runway was Stephenson himself. Bohr had a weak pulse, but at least he was alive. Somehow, the oxygen supply had failed.

In due course Bohr was nursed back to good health. Some days later he was in London, being visited by the great and the good of the British nuclear initiative.

'Professor Bohr was a gentle soul,' Stephenson remarked. 'He genuinely believed in Gandhi's philosophy of opposing evil with humility, of resisting violence with intellectual weapons. He had to come out of Nazi surroundings to comprehend the scale of the wickedness we were dealing with.'

A few days later Bohr met Churchill. He was bombarded with queries about Hitler's plans to shower London with thousands of *Vergeltung* (vengeance) weapons. Could an atomic or radiological warhead be fitted to such rocketry, as the Allies feared? Had the Nazis mastered such technology? Bohr couldn't answer. Ensconced within the ivory tower of his Copenhagen laboratory, he hadn't even known about the Third Reich's development of the V1 and V2 technologies. Yet here in Britain expert teams equipped with radiation detectors were set to deploy on the city streets, in case the *Vergeltung* weapons rained down such an apocalypse.

Churchill did little to hide his frustration. He scolded Bohr's passive and unwitting collaboration with the enemy, not to mention his wilful ignorance about the true nature of Hitler's ideology. He had been cosseted and stroked by the Nazis, and he had chosen to believe in their hollow words and flattery. Bohr was told that he was needed in the US as soon as possible to help perfect the Allied bomb.

'We cannot fight one barbarism with another barbarism,' he objected.

'We won't survive to fight for anything if we neglect this new weapon,' came the counter-argument. 'The freedom to behave in a civilised manner must be defended, and sometimes that means using violence.'

Bohr was persuaded to fly to America. He would go there to work on the Manhattan Project under an assumed identity – travelling as a 'Mr Baker'. Reluctantly, and after a long campaign to enlighten him, Bohr had become another of the Baker Street Irregulars.

As Bohr flew west to the USA, so a US Air Force armada thundered eastwards, darkening Norway's skies. It was 16 November 1943, and in the nine months since Operation Gunnerside the Germans had moved heaven and earth to get the SH200 production up and running again. Their success in doing so, and the transformation of the Vemork works into an utterly impregnable fortress, had convinced the Allies that only an air raid could stop them now.

General Groves had got his way, and a USAAF bombing raid was put into operation. The armada of 460 bombers – Flying Fortresses and Liberators – included some executing diversionary raids, while the main body headed for Vemork. At around 11.30 a.m. – when most of the workers should have broken for lunch, thus lowering the risk of casualties – the lead aircraft opened their bomb doors. Over the next thirty minutes hundreds of 500-pound bombs fell in and around Vemork.

Direct hits were scored on the railway along which the Gunnerside force had made their clandestine approach, on the pipelines snaking down the mountainside, and on the suspension bridge that spanned the gorge. Four bombs struck the heavy water building itself, but with the SH200 plant secreted in the basement, they did little or no damage to the key infrastructure. The all-important high-concentration cells were not even touched.

Due to a navigational error, dozens of bombs were dropped on the fertilizer plant at Rjukan. In total, twenty-two civilians were killed in the air raid, which enraged the Norwegian government in exile. They had not been informed that an air attack was scheduled to take place. They complained that the raid was 'out of all proportion to the objective sought', especially as not a single drop of SH200 had been destroyed.

With Haugland having left the Hardangervidda, Einar Skinnarland remained Wilson's sole communications link on the ground. In contrast to his own government's bitter complaints, Skinnarland sounded a positive note on the USAAF raid: 'Great enthusiasm for the results of the attack and for the accuracy . . . All pipelines for about 100 metres . . . badly damaged . . . Suspension bridge fell down and the gas pipes and electric cable to Rjukan are broken . . .'

Certainly, the USAAF attack did achieve one concrete result in the battle to defeat the Nazi bomb: it convinced the Germans that continued attempts at SH200 production in Norway were futile. They didn't possess the fighter aircraft to defend the Vemork plant should a second and more accurate bombing raid be launched. Thus the decision was taken to remove both the SH200 stocks and the means to produce them to the comparative safety of the Fatherland.

Skinnarland alerted London to the Nazis' intentions. Wilson read his message with growing unease.

Recently, the Allies had secured air reconnaissance photos of the Haigerloch-Hechigen area of southern Germany. These revealed that structures were under construction that had all the appearances of nuclear reactors. With Berlin increasingly being targeted by Allied bombing raids, this was the area into which the *Uranverein* were known to have retreated with their precious uranium pile.

In their intelligence assessments the Allies were working on the assumption that the Germans had a 100-kilowatt reactor up and running, which would produce enough 'fission products' to 'manufacture 4–8 bombs in a year'. The fear was that the Reich would either develop a fully fledged nuclear arsenal, or in desperation strike quickly by showering its enemies with some kind of radioactive warhead. The race for nuclear supremacy had become a brutal 'war of nerves', in which both sides were largely in the dark regarding the other's capabilities.

'One or more research institutes have been set up in the neighbourhood of Hechigen . . .' Allied intelligence reports concluded. 'Heisenberg is known to be working there . . . Information has also been received that Hechigen and the neighbourhood district are "prohibited areas" under military control . . . Heisenberg was in charge of experimental work on the production of a U.235 bomb . . . he was stated to have half a tonne of heavy water, and to be due to receive a further tonne.'

If Vemork's SH200 could be married up to the *Uranverein*'s new Haigerloch-Hechigen facilities, it could prove disastrous. At all costs, its shipment to Germany had to be stopped. Hence Knut 'Bonzo' Haukelid's February 1944 foray into Rjukan – a lone figure moving south on skis, and with sabotage in mind.

Haukelid remained the only fully trained SOE agent in the

region who was in a position to act – a reluctant Einar Skinnarland being charged with maintaining the all-important radio communications link with London. But from the very start Haukelid had questioned the merits of mounting any fresh sabotage attempt.

After Gunnerside, all the windows and doors into the SH200 plant had been bricked up, leaving just the one entranceway, which was heavily guarded at all times. A battalion of commandos would have trouble fighting their way in there, and Haukelid was alone – apart from a handful of locals recruited at short notice.

He had other reasons to feel daunted and dispirited: this war had cost him dearly. Recently he'd received a letter from his young wife, Bodil, asking for a divorce. Their wedding earlier in the war had been a rushed affair, after which Haukelid had disappeared to fight. Bodil was in Sweden and too much time and distance lay between them. She was seeing another man, she told him. Haukelid had given so much to the struggle. He'd fought for survival for eighteen months on the Vidda. His mother had been arrested, and his father was still in Gestapo custody facing untold horrors. His friends had been tortured and killed.

And now this: his wife of a few short years was leaving him.

Haukelid's mood was dark. On Gunnerside, he'd been part of a well-trained, well-armed, ultra professional outfit. Now he was alone, apart from one or two local resistance men, and the Germans were on the very highest state of alert. He rated his chances of survival at about zero, and either way he was sure to have the blood of locals on his hands, for the Germans were bound to react with untold savagery.

He'd radioed such misgivings to Wilson. Even if the SH200

stocks could somehow be destroyed, which he very much doubted, the risk of local reprisals was too great. The residents of Rjukan had been warned that if there were to be another sabotage attempt, they would reap the whirlwind. As Haukelid made clear, he did not want to be the author of that storm.

Wilson was under intense pressure from Churchill and Roosevelt; the British prime minister had made it clear that the SH200 shipment had to be stopped, and at all costs. His response to Haukelid was uncompromising, and it brooked no dissent. 'Case considered. Very urgent that heavy water be destroyed. Hope this can be done without too serious consequences. Send our best wishes for good luck in the work. Greetings.'

Despite Haukelid's clear misgivings, Wilson kept the faith. He reckoned that one such man in the Vidda was worth a hundred regular soldiers elsewhere. Somehow, Haukelid would find a way.

For his part, Haukelid had spent long enough in London to grow fond of the great city. He'd been drawn to its unique charms, not to mention the bulldog spirit of its wartime residents during the Blitz. If the Nazis succeeded in building their bomb, nothing the Luftwaffe had ever done to destroy London would equal the cataclysm that would follow. He had no choice but to act.

Using his local contacts at the plant, Haukelid studied how the Germans intended to move the stocks of heavy water. Steel drums were to be loaded aboard railway cars, to be shipped along the railway to Rjukan town and onwards to a ferry. The ferry boat would steam across the nearby Lake Tinnsjo, taking the drums by stages to a seaport, from where they would be shipped onwards to Germany.

At all stages General von Falkenhorst's exhortation – *When you have a chest of jewels like this, you plant yourself on the lid with a weapon in your hand!* – was to be adhered to. A crack unit of German troops would shadow the SH200 shipment every step of the way. Spotter planes would fly searches above the Vidda, keeping eyes out for suspicious movement or ski tracks, and Gestapo agents had flooded Rjukan town.

Even so, Haukelid sought out the enemy's weak point. Eventually he figured he'd found it in the Norsk Hydro ferry, the vessel scheduled to carry the drums of SH200 across Lake Tinnsjo. He reckoned the SF *Hydro* – a flat-bottomed ugly duckling of a boat – was the one chink in the Nazis' armour.

The SF *Hydro* was an ancient-looking, steam-powered vessel with a pair of vertical funnels set amidships. A rail car ferry, she was used primarily to shuttle goods to and from the Vemork and Rjukan works. Launched in 1914, and with a weight just short of 500 tonnes, she was already pushing thirty years old. With parallel tracks laid across her flat deck she could carry a total of twelve rail cars, plus 120 passengers.

Haukelid felt certain that the elite German troops charged to guard the SH200 shipment would do von Falkenhorst's bidding to the letter: they would sit atop the crown jewels – the precious barrels of heavy water – all the way. But paradoxically, that was both their greatest strength and also their greatest weakness.

The day the SH200 barrels were loaded aboard her the SF *Hydro* was sure to be crawling with German troops, but that didn't render her immune to sabotage. Far from it.

He just needed the means to execute the kind of attack that he had in mind.

Chapter Thirty-Two

Bonzo Haukelid stepped onto the streets of Rjukan looking almost like a court jester. He was wearing a borrowed bright blue suit, mirror-shiny dress shoes, and dangling from his arm was a most incongruous object for Rjukan in the tense late February of 1944. The streets were crammed with German troops and Gestapo officers checking ID papers, but Haukelid had what amounted to a free pass through the chaos and suspicion: a violin case.

There was a visiting orchestra in town, which was scheduled to perform an opera that evening. The conductor was the well-known Norwegian composer, Arvid Fladmoe, and the venue was expected to be packed. Rjukan's foremost residents and the Nazi bigwigs would be rubbing shoulders in the audience. Haukelid had decided to pose as one of the musicians, but his violin case was packed with a Sten gun, and he had grenades stuffed into various pockets and bags.

It was a Friday, just two days before the Sunday on which he knew from his source at Vemork that the heavy water was scheduled to be moved. The ferry was still unguarded, but that would all change. He was executing a vital recce mission, for he needed to work out exactly when the SF *Hydro* would be above the deepest part of the lake. If he was to sink her, he wanted to make damn certain the Germans weren't able to salvage her precious cargo.

He caught the train to the docks and boarded the SF *Hydro* as a foot passenger. To any casual observer he was just one more visiting musician taking a sightseeing trip amidst breathtaking scenery. The twin funnels belched black smoke and the SF *Hydro* chugged into motion. On her deck the rail cars were chained down, to prevent them from shifting about during the journey. Haukelid guessed they were loaded with fertilizer, destined for export.

He kept an apparently casual eye on his watch as the ferry steamed out. In truth, he was timing everything to the split second: how long it had taken to load the cargo; how long for the passengers to board; how long to reach the moment of departure, and from there until she neared the deepest spot in the lake, where the depth plunged to over 300 metres. Irretrievably deep, as he liked to remind himself, grimly – both for the cargo, and for the hapless passengers who might happen to be travelling on her that coming Sunday.

Haukelid sweet-talked the chief engineer into giving him a tour of the vessel. All the while he was looking for the best place to plant a bomb, and wrestling with his guilt: his present guide might well be one of his future victims. By the time he was done he was certain of his plan. He'd plant the charges in the bow, enabling the cold lake water to flood in. The bow would sink and the stern would rise, rendering the ship's propellers useless. The SF *Hydro* would be helpless, and she'd plummet to a dark and watery grave.

Yet in a sense Haukelid was still trying to seek the best of both worlds: he wanted to bury the heavy water quick and deep, while allowing enough time for the passengers to escape the stricken vessel. He'd work that out later. He had his timings. Now, to build his bomb.

Haukelid's chief co-conspirator was Rolf Sørlie, Helberg's Rjukan contact who had marked up the map to help guide the Gunnerside assault force in. Sørlie had in turn recruited Knut Lier-Hansen, someone that Haukelid had warmed to right away. A former Norwegian sergeant, craggy-faced Lier-Hansen was almost as much of a daredevil and rebel as Haukelid himself.

With Einar Skinnarland poised over his radio set on the Vidda, Haukelid had his team. Everything depended now on the bomb maker, who was perhaps as unorthodox an explosives man as it was possible to get. A 67-year-old pensioner, Ditlev Diseth had once worked for Norsk Hydro. He now had a clock repair shop, the backroom to which looked like a cross between a mad inventor's workshop and a pawnbroker's: boxes were piled high with cannibalized watches, springs, wires, wireless parts and old clock housings.

Diseth had already been arrested by the Gestapo as a suspected resistance sympathizer, but they hadn't been able to hang anything on the tough and wizened patriot. A good friend of Sørlie's, Diseth had offered a suggestion as to how to blow up the SF *Hydro* at a particular point on Lake Tinnsjo. It was as simple as it was ingenious: they'd sink the ferry using two old-fashioned alarm clocks, with mechanical hammers on top that struck a bell.

With the bells removed, the hammers would still activate once the time for the alarm to sound was reached. If they completed an electrical circuit, the current in turn could ignite detonator caps, which could trigger the explosion. Diseth welded four nine-volt batteries to each alarm clock, to provide the current; when the hammers closed, the circuit would go live and trigger the detonation of the charges.

Diseth's DIY time bombs would be positioned in the *SF Hydro*'s bow. The alarm clocks would be set to go off at the exact time when the ferry reached the deepest part of the lake. From his training with the SOE Haukelid had calculated the weight of explosives – nineteen pounds – required to blow out 121 square feet of the ship's hull. That should sink her in four to five minutes, which should enable the passengers to jump to safety, yet without allowing the captain time to run the SF *Hydro* into shore, so saving her cargo.

It was a little after midnight on the morning of the ferry sailing. As the ice snapped like gunshots beneath his feet, Haukelid felt like some kind of lumbering human bomb. He had a string of Nobel 808 sausages slung around his waist and shoulders, his pockets were stuffed full of detonators, clocks and grenades, and all was hidden beneath a huge and voluminous greatcoat.

There was a hard, frozen crust to the snow as he, Sørlie and Lier-Hansen advanced towards the darkened ferry port. Haukelid led the way, hands swinging free at his sides. They stole through the shadows of Mael harbour, where the terminus of the railway also marked the berthing place of the target for tonight.

Once they were close but still in the cover of some sheds, Haukelid waved them down. In a crouch, they studied the target. The night was deathly still and clear, moonlight edging around high clouds. Incredibly, not a single guard appeared to be in sight.

Before leaving for tonight's mission, the three piratical raiders had paid a visit to the rail yard, just to make sure the SH200 was on the move. They'd crawled to a cliff edge and gazed down upon a floodlit scene. Silhouetted in the harsh light were rail cars piled high with steel barrels, and with several dozen crack German troopers standing guard.

'We'd need the whole of the Linge Company to hit that,' Haukelid had growled. 'There's no option but to blow the ferry. Blast it.'

Haukelid cursed some more. He didn't like what they were about to do. His co-conspirator, Sørlie, had a family friend booked on that Sunday morning's sailing. Or rather, she had been scheduled to take it. The quiet administration of some laxative had convinced her it was not a good idea to travel. But none of them could be sure who exactly would be boarding the SF *Hydro* – friends, relations, fellow townsfolk – prior to her departure.

They'd also received some decidedly ominous warnings. A member of the resistance who spoke fluent German worked at the Rjukan telephone exchange. She'd overheard a conversation between two enemy commanders: Gestapo headquarters had been alerted that 'the most fantastic sabotage' attempt was about to be attempted.

After a life spent hunting in the shadows, Haukelid's instinct for survival was razor sharp. He could sense the tension; the noose tightening. The Germans knew something was in the air. Yet still the SF *Hydro* appeared to be unguarded. Was it a trap, Haukelid wondered? Surely it had to be. The moment they moved out of hiding figures would spring from nowhere. Perhaps they were already under secret observation?

Well, if so, they would go down fighting.

Haukelid rose to his feet. Cat-like, he stalked ahead. Tension pulsed through his temples. The gangplank was but yards away, and still no one had shown themselves. It all seemed too easy. He paused and signalled for the others to join him: pirates, about to walk the gangplank and board her.

With a deep sense of unease three figures flitted up the walkway. They stole aboard, silently crossing the flat deck. Haukelid's attention was drawn to the crew quarters, from where there came the sound of voices and raucous laughter. He crept to the window and peered inside. A card game. Poker. Almost the entire ship's crew, by the looks of things, although surely there would be some manning the engine room.

Haukelid backed away, signalling to the others to follow. They crept down some iron steps to the third-class accommodation on the lower deck. Haukelid searched for the hatch that would give access to the bilges. They needed to drop through that and creep forward to the bow, then plant their time bombs. To have got this far unchallenged still felt too easy.

Suddenly he heard footsteps. Moments later a figure was framed in the light of a thrown-open doorway. Whoever it was must have sensed movement – a human presence – and broken off from the poker game. Haukelid melted into the shadows. He feared very much that the game was up; the trap had been sprung.

A voice called out a challenge. 'Who's there? Is that you, Knut?'

Cool as a cucumber, Knut Lier-Hansen replied: 'Yeah, it's me. With some friends.'

Lier-Hansen had recognized the challenger. It was John Berg, the ship's night watchman; they knew each other from the local sports club. Haukelid and Sørlie stepped out of the shadows so that the watchman could see them. He eyed the three figures, their coats bulging suspiciously. There was a long beat of tension, an unspoken question hanging heavy in the air: *what are you doing sneaking around my ship?*

'The thing is, John, we're expecting a raid,' Lier-Hansen volunteered. 'The Gestapo. Got a few things we need to hide.' He glanced around the ferry. 'It's as simple as that. Any suggestions?'

The watchman brightened. 'No problem. Why didn't you say so? . . .' He knew Lier-Hansen was a member of the local resistance, and it wasn't the first time that he'd been asked to carry arms and even personnel for those secretly fighting the German occupiers. He gave a nod towards the hatch, and jabbed a thumb towards the ship's hold. 'Won't be the first time something's been hidden below.'

It was all the encouragement that Haukelid needed.

As Lier-Hansen kept up the conversation, Haukelid and Sørlie lifted the heavy steel hatch and slid into the cold darkness. Down the iron rungs they went, until the freezing and oily bilge water was up to their knees. Crouched low and with only a torch to guide them, the two pirates crept ahead. They felt their way forward until they reached the bow – a low, cramped area utterly devoid of light.

Without the light, neither man would have been able to see their hand in front of their face. Haukelid glanced at Sørlie. He could see that his fellow pirate was perspiring. Haukelid was too. This was the sweat of fear. They had voluntarily entered a narrow steel coffin, and if German troops arrived right now to secure the ship, they would be trapped.

Dead men.

Sørlie held the torch as Haukelid got to work. First, he pressed the sausages of Nobel 808 against the plates of the hull, at the lowest point that he could reach, to form a circle of the correct circumference. Next, he fixed detonators to either end of the sausages, attaching their free ends to the fuses, and taping those to one of the ship's ribs. That done, he taped the two alarm clocks next to the detonators, set to go off at 10.45 a.m. – the moment Haukelid feared the ship would turn into a tomb.

He was worried about the amount of time this was taking. How long did someone need to hide a few things below decks in such a ship?

'They're still above,' Sørlie whispered, referring to Lier-Hansen and the watchman. 'Knut's talking his head off. It's all right.'

His hands numbed from the cold, his eyes stinging with sweat, the kneeling Haukelid started upon the most dangerous part of the job: setting the timer device live. He connected the wires from the alarm clocks to the detonator caps. If he made one mistake – if his greasy hands slipped, if he knocked one of the clocks and forced it to go off accidentally – he would blow them all to kingdom come.

The job seemed to take for ever. Haukelid's sense of nervous anxiety seemed to blind his mind to how he was to get this done, but at last he was satisfied. He looked up at Sørlie and nodded.

'Thank God,' Sørlie whispered, backing away from the charges.

As quickly as they could the two men retraced their steps to the hatch. Above them, the soft murmur of voices marked where Lier-Hansen was still deep in conversation with the night watchman. Haukelid and Sørlie emerged into the light, smeared in oil and soaked to the skin.

Haukelid offered the watchman a hand to shake, thanking him for being a good and loyal Norwegian. He felt like Judas, but what else was he to do?

'If we had cracked him over the head and carted him ashore . . . his absence would have raised the alarm,' Haukelid noted, 'and the whole operation would have been wrecked. I just had to console myself with the . . . hope that he was a good swimmer.'

The three saboteurs left the ferry just as the shrill whistle of an approaching train cut through the air. Now was the parting of the ways. Sørlie threw on some skis: he was heading into the mountains to rendezvous with Einar Skinnarland. Haukelid would head east by road and train to Oslo, and from there he would take the quickest route to Sweden. And Lier-Hansen would return to his life in Rjukan as if nothing had ever happened.

There were hurried handshakes all round; soon this place would be crawling with German soldiers.

'I'll be back soon,' Haukelid promised.

In the bowels of the SF *Hydro* two clocks ticked away.

Time passed.

With sunrise a steam train chugged into the rail terminus. The entire length of her was bristling with men with guns. Sitting tight, guarding the jewels as instructed. Under watchful eyes, the flatbed rail cars were shunted aboard the SF *Hydro* and lashed down to stop them shifting about once the vessel had set sail.

Not that there was much obvious danger of the ferry's cargo being disturbed today: it was a beautiful, millpond-calm morning. The February waters of Lake Tinnsjo were like a mirror. Ahead of the SF *Hydro*, thick fir woodlands crowded down to the waterline, framing the reflected blue of the sky in shades of rich, dark greens.

With the last of her cargo loaded, this morning's passengers thronged aboard. They included the composer Arvid Fladmoe – a genuine sightseeing musician – plus several dozen local men, women and children. On the ship's bridge Captain Erling

Sorensen prepared to set sail. He'd made this journey hundreds of times before, and this was a perfect morning for such a crossing.

At just after ten o'clock the mooring lines were cast free, and the ferry chugged out, heading east and then almost due south along the thin but crooked finger of the lake. The journey should be no more than twenty-four kilometres, and apart from the heavy German military presence aboard ship all seemed normal.

But below decks the clocks ticked.

Just before 10.45 a.m., Captain Sorensen stepped out of the wheelhouse and began to descend the ladder to the main deck. No sooner had he set foot on the iron steps than a muted roar sounded from the front of his ship. He felt the entire vessel shudder from end to end, as if she had somehow run aground, but the captain knew that this was one of the deepest stretches of the lake.

He turned around and hurried for the bridge. Whatever might have happened, he could see thick smoke billowing out of the bow section.

'Steer for land!' he yelled at the helmsman. 'Make for land!'

It was already too late. As the man at the wheel spun the spokes through his hands, trying to turn the cumbersome ferry ninety degrees to starboard, she began to keel violently. Dragged down by the sheer volume of water gushing into her ruptured hull, she was dropping at the bow, her stern rising alarmingly. Below decks the lights went out. Steam hissed from hot pipes as they made contact with the icy water. Terror-stricken passengers screamed with alarm.

'A bomb! We've been hit by a bomb!'

Sorensen could see already that his vessel was lost. The bow was going under and they were a good 500 metres from the shore.

He gave the order to abandon ship. With the help of his crew he managed to free one of the lifeboats, which plummeted into the waters of the lake. For a moment longer Sorensen himself tried to wrestle with the ship's wheel, but it was pointless.

The SF *Hydro* was doomed.

Sorensen clambered out of the wheelhouse. From the steeply angled deck figures were leaping into the lake. A series of deafening cracks rang out like a volley of cannon fire. The first of the rail cars broke free of its moorings. Sorensen watched in horrified fascination as it slid forwards on the rails, left the end and landed in a huge plume of spray. Further shattering percussions split the air, as ten more rail cars followed suit, breaking free on the keeling deck and rolling overboard.

The bow was completely submerged. The stern rose higher, the ship's screws spinning around uselessly. Sorensen had only seconds to jump, or he would be going down with his vessel. He had no idea if all the passengers and crew had abandoned ship, but tarrying a second longer wouldn't help. He leaped.

Moments later the ferry went down. For a second she almost seemed to stand on her head, before the dark waters claimed her. She was 174 feet in length, but the lake was far deeper; by a factor of eight, in fact. Tinnsjo swallowed the SF *Hydro* and her cargo of seventy barrels of SH200, almost without trace.

The overcrowded lifeboat bobbed about on the calming water. Composer Fladmoe was pulled aboard, along with the sodden violin case that he'd managed to salvage, but women and children were given first priority. To either side figures clung onto the debris – suitcases, packing crates, oars, lifebelts – that floated on the lake's surface. Amongst the flotsam were two steel barrels, which were partially full of heavy water.

From the shore, farmers and villagers launched rowing boats to pluck the survivors from the ice-cold water. Of the fifty-three passengers and crew aboard the ill-fated *SF Hydro*, twenty-seven survived – including the ship's captain and four German soldiers. Their task had proved an impossible one: the heavy steel drums had plummeted hundreds of feet to the dark depths, where no sentries, no matter how dedicated and diligent, could ever hope to safeguard their contents.

It was 11 a.m. in Norway – 10 a.m. in London – as the SF *Hydro* settled into the thick, swirling sediment of the lake bed. Wilson would have to wait until the following day to receive news of the sinking of the ferry, and with it the nuclear dreams of Hitler's Reich. That Monday evening the headlines in the Oslo newspapers declared: 'Railway Ferry Hydro Sunk in the Tinnsjo'.

Haukelid read the news with mixed feelings. He was ensconced in an Oslo safe house, awaiting onward transport to Sweden. 'What would happen now?' he wondered. 'How many Norwegian lives would be lost through this piece of devilry? The explosion on board the ferry must cost lives, and the reprisals at Rjukan certainly no fewer.'

The news reports filtered through to Wilson, but a ferry sent to the bottom didn't necessarily mean that the heavy water had been put beyond the reach of the Nazi regime. For confirmation of that Wilson needed to hear from Grouse One. Einar Skinnarland radioed through verification the following day: 14,485 litres of heavy water, much of which was at 99.5 per cent concentration, had been sent to the bottom of Lake Tinnsjo – rendering it beyond any hope of salvage.

On 24 February 1944 – three days after the sinking – Wilson

telegraphed a brief message to the rump of his team on the Vidda: 'Congratulations on good work.'

A man of few words, Wilson only said what he thought was necessary. He'd pledged to win the heavy water war. The former Scoutmaster and tiger hunter had grabbed the Babu by the horns, put images of Glenalmond firmly at the forefront of his mind, and achieved the seemingly impossible. The sinking of the SF *Hydro* was the final chapter. Using just a handful of SOE agents, Wilson had got the job done, and against all odds.

'So ended the Battle for Heavy Water,' he would remark, one in which, 'the Allies could not afford to take any risks . . . I count myself most fortunate that I was given the opportunity to do what I could for the Allied cause and for the sake of freedom of the individual. Our hopes for a better world . . . who knows what history may say in later years.'

In his own writings on the SF *Hydro* sinking, the then chief of the SOE, Brigadier Colin McVean Gubbins, would say of Haukelid: 'His action was one of the most courageous, successful and complete ever carried out in Norway . . . He foretold . . . precisely what eventually happened, even to within minutes of the explosion.'

William Stephenson – Churchill's spymaster – went even further: 'If it had not been for Haukelid's resolve, the Germans would have had the opportunity to devastate the civilized world. We would be either dead or living under Hitler's zealots.'

Of the Norwegian and wider resistance, Brigadier Gubbins would state: 'No nation has a monopoly on courage . . . This fact both Germans and Japanese overlooked; they expected by execution and torture, by reprisal and concentration camp, to stifle all opposition and bring all peoples to their will, to work for them as slaves. Every oppressed nation gave them the lie.'

In May 1945, Churchill, the man who more than any other had made such resistance possible, sponsored the placing of an article in the media summing up the battle for wartime nuclear supremacy. It was splashed across both the front and back pages of the *Daily Express*, underlining its importance. Headlined 'Secret Army Fought Nazi Atom Bomb', the full text is included in the following pages, but the first two paragraphs pretty much say it all:

> It can be revealed today that for five years British and German scientists fought their own war-within-a-war. They fought to perfect the Atom Bomb, which, with the most explosive force in the world, would have given either side walkover superiority.
>
> But it was no war of theorists only. British and Norwegian paratroopers fought it out, too, with Wehrmacht men and their quisling supporters in the white hell of the storm-swept Hardanger Plateau in Norway.

Some weeks later Churchill made a public announcement summing up the wartime race for nuclear supremacy:

> By God's mercy British and American science outpaced all German efforts . . . The possession of these powers by the Germans at any time might have altered the course of the war . . . In the winter of 1942–43 most gallant attacks were made in Norway . . . by small parties of volunteers from British Commandos and Norwegian forces, at very heavy loss of life, upon stores of what is called "heavy water" . . .

what became known as the 'Robo-Blitz'. The V2 followed three months thereafter. While means were put in place to counter the V1 threat – ground-based anti-aircraft gun batteries, and fast fighter aircraft – no such defences were possible against the V2, which plummeted from the outer limits of Earth's atmosphere at speeds of over 5,000 kph. The only option was to hit the launch sites, but the Germans' response to that was to develop mobile launchers.

The big question to those in the know was whether Hitler had developed the ultimate weapon – a V2 nuke. At the same time the British and Americans worried about the Russians' nuclear ambitions, and how to ensure they seized Nazi Germany's technology and scientists ahead of the Red Army. Indicative of the Russians' ambitions in this field, in the autumn of 1944 they made several approaches to Niels Bohr in an effort to convince him to move to Moscow and carry on his scientific work there.

As British and American forces rolled into occupied Europe, Roosevelt and Churchill were warned of the grave danger of key German nuclear sites and expertise falling into Russian hands. Elite units were formed – the American Alsos Mission and the British Target Force – tasked with moving forward with front-line units to secure, or if necessary destroy and thus remove from Russian reach, German nuclear technology and know-how.

At the same time, the fear of a desperate last-gasp use of nuclear weapons or radiological devices persisted, amidst widespread reports of intense German activity in this field. The Allies were playing a difficult double game: they wanted to deter at all costs the Germans from using such weapons, while ensuring they captured their facilities intact and their experts alive.

On 5 March 1945 the British and Americans realized that

the Germans' Oranienburg uranium-refining facility would very likely fall into Russian hands. Senior commanders ordered a massive USAAF bombing raid to deny it to the Russians. On 15 March 1945 the Oranienburg plant was obliterated.

Churchill made it clear that all necessary measures were to be taken to ensure the Nazis' secrets were secured by the Allies. When it became clear that the crucial Haigerloch and Hechigen areas – the site of the Germans' newest research facilities and their suspected nuclear pile – were slated to fall to Free French forces, drastic measures were proposed.

In Operation Harborage, British and American forces would hook around ahead of the French front line to seize the area before the French were able to get there. Alsos, the American's specialist unit, was charged to seize whatever technology, paperwork and expertise they could lay their hands on, and to blow up whatever remained.

Meanwhile, in Denmark, the very active resistance network alerted London to a new potential threat: the papers resulting from the long years of research by Niels Bohr were said to have been moved to Gestapo headquarters in Copenhagen. They might conceivably aid a last-gasp Nazi nuclear effort. In the same building key leaders of the Danish resistance, captured in recent raids, were incarcerated. If they talked, the 15,000-strong Danish resistance movement would be in grave jeopardy.

On 21 March 1945 a daring raid on Copenhagen, code-named Operation Carthage, was mounted, using an RAF Mosquito squadron. The daylight attack was flown at such low level that aircraft crashed into rooftops. But it proved spectacularly successful: the target building was turned into a raging inferno and the cells holding the Danish resistance leaders were blown open, with most managing to flee. Though civilians were also killed in the attack, and casualties amongst the Gestapo were lower than might have been expected (many happened to be attending a funeral), the last vestiges of Bohr's potentially dangerous legacy had been laid to rest.

As the Mosquitoes pounded their target in Copenhagen, so US troops thrust deep into what was scheduled to be the Russian zone of occupation. Declaring 'to hell with the Russians', they seized approaching 1,000 tonnes of uranium ore, and shipped it out to the US ahead of the advancing Red Army. And on 22 April 1945 British and US forces forged ahead on Operation Harborage, overrunning the Hechigen and Haigerloch facilities on the fringes of the Black Forest.

Hidden in a cave beneath the ancient church at Haigerloch they discovered an atomic pile, consisting of a latticework of 664 cubes of uranium suspended in a heavy water chamber, plus a veritable labyrinth of associated laboratories. They also seized the cream of Germany's nuclear establishment, including Otto Hahn, Kurt Diebner and Werner Heisenberg.

British and American nuclear experts calculated that the Haigerloch pile was lacking some 700 litres of heavy water, which would have allowed it to 'go critical'. This was approximately the amount sabotaged by Haukelid's crude alarm-clock time bombs, when the SF *Hydro* was sent to the bottom of the Norwegian lake (taking into account the further refinement of the SH200 to 100 per cent pure deuterium oxide).

On 23 April 1945, US General Groves – the head of the Manhattan Project – was finally able to conclude that the actions of the Allies had removed 'definitely any possibility of the Germans making any use of an atomic bomb in this war'.

Kurt Diebner, one of the most senior *Uranverein* scientists, had believed they would have enough SH200 for a working reactor by the end of 1943, so enabling the building of a Nazi nuclear weapon. He would subsequently write of the war years: 'It was the elimination of German heavy water production in Norway that was the main factor in our failure to achieve a self-sustaining atomic reactor before the war ended.' That reactor would have been their path to the bomb.

On 8 May 1945, even as the final signatures were being put to the deal under which Germany would surrender, British and American commanders were plotting a thrust into Czechoslovakia to overrun the Joachimsthal uranium mine. And in Norway some 50,000 resistance fighters – the Norwegian home forces, also known as the 'Milorg', and with Grouse and Gunnerside veterans amongst their number – took back control of their country from the German occupiers.

Late on the evening of the same day *Reichskommissar* Josef Terboven drained a bottle of brandy and lit the fuse to a heap of explosives, ending his life and his hated rule over the Norwegian people. Beside him was the body of SS General Wilhelm Rediess, who had shot himself dead shortly beforehand.

Few would lament their passing.

By the summer of 1945 ten of the *Uranverein*'s top scientists were installed at Farm Hall, a private country house near Cambridge. Unbeknown to them, the entire building was wired for sound, and all of their conversations were being recorded in an effort to ascertain if any of the Nazis' nuclear secrets had escaped the British and American dragnets.

On 6 August the first of the atom bombs was dropped on the Japanese city of Hiroshima. That evening the news was announced on the BBC. The former *Uranverein* scientists listened to the broadcast in disbelief, tinged with not a small degree of cynicism. Surely, they argued, this had to be Allied propaganda to force the Japanese to surrender. None amongst them was able to believe that the Allies had succeeded in building an atom bomb.

As reality began to sink in, they started to criticize the Allies for using such a terrible weapon, and to field their own excuses for not getting there first. Their laboratories were forever being bombed by the Allies. They had worked under too much pressure; those in charge were forever pressing for 'immediate results', which were impossible to achieve. They never had the supplies they needed – chiefly the heavy water – to make a weapon feasible.

As an official British government report, broadcast on the BBC to a grateful nation, would conclude of the German nuclear effort: 'Germany's use of the atomic bomb, which the War Cabinet with their inner knowledge had so much dreaded, was delayed. Before her researches were complete, she was a beaten nation.'

But in Norway there remained unfinished business: those who had died so that the Nazi nuclear dream might be vanquished still needed to be avenged. Across Norway, British and Norwegian officers working for the War Crimes Investigation Teams hunted for evidence, and the guilty. In the spring and summer of 1945 Norwegian Arne Bang-Andersen – a former policeman and resistance fighter – set about tracking down those Germans responsible for the Operation Freshman executions.

Over the following months, he and a team of British investigators managed to establish the fate of every single one of the missing Sappers. The survivors of the glider crashes had been killed as a direct result of Hitler's Commando Order. Some – those more fortunate – had been shot. Others were executed with varying degrees of cruelty – by agonizing injections, strangulation or hanging, amongst other means. Some of the corpses had been thrown into mass graves, while others had been dumped at sea. Those bodies that could be were disinterred and reburied with full honours, and memorials were established to commemorate the Sappers' sacrifice. As an official report into Operation Freshman concluded, it was 'a most gallant attempt that had failed.'

Those Germans responsible were duly brought to trial. They pleaded various defences and tried to blame each other in an effort to save their own skins: they were acting under orders; they were fearful of Gestapo reprisals. Regardless, all were sentenced to death or life imprisonment.

In May 1946 the trial of one of the senior officers, General Karl Maria von Behren, the commander of the area where the first glider crashed, got under way. Von Behren was found not guilty, but the overall architect of the killings would not get off so lightly. General von Falkenhorst stood trial in July 1946, charged with overarching responsibility for the Freshman murders, and that of the Musketoon captives.

Von Falkenhorst argued that he was acting on orders laid down by Hitler himself – the so-called 'defence of superior orders'. Von Falkenhorst's plea failed, for the Commando Order was judged to have been illegal, and he had in any case modified the order when passing it down to his officers. In late July 1946 von Falkenhorst was sentenced to death, but that was commuted to life in prison after a plea for clemency was heard. He was released from prison on humanitarian grounds in July 1953 and died in July 1968.

After the war the production of heavy water was resumed at Norsk Hydro's Vemork facility, and in a sense the war over heavy water had one last skirmish to play out. The British government sought to restrict the countries to which the heavy water could be exported, keeping it well out of Russian – and even French – hands. It was feared that the French might sell the heavy water or related technologies to the Russians, or share it with them because of common political aspirations. That battle would rumble on for several years.

The Joachimsthal uranium mine, in Czechoslovakia, was overrun by Russian forces at war's end. After the 1948 takeover by the Communist Party in Czechoslovakia, prison camps were established in the town of Joachimsthal. Opponents of the new regime and its ever-closer links to Soviet Russia were forced to work in the uranium mines under brutal conditions. Life expectancy for those miners was forty-two years. Uranium mining ceased there in 1964.

Some commentators have argued that Nazi Germany failed to win the race for nuclear supremacy because the *Uranverein* scientists were on the wrong track – a heavy-water-based plutonium reactor was not the route to a nuclear weapon. This is incorrect. Of the two bombs dropped by the Americans on Japan, one – 'Fat Man', unleashed over Nagasaki – was an implosion-based weapon with a solid plutonium core.

The plutonium to build the Fat Man bomb was produced in heavy water reactors, using heavy water from both American plants and the Canadian facility, in Trail, British Columbia. Heavy water remains an essential component in some types of reactors today, both those that produce nuclear power and those designed to produce raw materials for nuclear weapons. Heavy water is produced by Argentina, Russia, the USA, India, Pakistan, Canada, Iran and Norway, amongst other countries.

Some of the brave individuals portrayed in these pages sadly did not survive the war years. Odd Starheim – Agent Cheese – returned to Norway in 1943 as part of a commando operation to hijack another vessel, as he had with the *Galtesund*. Sadly that ship, the *Tromosund*, was sunk at sea by German warplanes with the loss of all lives. Likewise, Lief Tronstad – the Professor – would not survive the war. Sent into Norway late in the fighting, he would be killed in a shootout in a hut on the Hardangervidda.

All those who had made up the Grouse and Gunnerside teams did survive the war. For their actions in sabotaging the Vemork heavy water plant they were given the following honours, amongst others:

1. Second Lieutenant Jens Anton Poulsson – Distinguished Service Order (DSO)
2. Second Lieutenant Joachim Holmboe Rønneberg – DSO
3. Second Lieutenant Knut Magne Haugland – Military Cross (MC)
4. Second Lieutenant Kasper Idland – MC
5. Second Lieutenant Knut Anders Haukelid – MC
6. Sergeant Claus Urbye Helberg – Military Medal (MM)
7. Sergeant Arne Kjelstrup – MM
8. Sergeant Fredrik Thorbjørn Kayser – MM
9. Sergeant Hans Storhaug – MM
10. Sergeant Birger Edvan Martin Stromsheim – MM

Haukelid was also given a DSO for his actions sinking the SF *Hydro* ferry, and a memorial was established for those innocent Norwegians who had died in the ferry's sinking. Einar Skinnarland was awarded the Distinguished Conduct Medal, and Captain and Professor Lief Tronstad was made an OBE (several months prior to his being killed in action). John Skinner Wilson was awarded an OBE, and also appointed to the chivalrous Order of St Olav by the Norwegian government. The Grouse and Gunnerside men were given an array of medals by the Norwegian government, and several other countries, after the war.

Those who had taken part in Operation Musketoon were also awarded their share of honours – Captains Graeme Black and Joe Houghton included. They were supposed to pick them up once they had been released from whatever POW camp they had been held in. But, since none would survive captivity, these awards were all made posthumously.

The Special Operations Executive itself fell victim to the immediate post-war years. On 15 January 1946 it was formally disbanded, the argument being that the SOE's revolutionary, distinctive and ruthless form or warfare-espionage may have been justified in the war years, but there was no role for such an outfit in peacetime. As the subsequent strife-torn decades would prove, this decision was doubtless somewhat premature.

After Gunnerside, Joachim Ronneberg had deployed to other missions in the Norwegian wilderness. Post-war he involved himself in broadcasting, becoming known as 'the Voice of Norway'. A television and radio producer, he also gave extensive lectures, including to the Norwegian Army and elite units of the British military. He is the only member of the Grouse and Gunnerside teams still alive at the time of writing.

Jens Poulsson served with the Norwegian resistance post-Gunnerside, recruiting and training extensively. After the war he served in the Norwegian Army, rising to the rank of colonel and becoming an expert in mountain warfare and Arctic survival. He settled in an area equidistant between Oslo and Rjukan, remaining a keen outdoorsman despite his advancing years. He died in February 2010, aged ninety-one, and his funeral was attended by the Norwegian king.

After the Vemork sabotage Claus Helberg returned to the Hardangervidda, serving as a radio operator and instructor in the Norwegian resistance. Post-war he became a prominent figure in Norway's tourism industry, and was an intimate of Scandinavian royalty and the political class. He never lost his love of the outdoors, and was something of a living legend in Norway. His death in March 2003 was mourned throughout the country.

Knut Haugland served out much of the war post-Gunnerside in Norway, working as a superlative radio operator. He played a pivotal role in several high-profile sabotage operations, escaping capture by the skin of his teeth on more than one occasion. After the war Haugland served in the Norwegian Army, and was chosen to take part in the famed *Kon-Tiki* expedition, led by Thor Heyerdahl in 1947. Six men sailed 6,000 kilometres on a thirteen-metre balsa wood raft, from South America to Polynesia, to prove theories about the global migration of early humankind. Haugland died in December 2009 aged ninety-two.

Knut Haukelid rejoined the Norwegian resistance after the SF *Hydro* sinking, and served with them for the remainder of the conflict. After the war he joined the Norwegian Army, rising to the rank of major in the Telemark Infantry Regiment. He later became a lieutenant colonel in the Home Guard of Greater Oslo. Haukelid reconciled with his wife, Bodil. He died in 1994.

Einar Skinnarland remained in the Hardangervidda following the SF *Hydro* sinking, working with the resistance. Post-war he emigrated to the USA, working as an engineer on construction projects around the world. He died in Toronto, in 2002. Modest to a fault, he rarely displayed any of his medals from the war years, keeping them locked away for posterity. One souvenir he did treasure from his time with the SOE was the case that had contained the suicide pill that he had carried with him during the long years of conflict.

After the war, John Skinner Wilson reverted to his role as a leading light in the Scouting movement. He would declare of his time at the SOE: 'These years marked a very special era in my life . . . this experience, varied as it was, gave a fresh impetus to my subsequent Scout work . . . I found that I had proved myself in a new and entirely different role and that at a comparatively advanced age.' He continued to play a very active role in SOE and Linge Company reunions until the day he died, at age eighty-two, whereupon a delegation from Norway attended his funeral.

'To those of us privileged enough to serve under him, the one quality which shone out was his utter integrity,' one of the Linge Company veterans would write of Wilson:

It was this which undoubtedly led our Norwegian comrades to accept and trust him in a way seldom given by soldiers of one nation to a commander of another . . . The success of

SOE operations in Norway . . . bear testimony to his wisdom and vision, not to mention the long hours of work he put in and to his mastery of detail of every operation. His influence on men going into the field was tremendous . . . A man of another generation who had all the best Victorian virtues and few of their vices, he was an inspiration to us all.'

Acknowledgements

In researching this book I was able to speak to and receive assistance from a number of individuals, many of whom were especially generous with their time and are mentioned in the Preface. My special thanks and gratitude are extended to all, and my apologies to those that I have inadvertently forgotten to mention.

In no particular order I wish to thank the following, who assisted in many ways (research, proofreading, hospitality, recollections and subject matter expertise): Tean Roberts, Simon Fowler, Paul Sherratt and Anne Sherratt, Hamish De Bretton-Gordon, David Lewis, Jack Mann, Kenneth C. McAlpine, Seán Ó Cearrúlláin and Astri Pothecary. The staff at several archives and museums also deserve special mention, including those at the British National Archives; the Imperial War Museum; the Churchill Archive Centre at Churchill College, Cambridge; Norway's Norges Hjemmefrontmuseum (NHM) and Rjukan's Norsk Industriarbeidermuseum.

Enormous gratitude is also due to Colonel Kev Oliver RM, Lieutenant Colonel Tony de Reya MBE RM, Lieutenant Colonel Rich Cantrill RM, Major Finlay Walls RM, Captain Lee Piper RM, RSM Paul McArthur RM, CSM Steve Randle RM and all at the Commando Training Centre Royal Marines (CTCRM), for hosting my various visits in connection with the book and related topics. I remain immensely grateful.

Huge thanks are also due to Jonathan Ball, and all at the Royal Marines Charitable Trust Fund, and to Alex Murray MBE RM, at Navy Command Headquarters.

My gratitude to my literary agent, Gordon Wise, and film agent, Luke Speed, both of Curtis Brown, for helping bring this project to fruition, and to all at my publishers, Quercus, for same, including, but not limited to: Charlotte Fry, Ben Brock and Fiona Murphy. My editor, Richard Milner, deserves very special mention, as does Josh Ireland. Your faith in my ability to tell this remarkable and important story is, I hope, rewarded by the writing that has resulted.

And of course, thanks are due as always to the ever-patient and supportive Eva, and the wonderful David, Damien Jr and Sianna, for not resenting Dad spending too much of his time locked away . . . again . . . writing . . . again.

Bibliography

Baden-Powell, Dorothy, *Operation Jupiter*, Robert Hale Limited, 1982

Bailey, Roderick, *Forgotten Voices of the Secret War*, Ebury Press, 2009

Bascomb, Neal, *The Winter Fortress*, Houghton Mifflin Harcourt, 2016

Berglyd, Jostein, *Operation Freshman*, Leandoer & Ekholm Forlag HB, 2006

Dalton, Hugh, *Hugh Dalton Memoirs 1931–1945*, Frederick Muller Ltd, 1957

Drummond, John, *But for These Men*, Award Books, 1965

Embury, Sir Basil, *Mission Completed*, Methuen & Co. Ltd, 1957

Gallagher, Thomas, *Assault in Norway*, Harcourt Brace Jovanovich, Inc., 1975

Groves, Leslie, *Now It Can Be Told*, Da Capo Press, 1962

Haukelid, Knut, *Skis Against the Atom*, William Kimber, 1954.

Irving, David, *The German Atomic Bomb*, Simon & Schuster, 1976

Mears, Ray, *The Real Heroes of Telemark*, Coronet Books, 2003

O'Connor, Bernard, *Churchill's School for Saboteurs – Station 17*, Amberley Publishing, 2013

O'Connor, Bernard, *Churchill's Most Secret Airfield – RAF Tempsford*, Amberley Publishing, 2010

Olsen, Olaf Reed, *Two Eggs on My Plate*, Companion Book Club, 1954

Powers, Thomas, *Heisenberg's War: The Secret History of the German Bomb*, Da Capo Press, 2000

Schofield, Stephen, *Musketoon,* Elmfield Press, 1964

Sonsteby, Gunnar, *Report from No. 24*, Barricade Books, Inc., 1999

Stevenson, William, *A Man Called INTREPID*, Lyons Press, 1976

Tickell, Jerrard, *Moon Squadron*, Allan Wingate, 1956

West, Nigel, *Secret War*, Coronet Books, 1993

Wiggan, Richard, *Operation Freshman*, William Kimber, 1986

Wilkinson, Peter and Astley, Joan Bright, *Gubbins & SOE*, Pen & Sword, 1993

Young, Gordon, *Outposts of Peace*, Hodder & Stoughton, 1945

Appendix

The Daily Express, 21 May 1945

SECRET ARMY FOUGHT NAZI ATOM BOMB
Four men hid three months in white hell

It can be revealed today that for five years British and German scientists fought their own war-within-a-war. They fought to perfect the Atom Bomb, which, with the most explosive force in the world, would have given either side walk-over superiority.

But it was no war of theorists only. British and Norwegian paratroopers fought it out, too, with Wehrmacht men and their quisling supporters in the white hell of the storm-swept Hardanger Plateau in Norway.

The Germans opened the fight in the summer of 1940. A few weeks after moving into Norway they seized the vast hydroelectrical works at Rjukan. These works, fed by the famous 'smoking-cascade' waterfall, supply electricity plentifully. And plentiful electricity was essential to the German plan and to the arms plant they intended to set up at Rjukan.

Their plan was to –

Split the Atom.

At Rjukan the Norwegians produced large quantities of a substance known as 'heavy water'.

Heavy water contains atoms of hydrogen twice as heavy as those contained in ordinary water, from which it can be made electronically.

The price of heavy water is about £1,500 to £2,000 a pound.

Scientists the world over had experimented with heavy water and they believed that if they treated the metal uranium with it, under great force, they could split the atom of uranium.

And in so doing they would release terrific energy – and produce a catastrophic explosion.

There are many technical difficulties but the Germans may have been near solving them.

All they needed was sufficient heavy water to go ahead with their experiments.

And with Rjukan in their hands they were ready to go ahead.

The manager of the works was –

Called to Berlin

There he was questioned by Speer, arms chief, and by scientists from the Wehrmacht laboratories. He told them as much as he had to – he was a patriot. Then, back in Norway, he told his friends what the German plans were.

By this time the Germans had the plant heavily enough

guarded to rule out sabotage – but no German capable of understanding them had yet seen the research records at Rjukan.

Leif Tronstad, professor of chemistry, patriot of Norway, burned them all.

Then, with the scientists who had worked with him, Tronstad fled to Britain.

In a little Scottish town he resumed his experiments. Army, Navy and RAF experts, and members of the Committee for Scientific Warfare worked with him. The race to produce the atom bomb was on.

In November 1942 the race turned into war. Twenty-five British specialists were chosen to go to Rjukan on the Hardanger plateau: their job –

Sabotage

They were going to wreck the laboratories and destroy if they could all the heavy water the Germans had made.

Ahead of the them went four Norwegians. Men who had been born in the icy desert of the Hardanger plateau. Three of them had come to England by way of Moscow, Odessa, Bombay and Capetown. The fourth, a young radio operator, came through Sweden. Four men of adventure.

They wore Norwegian uniform under white camouflage. They took with them a radio. And with their load of equipment, with their white-painted skis and their white-painted tommy guns they parachuted onto the plateau.

In the daytime they lay low, somewhere, somehow, amidst

the snow. By night they sent weather reports to Scotland and explored the roads and tracks.

December came in with heavy storms. And there was no news from England until the day the heavy clouds broke, the wind dropped and they got what they called 'crack signals.'

Two Halifax bombers were on the way: behind them, gliders. And in the gliders 25 British paratroopers.

It was all clear until sunset. Then a gale broke. The worst gale that even these men of the plateau had ever seen. The snow, whipped by the Arctic wind, blinded them: they were almost senseless in the driving, crushing cold.

For hours they struggled to keep burning the beacons which were to guide in the bombers. From a hole in the snow they waited, and they watched. And they listened – and there was the drone of the planes.

The first plane came in. One engine – maybe more – had been knocked out. She was battling with the gale. And this plane had in tow the glider in which was the equipment that they needed.

It was hopeless trying to land the glider. It did not take the pilot long to learn that. So, with the wings battered and ripped by the moaning storm, his engines crippled, he headed back towards the sea.

A few minutes later the plane crashed.

The second plane came in. The pilot had seen nothing of the first. And into the storm he let go his glider. With its 25 paratroopers aboard this glider came down near Stavanger, not how or where they had planned, but to a –

Forced Landing

There they were, these 25 men, in the middle of the winter night, in that terrific storm, on desolate Hardanger Plateau. No food, ammunition or tents and hardly knowing where they were.

They struggled along for days. Then, after rest at a lonely farm, they asked the farmer to tell the Germans 25 British soldiers were ready to surrender.

The Germans arrived. The British downed their arms before the farm and, all wearing Army uniforms, awaited them with a white flag made from a towel.

A German officer shouted a command. Tommy guns rattled, and the Britons who had surrendered were dead.

The Germans examined the maps and notes in the pockets of the dead Britons. They acted quickly.

More than 6,000 Germans, led by SS and Gestapo officers, were rushed to Rjukan.

Terboven, the Nazi boss of Norway, arrived by plane to supervise the combing of the plateau. Huts and farms were burned down so there should be no shelter for saboteurs.

All civilians were evacuated. Scores of ack-ack guns were set up around Rjukan. Barrage balloons were brought in.

The four Norwegians still hiding on the plateau got their orders by radio from Scotland. 'Stay where you are. We will come back.'

By then they were starving. But on Christmas Eve one of them shot a reindeer. So they lived on through bleak January. In the middle of February the 'crack signal' was heard again, and six men parachuted down.

But they dropped 25 miles from the fixed rendezvous. It took a week for the two groups to meet. Then, on 23 February 1943, they left for Rjukan.

Professor Tronstad, now a Major in the Norwegian Army, had given them three plans. Which plan they used depended on conditions.

The attack had been rehearsed in Scotland.

They found the main entrance to the factory closed and heavily guarded, so they decided on –

Plan No. 3

They crept along high-tension cables to the plant. Six went in. The other four covered them with tommy guns.

The six men were attaching explosives to the safe where the Germans kept their radium and uranium, when a workman entered the laboratory.

They said to him: 'Get out and keep quiet. We want to destroy the plant – we do it for Norway.'

The man wiped his forehead and said: 'Well, boys, I hope you do it properly.'

Twenty minutes later the Germans had no more heavy water, no uranium, no radium, and no laboratory.

The paratroopers skied 500 miles over German-occupied Norway and escaped.

Seven months later the Germans had their plant repaired. Then it was –

Bombed by the RAF

The Germans brought in new plant. By April 1944 they had made 12 tons of heavy water, and were going to ship it over Lake Tinsjoe and into Austria, where the first atom bomb would be made.

The day 12 wagons loaded with heavy water left the plant, three men came from Hardanger Plateau to Lake Tinsjoe.

The wagons were surrounded by German soldiers and SS men. The only chance to destroy the precious cargo was to sink the ferry in the middle of the lake. And they did. A magnetic demolition charge with a time fuse was attached underwater to the hull of the ferryboat and she went down.

The secret battle of Rjukan was over.

Index

Ellman, Captain 113
Erling, Captain 383–4

F

Fairclough, Jack 12–13, 48–9, 50,
    54–5, 154
Falkenhorst, General Nikolaus von
    53, 74, 149–50, 155, 156, 173,
    219, 233, 234, 236, 238, 336–7,
    339, 345–6, 373, 396
Fasting, Andreas 'Agent Biscuit' 94–5,
    101, 103, 104, 105, 106, 113
'Fjellsangen' poem code 192
Fladmoe, Arvid 375, 383, 385
Fort William hydro station 137
France/Free French forces 2, 392,
    397
Free Norwegian Forces 15
Frisch, Otto 77–8
Frisch-Peierls Memorandum 77

G

Galtesund hijack 100–1, 103–15
Germany/German Forces
    Allied intelligence 84–91
    army in Glomfjord 28, 34–5, 37–9,
        41–2, 44–9, 50–5
    capture and interrogation of
        Musketoon raiders 49, 50–3,
        149–54
    capture survivors of Freshman
        216, 217, 223, 224, 233–4,
        247–8, 395–6
    Colditz Castle (Oflag IV-C)
        150–2
    control of Czechoslovakia 61–2
    invasion of Belgium 75
    invasion of Denmark 73
    invasion of Norway 15, 53, 73, 74,
        102, 116, 141, 144, 227–8,
        324
    Operation Eagle/hunt for

Gunnerside saboteurs 346,
        348–54, 355
    plans for racial purity 82, 237
    Rjukan town raid 234–5, 236,
        237–8
    search for Freshman and Grouse
        suspects 218–19, 234–5, 236,
        237–8, 240, 243, 245–6
    secret weapon propaganda 64–5,
        363
    security across Norway tightened
        155–6, 157
    strength and extent (June 1942)
        132
    V1 and V2 rockets 158, 361, 368
    see also Falkenhorst, General
        Nikolaus von; Gestapo;
        Hitler, Adolf; Luftwaffe;
        nuclear capabilities/bomb
        development; Operation
        Eagle; Rediess, General
        Wilhelm; SS; Terboven,
        Josef; Vemork heavy water
        facilities
Gestapo 53, 86–9, 95–6, 116, 219,
    228, 234, 235, 238–9, 243, 245,
    345, 356, 365, 377
Gibson, Squadron Leader 268, 269,
    270
gliders 174–6, 177, 179, 197,
    199–200, 202, 205–6, 207,
    208–11, 223–4
Glomfjord hydro station and
    aluminum factory 25–7, 30–47,
    57, 148
Goebbels, Joseph 98, 235, 236, 289,
    363
Goudsmit, Samuel 263–4
Granlund, Sverre 15–16, 17, 20–1,
    36–8, 47, 48, 49–50, 54–5,
    154
Grini concentration camp 143, 356

Groves, General Leslie 265, 362, 369, 393

Gubbins, Brigadier Colin McVean 56, 214–16, 229, 289, 387

H

Hahn, Otto 60, 393

Haigerloch–Hechigen district, Germany 371, 392, 393

Halifax bombers and crews 162, 163, 165–7, 173, 174, 177, 195–6, 202, 203–7, 208, 210, 211, 268, 269, 270, 274–5

Halvorsen, Frithjof 105

Hampton, Colonel Charles 214, 221

Hardangervidda *see* Vidda (Hardangervidda)

Harteck, Paul 62–3

Hassel, Ase 355, 356–7

Haugland, Knut 145, 147, 166, 185–7, 188, 191–3, 194, 197–8, 200, 204–5, 211, 216, 217, 218–19, 237–8, 239–40, 243, 244, 245–6, 259, 265, 271, 275, 284, 292
  in hiding post attack 337, 344, 346, 359
  post-Gunnerside career 400
  recommendations and honours 360, 398, 399
  see also Operation Grouse

Haukelid, Knut 'Bonzo' 225–30, 248, 262, 270, 271, 272, 280–1, 283, 284, 297, 310
  attack on Vemork plant 313, 314, 315, 323–4, 329–30
  escape and in hiding post-attack 331, 344, 346, 359, 365
  post-SF *Hydro* sabotage career 400–1
  recommendations and honours 360, 398
  Vemork/SF *Hydro* sabotage

mission 365, 371–82, 386, 387, 393, 398
  see also Operation Gunnerside

Haukelid, Sigrid 225, 226

heavy water supplies 397–8
  Allied 131, 134, 159, 263
  German 67, 68–9, 70, 71, 75, 90–1, 93, 115, 127–8, 129, 158, 160, 182, 191, 237, 248, 347, 362, 363, 371, 388, 393 (*see also* SH200; Vemork heavy water facilities)

Heisenberg, Werner 63, 68, 74, 129, 157–8, 371, 393

Helberg, Claus 141, 143–4, 147, 166, 167–8, 187, 188, 193, 205, 219, 243, 244–5, 281, 287–8, 290–1, 293–6, 297, 299–300
  approach to Vemork plant 301–2, 304–5, 306, 309, 310, 311
  escape 330, 331–2, 335, 336, 338, 344, 348–54, 355–9
  Operation Eagle pursuit across Vidda 344, 348–54
  plans escape 290, 295–7, 299–300, 314
  post-Gunnerside career 400
  recommendations and honours 360, 398
  see also Operation Grouse

Henneker, Lieutenant Colonel 178–9, 182, 196, 200, 201, 202, 208, 211, 212, 223

Henschel, Oberst Franz 52–3

Hewins, Ralph 342

Heyerdahl, Thor 400

hijack of *Galtesund* 100–1, 103–15

the Hird 228

Hiroshima 394–5

Hitler, Adolf 53, 59, 235
  chemical weapons programme 67–8

418

Rebecca/Eureka homing beacon
system 177–8, 196, 197, 204,
211, 216, 271
Red Cross 151
Rediess, General Wilhelm 236–7,
238, 337, 338–9, 340, 345–6, 355
Reich Main Security Office 153, 156
Reich War Ministry 62
reindeer hunting 252–7
reindeer moss 242
resistance and intelligence network,
Norwegian 73, 84–91, 94–9,
116–21, 233, 234, 238–9, 290,
377, 379, 394, 395, 396, 400–1
see also Skinnarland, Einar; Sorlie,
Ralph
Reuters 57
Rjukan town 101, 102, 234–5, 236,
237–8, 292–3, 339, 373
Rommel, General Erwin 132
Ronneberg, Joachim 214, 221–3,
224–5, 229, 231, 232, 246–7,
259–61, 262, 266, 267–8, 270,
272–4, 275, 276–80, 285–8, 292,
295, 297–9, 301, 389
approach to Vemork plant 303–4,
306, 309, 310–12
attack on Vemork plant 313–14,
315–22, 324–9
escape 331–2, 335, 337–8, 344, 359
post-war career 399–400
recommendations and honours
360, 398
see also Operation Gunnerside
Roosevelt, Franklin D 64, 82, 131,
132, 133–4, 158, 219–20, 248–9,
360, 361, 362, 363, 391
Rorvig, Sofie 89–90
Royal Air Force (RAF) 111, 112, 123,
135–6
see also Halifax bombers and
crews; Whitley bombers

Royal Engineers 'Sappers' see
Operation Freshman
Royal Society 76
Russia/Red Army 391–2, 393, 397

S
Sachsenhausen concentration camp
153, 235
Saheim heavy water facility 93
Saint-Nazaire raid (Operation
Chariot) 10, 11, 152
Santhal tribes, India 56
Secret Intelligence Service (SIS) 58,
129
Seuss, Dr Hans 191
SH200 68–9, 75, 90, 93, 119, 128,
129, 130, 134, 160, 237, 248,
363, 370, 371, 393–4
see also heavy water supplies;
Vemork heavy water
facilities
Shetland Bus flotilla 4, 95, 97–8
Skinnarland, Einar 100–5, 106, 111,
113, 115, 117–20, 122, 123–7,
129, 131, 136, 147–8, 157, 189,
218, 219, 237, 243, 245, 246,
265, 292, 337, 346
in hiding post-attack 337, 346,
359, 365
honours awarded 399
post-Gunnerside career 401
post-Gunnerside communications
with SOE 370, 377, 386
Skinnarland, Torstein 126, 148–9,
187, 237, 243
Skylark B 116–17
Smith, Miller 'Dusty' 12, 23–4, 48–9
Sorensen, Captain 384–5
Sørlie, Rolf 290, 377, 378, 380, 381–2
Special Operations Executive (SOE)
14, 58–9, 70, 85, 128–9, 130–1,
135–6, 140, 159, 162, 214–16,

THE ROYAL MARINES CHARITY

Royal Marines have always been the first to understand, first to adapt and respond and the first to overcome – that's the Commando Mindset but today Royal Marines and their families are fighting battles they cannot win alone.

We are the Royal Marines' own Charity and are uniquely placed to understand, respond and react, enabling Marines and their families to overcome their challenges including life changing injury, life limiting illness, mental disability, transition to civilian life and even poverty.

We can target your support across every need to ensure no one is left behind.

Our Vision
Royal Marines and their families supported through life.

Our Mission
To provide the best possible through life charitable support for Royal Marines, their families, veterans and cadets.

Our Purpose
We are a single, unified and integrated charity for the Royal Marines extended Corps family, where cadets, the serving Corps, veterans and families are supported through life with benevolence, comradeship, transition support and amenities, underpinned with a cohesive sense of heritage and esprit de corps.

To support Royal Marines in need and donate today please text TRMC28 £amount to 70070. Alternatively if you are interested in fundraising for the charity or leaving a gift in your Will please call 023 9387 1566.

The Royal Marines Charity
Building 32, HMS Excellent
Whale Island
Portsmouth
Hampshire.
PO2 8ER

E jo.whitwood@theroyalmarinescharity.org.uk
T 023 9387 1567
W www.theroyalmarinescharity.org.uk

The Royal Marines Charitable Trust Fund operating as The Royal Marines Charity is a charity registered in England and Wales (1134205) and is a charitable Company Limited by Guarantee (07142012) registered with Companies House. Registered Office: Building 32, HMS Excellent, Whale Island, Portsmouth, PO2 8ER

A PROUD PART OF

ROYAL NAVY & ROYAL MARINES CHARITY